GAMES GIRLS PLAY

CAROLINE SILBY, Ph.D.
with SHELLEY SMITH

St. Martin's Griffin
New York

GAMES GIRLS PLAY

UNDERSTANDING AND GUIDING
YOUNG FEMALE ATHLETES

www.stmartins.com

Book design by Michelle McMillian

Frontispiece photo by Photodisc Inc.

Library of Congress Cataloging-in-Publication Data

Silby, Caroline
    Games girls play: understanding and guiding young female athletes / Caroline Silby with Shelley Smith—1st ed.
        p. cm.
    ISBN 0-312-26163-2 (hc)
    ISBN 0-312-27126-3 (pbk)
    1. Sports for women. 2. Sports for women—Coaching. 3. Women athletes—Psychology. I. Smith, Shelley. II. Title.
GV709.S515 2000
796'.082—dc21   00-027849

First St. Martin's Griffin Edition: October 2001

10 9 8 7 6 5 4 3 2 1

For the special women in my life,
Nana, Mom, Lis, and Anne.

—CAROLINE SILBY

For the girls of my friends, the girls who play with and against
my daughter, Dylann, every weekend; and especially for sixteen-
year-old Susanne Nicholas, who beat cancer and a lot of volley-
ball teams at the same time.

—SHELLEY SMITH

Contents

Acknowledgments

I am blessed to have some very special people in my life who helped teach me the true value of sport and encouraged me to teach it to others.

My greatest assets, my parents, Barbara and Howard Silby. Howie and Babs have been my role models, cheerleaders, teachers, mentors, and butt-kickers (as needed). Together we negotiated the sport process as best as we knew how and although mistakes were made along the way we worked through them together. Their tenacity, intelligence, warmth, humor, and openness to life are the qualities I love about each of them. They have inspired me to approach my career with passion and to live my life with integrity. The best parts of me are the lessons I learned from them.

My sister Lis is definitely my most ardent supporter. It's been like that since we were kids. Lis was and still is the performer of the family and through our "sisterly sisters" acts she helped me tackle my shyness. I encouraged her to get out of bed at five A.M. to skate and she reminded me that there was more to life than just sports. I feel so blessed that Lis and her husband Misha allow me to share in the lives of their extraordinary children, Kathryn, Drew, and Nicholas, and that they always—without question—let me home in on really fun family vacations.

Nana is my ninety-year-old grandmother who never really understood why I got up at five A.M. to figure skate or why my parents allowed it. Although sports mystified her, she did spend many days in cold silent ice rinks watching me go round and round. Nana is my mother's mother and in my family there is a special bond among the girls. I can talk to my Nana about anything and she listens. I mean she *really* listens. To this day, Nana continues to be open to learning and is the rock that keeps four generations of our family together. She has waited patiently for this book to become a reality and I hope someday she can read it with her ears.

Anne Batdorf Militano is my dear friend and former figure skating coach. Of course, without her expertise I could not have developed my talent. Yet, when I reflect back on skating, it's not the medals won that I value. It's the incredible gift of having an adult outside of your immediate family see you as special and lovable. And that person is Anne.

When I was just a teenager my parents provided me with the great opportunity to work with sports psychologist Dr. Bruce Ogilvie. I distinctly remember thinking that he had the coolest job of anyone in the world. Up to that point in my life, I had toyed with the idea of becoming a fabric cutter, a thoracic surgeon, and a reporter. So, Dr. Ogilvie had some stiff competition, but nonetheless our work together inspired me to get a Ph.D. in sports psychology.

Thank you to Dr. Bob Rotella, Dr. Linda Bunker, and Dr. Courtland Lee for teaching me how to understand and guide athletes. Shelley Smith for her collaboration on this book and helping me understand how to put my voice into words. My editor Carrie McGinnis for jumping into this project and making it a reality. My agent Michael Carlisle for believing in my work and opening my mind to the world of publishing. Drs. David Coppel, Gayle Davis, and Sean McCann for allowing me to learn from them. Dr. John Anderson for his powerful wisdom. John LeFevre for passing my third test and for his guidance through the years. And Nancy Marshall because her dedication and commitment to young female athletes is an inspiration.

I extend warm appreciation to all the parents and coaches that have given me the opportunity to work with their athletes and daughters.

Finally, I applaud the young female athletes whose passion toward their pursuits continues to amaze me. Thank you for allowing me the great privilege of contributing to your development as athletes and young women. I expect great things from you all.

—Caroline Silby

Working on this book with Caroline Silby helped me deal with my own situation with my teen-aged daugher, Dylann, a gifted student and a talented athlete. She began playing soccer and basketball when she was about five years old, and as she grew and progressed, she faced many of the problems that we talk about in this book. Working with Caroline helped me help Dylann, and for that, I'm eternally grateful.

I'd also like to thank Dylann's father, Mike Tharp, and several of the fathers of players on the Torrance United Storm soccer team, especially Pat Grimes, for providing much of the material in the chapter, "Parenting: When Mom and Dad Need Guidance." I say this only half in jest. I know they are good men who mean well, they just need a little redirecting from time to time.

Many thanks to all the players on Dylann's various teams throughout the years, especially the Torrance United Storm, which was a special group that represented so many of the good things that come from sports participation. It aslo helped that our newsletter often featured headlines like: "Girls Make Finals (parents make margaritas)." I hope every young girl and their parents can find a team like that.

Thanks to Dylann's coaches, some of whom have been great—and some less than great—but all who gave their time and efforts to making her a better athlete and teammate. Special appreciation goes to coaches Paul Watson, Hal Pope, Pat Donlon, A.J. Johnson, Ivory Ocean, Byron McCollum, Mark Monroy, Steve Thornton, Dave Akamine, Steve Alyea, and Tom Intagliata.

As always, much appreciation to those who must put up with me on a daily basis at ESPN, and to my parents, Ron and Luanne Smith, as well as my sister, Zoanne, and her husband, Jubal, and their three little ones. Thanks to my best friends, Team Samuelson: Hiller, Roemer, Walsh, Whitman, Kunz, Nicholas, Norton, and Pleasant. Also gratitude to Kelly Neal, Lesley Visser, Heather Faulkiner, Anne Marie Jeffords, Vanessa and Rachel Tharp, Keyshawn and Shikiri Johnson and their two little ones, Reynaldo Spalding, Jeff Fellenzer, and Rod Baker.

Dylann has truly benefited from playing sports and I am extremely proud of the way she's handled the obstacles thrown at her. Because of that, because of sports, she is a stronger, more confident, responsible young woman. I wish this for every daughter.

—Shelley Smith

Introduction

Whenever I was feeling depressed or discouraged, I would come and cry out my heart to you and you didn't judge me. You understood and let me know you cared. You gave me the courage to face my problems and the strength to work through them. You have helped me see that everything in life is not just black and white, that I have to find a balance and what is right for one person may not be right for me. You have helped me to look at my positive aspects and to not always be so hard on myself. When I have come to you not knowing what I should do next or which way to turn, you did not simply tell me what I should do but instead you discussed my options with me and let me decide what I could do and when I was ready to do it. With your support and guidance I have become a much stronger person and I feel I can cope better now with my problems. You are not only an inspiration but a true friend. . . .

—Letter to Dr. Silby from a former client

Dominique Dawes was leading in the all-around gymnastics competition during the 1996 Olympic Games in Atlanta, and up next was one of her best events—the floor exercise. Throughout the competition she had been performing magnificently, and she knew the gold medal was within reach; all she had to do was continue to perform with the same confidence and expertise.

But then the unthinkable happened: Dawes stepped out of bounds during the routine, a mistake that cost her the all-around gold.

Dominique easily could have fallen apart, but instead of collapsing in the face of disaster, she stayed strong and survived. She refused to allow her extreme disappointment to control her thoughts. Two nights after making that crucial mistake, she won the individual bronze medal in that very same event.

The reason why she triumphed in the face of adversity, turning an obstacle into a challenge, was because she had practiced dealing with the numerous internal and external pressures of athletic competition. Quite simply, she had trained her mind as well as her body.

Over the years, Dominique and coach Kelli Hill spent countless hours in the gym developing her tremendous physical talent while also building her confidence. The training paid off, and Dominique spent seven years at the highest level of her sport. It was the process of getting to the top and staying there that showed Dominique how important it was to develop and strengthen her mental agility so as to support and enhance her physical capability.

Dominique and I worked together to help her develop the necessary mental skills that would allow her to trust her well-trained body at critical moments. Dominique learned through daily mental practice how to use her thoughts, feelings, and reactions to move herself closer to achieving her goals. She said, "For a long time, I never thought I was one hundred percent mentally prepared for competition. So, I learned how to control my emotions more, and stay positive and confident."

Throughout Dominique's career, there was evidence of her consistent dedication to strengthening her mind as well as her body. Before the Olympic trials, Dominique stated, "I think people will be looking up at me and I don't want to be looking down on myself. In school, if I made a mistake I'd say, 'Oh, that's okay' and I'd work it out. But in gymnastics, if I made a mistake I would think, 'I'm not good enough.' I learned it's not the end of the world if I'm not able to be perfect every single day." These were realizations that would help her win the 1996 Olympic trials.

What took place for Dominique was a shift in the way she saw herself and her situation. That shift changed her thinking, which changed her performance. It was a process, and it's ironic that of all the in-depth conversations we had about factors effecting performance, it was a two-minute example of how she successfully dealt with school pressures that seemed to open her mind to a new way of thinking.

It was clear to those close to Dominique that she had incredible mental strength, some of which was not developed through the years of national and international success, but through dealing effectively with the daily struggles encountered by elite athletes. One day, Kelli Hill observed, "If Dominique made a little error, she wouldn't be able to continue. She would just stop and think, 'the routine's over.' The most time we've spent is working on her ability to recover. Now if she makes a mistake, she just goes on."

And on she went to win Olympic gold and bronze, appear on Broadway in *Grease*, attend college, compete as a professional gymnast, give motivational speeches, and act as a spokesperson for children's issues. I watched as Dominique stood on the podium with Olympic gold draped around her neck and realized that although I admired her for the tremendous commitment she had made to becoming a great athlete, what truly inspired me was the commitment she made to developing herself as a person. Through gymnastics, Dominique came to learn about herself.

Dominique's story is representative of the kinds of situations young women athletes are faced with on an increasing basis. The success of the 1999 U.S. women's soccer team, which beat China in the finals in front of ninety thousand screaming fans—the largest crowd ever to witness a women's sporting event—and more than forty million television viewers, vividly brought to life the claim that women's sports have never been stronger or filled with such promise and potential. Dreams of athletic prominence and dominance are no longer just dreams; they are realities, because young women are becoming athletes in record numbers, advancing to collegiate, Olympic, and professional levels. And yet, as the popularity and image of women's sports has skyrocketed, so have the pressures and problems:

- An eleven-year-old softball player's confidence is dwindling because of her lack of playing time.
- A thirteen-year-old gymnast buckles under the weight of high expectations.
- A mother of a fourteen-year-old athlete anguishes over whether to allow her daughter to train away from home.
- A ten-year-old soccer player is afraid that everyone will laugh at her when she gets in the game because she's not as talented as the other girls.

- An eleven-year-old swimmer feels pressure from her mother, who is counting on her daughter's potential as an athlete to pay for college.
- A sixteen-year-old figure skater performs poorly under pressure and worries she will lose her parents' support.
- A fourteen-year-old volleyball player can't handle her father's tirades during her matches and the car ride home, when he critiques every shot.
- A thirteen-year-old tennis player gets so angry with herself when she makes a mistake that her practices are unproductive.

There are more serious issues, too:

- A fifteen-year-old softball player wants to improve her performance; a friend suggests she "bulk up" by taking steroids.
- A sixteen-year-old volleyball player is sexually harassed by her coach.
- A fourteen-year-old moves to a new school and makes the basketball team, only to find out that almost everyone on the team is lesbian and she isn't.
- A sixteen-year-old ballet dancer, under enormous pressure from her instructors, stops eating.

It is true that sports can provide vast benefits to young women. Research conducted by the Women's Sports Foundation and the National Collegiate Athletic Association (NCAA) shows that girls who play sports are likely to do better in school and have higher self-esteem than are those who don't; moreover, they are less likely to do drugs, join gangs, or even become sexually active. Sports are a way for a young woman to feel connected to something and to express and learn about herself as well as others. But a young woman doesn't derive those benefits simply by signing up for a team or taking lessons.

That's where parents enter the picture. And that's where I come in.

As a sports psychologist, I work with young women all over the country helping them learn how to deal with issues they face as athletes—and as young women—by using the most powerful training tool they have: their mind. By shaping the way they view themselves and various situations, athletes can reap all the benefits of sports participation no matter what their ability level. And athletes with exceptional ability can use the same techniques to reach even further heights.

My own experience as an athlete taught me how important it is to use athletic participation and sports not as a goal but as a process to becoming a stronger person. I began my quest to become an elite athlete at the age of six and ended the journey when I was nineteen years old as a member of the national figure skating team and having participated in the Olympic trials. It was through my sports involvement that I experienced the proudest and yet the saddest moments of my life.

When I began skating, I didn't know about the Olympics or winning or the freedom you feel gliding and jumping. All I knew was that my older sister, Elisabeth, loved to skate, and my whole world revolved around being exactly like my sister. I took to the ice, racing around, willing to try anything, and I found that people stopped to watch me. They talked about talent, potential, training, Olympics—words that had no meaning to me, but words that would later drive me to excel.

When I was eleven, I moved away from home in order to train. I liked the way my skating improved when I was at a training center and I begged my parents to let me go. I even arranged for a family friend to let me live with her. I thrived on the attention and admiration I received for being proficient at sports. I wanted to find out how good I could be at skating, and visions of national team uniforms provided me with unlimited motivation.

And then I experienced failure. I went through a period of time where I just couldn't perform as I did in practice. I kept skating dreadfully at important competitions. I remember getting in the car to go home with my father and just sobbing. He held me and told me it was okay. He didn't ask me why I had performed poorly and he didn't tell me how to feel. But I told him I wanted to quit skating. The failure hurt too much, and the payoff didn't seem worth the pain. He couldn't understand why I felt like such a failure. I explained that I could never be as successful at skating as he and my mother were in their careers. I had seen my father create one of the largest neurology practices in the country and my mother build her own political fundraising business and later become a White House appointee. How in the world could I live up to their accomplishments?

I later realized that the problem was not my failure but how I reacted and processed the failure. All I was seeing was the accomplishments themselves. I wasn't placing any value on the qualities about my parents or myself that enabled each of us to create success. Therefore, skating only seemed worthwhile if I won and won often. Unfortunately, I was going through a developmental stage physically and emotionally that had stalled my ability to win. I was allowing my athletic experiences to alter the very way I saw myself. I went from feeling special, successful, in control, empowered, approved of, and directed to feeling awkward, different, unsuccessful, out of control, powerless, unapproved of, and lost.

My father tried to encourage me with his favorite story of the tortoise and the hare. "Just keep at it. You'll get there," he said. I did keep trying, but hard work didn't seem to be the answer. My physical skills continued to improve and my performances continued to decline. It seemed the better I got in practice, the more everyone talked about my tremendous potential, and the more incapable I felt of meeting those grandiose expectations. It was my mother who decided that I needed to learn skills beyond the physical part of skating. She introduced me to the field of sports psychology.

It was 1978, and although sports psychology had emerged in the early 1900s, sports psychologists had only begun working as consultants to teams in the sixties. My parents scouted around and found Dr. Bruce Ogilvie, often known as the "father of sports psychology" for his groundbreaking work with athletes and teams. I flew off to California to meet Dr. Ogilvie and to learn how to perform. But I learned much more than that.

From the first time I talked with Dr. Ogilvie, I knew my skating had to have a purpose other than medals and applause. Over time, I learned to value the process of sports. I learned to enjoy the sport itself, accept failure as a part of the process, use failure as an opportunity to learn and move forward, and find the life lessons in sport that I could carry with me forever. As I ended my sports journey, my whole outlook had changed. Skating no longer defined who I was, rather, it would take me to where I wanted to be. I never achieved the ultimate Olympic dream, but was not devastated by this; instead, I take pride in my athletic accomplishments and believe that sports provided numerous challenges, which I see as life's way of pausing to teach me a lesson I needed to know to get to where I inevitably wanted to go.

It was the combined efforts of Dr. Ogilvie, my parents, and my coach, Anne Militano, that helped me to open my mind to the many life benefits I had received through sports participation. When people apply the principles of sports psychology, they can affect not only an athlete's performance but also the very way she sees herself and her sports experience. So what exactly does "training her mind" mean? Ask any athlete, and she will attribute at least half of her sports experience, including performance success and failure, to her mental skills and attitude. However, most athletes—like Dominique Dawes—admit that they spend as little as 10 percent of their training time preparing themselves mentally and more often don't even know what mental training entails.

Simply put, sports psychology is a field that examines personal and environmental factors and applies techniques to affect the way one feels, thinks, and ultimately performs. Mental aspects of performance such as perceptions, thoughts, attitudes, beliefs, expectations, and emotions are influenced by the development of a set of mental skills that when strengthened can enhance and support physical capabilities. Training an athlete's mind begins with assisting an athlete in identifying those factors about her sports and performance that are under her control. The factors that are under an athlete's control are critical to shaping successful and rewarding sports experiences. It sounds simple, but athletes have extreme difficulty recognizing how they control their own performances. On the other hand, they have little difficulty distinguishing factors about their performance that are outside of their control or cause them worry. It's important to help athletes separate what I call "external" factors—aspects of performance outside of an athlete's control—from the "internal" factors—aspects of performance under an athlete's control.

External Factors in Athletics—Aspects She Can't Control:

What her parents say or do
What her coaches say or do
What her friends say or do

Conditions of the field or gym
Equipment being used
Crowd attendees or crowd reaction
Referee calls or scoring by judges
What teammates do or say
Event scheduling
Event outcomes (winning, losing, hitting, missing, placement)
Injuries

Internal Factors in Athletics—Aspects She Can Control:

What she thinks about
Goals she sets
Her focus
How she perceives herself and her situations
How she reacts to others and her situations
Her emotions
How confident she feels
How hard she tries
Her body language
The images she sees in her mind
How she prepares for competition

The internal factors must be used to deal with and respond to the external factors. An athlete who worries and worries about winning the game will quickly feel stressed. However, if she shifts her attention to an internal factor under her control such as her thoughts, she can choose to think about something that will help her create the win. By doing so, she puts herself in control of the situation and provides herself with the best chance of getting the desired outcome.

Training the mind is all about strengthening internal factors to assist athletes in better responding to their external worries. Yet these internal factors are too often overlooked or undervalued. The most precious gift parents can give to their athlete is to place great importance on the internal strengths and celebrate the qualities about their daughters that help them control their own performances. These internal factors are the true life lessons of sports and can be applied to a lifetime of endeavors.

Athletes typically go through stages in their acquisition of mental skills. The process of strengthening one's mind works like this:

1. Athletes are introduced to a sports psychology skill (e.g., visualization)
2. Athletes are taught to acquire the skill and practice it
3. Athletes are taught to apply the skill during practices, games, and competitions
4. Athletes work to consistently apply the knowledge and skill
5. Athletes refine the skill to suit their needs and meet specific demands

Once understood, however, getting athletes to use theories and skills from the field of sports psychology is another challenge. Many athletes have a great deal of pride and are accustomed to taking full responsibility for their actions. As a result, it is often difficult for them to admit that they might need help. Sometimes they believe that strength means solving their own problems. It is important to explain to athletes that my work involves assisting them in identifying their internal strengths and finding ways to apply those very strengths to enhance their sports experience. It's not about having a problem but maximizing one's strengths in order to be prepared to face a multitude of challenges. An athlete who is open to mental skills training is an athlete who is trying to give herself the best chance of making her dreams come true.

In order to reinforce this point, I encourage athletes to talk about their successes. Instead of addressing the specific problem by asking, "What's wrong?" I ask, "What would you like to improve?" That gets an athlete immediately thinking about solutions, and I invite her to then discuss times she's been successful in that area.

For example, a young hurdler told me she was having problems in races. She had been running great times in practice, but hadn't come close to those times in the last three meets. I asked her to think of a race where she had run a great time. I asked her to describe the race to me in detail, including what she was thinking and feeling. I pointed out the essential pieces of her emotions, thoughts, and behaviors (internals) that she seemed to have trouble identifying for herself. That got her in tune with thinking about things under her control and shifted attention away from the problem and toward the solution. Once she recognized that she did indeed possess the necessary skills to race well, it was a matter of getting her to apply similar thoughts, feelings, and perceptions to create new successes. By allowing athletes to talk about how and why they've succeeded, their self-perception changes. As they talk, it becomes apparent to them that they do indeed possess some of the necessary skills, strengths, and abilities to meet their challenges. Athletes begin to see themselves in a whole new way.

I also take great care not to stifle an athlete's thoughts and feelings. I may not agree with them, but I listen rather than judge, validating what she's feeling, rather than saying it isn't so. I heard a young girl cry to her mother once, "My arm really hurts." Her mother responded, "No, it doesn't." Instead of discounting her daughter's feelings, she could have said, "I can see that it is really hurting you, but it was a safe fall. You are going to be okay."

Once I validate an athlete's feelings, I find that her comfort level increases and she becomes more receptive to listening to what I say next. It also helps pave the way for asking questions. Too often, athletes are told what to do, when to do it, how to do it, and how well they did it. The result is that they lose their own voice. This fact seems to be especially apparent in adolescent girls. Anyone who knows an adolescent girl has probably observed her struggle to balance what she wants and who she is with what others want for her and think of her. At a time when everything about her is changing from her body to her thoughts, she finds herself confused by what she should be and do. Society provides norms about what she "should" look like and how she "should" behave, but these standards only serve to confuse her more. And at a time when she needs guidance, she distances herself from her support system, the family. She struggles to figure it all out, to feel independent and self-assured, but she may feel so lost and confused that she loses her own voice and becomes what she is told to be.

I try to assist young women in differentiating between their own voice and the voices of coaches and parents. I value her opinions and ask questions such as, "How does that fit for you?" or "What did you think about that?" It is critical to the emotional growth and happiness of young women that they differentiate between what they think and feel and what others think and feel. They must be encouraged to take the risk to identify their own needs and strive to meet them. As Mary Pipher puts it in her book *Reviving Ophelia*, "We reestablish each woman as the subject of her life, not as the object of others' lives. . . . Each woman wants something different and particular and yet each woman wants the same thing—to be who she truly is, to become who she can become."(1)

WHY FEMALE ATHLETES?

Today, 2 million girls play interscholastic sports and take the comment "You play like a girl" as a compliment. Slowly but surely female athletes are getting the recognition they deserve and as a result people have taken notice that girls do not experience sport in the same way as boys. The differences are evident at playgrounds across the country, where boys will tend to play organized games such as basketball while girls will be more likely to form small groups to talk. In the early years of sports, girls' reasons for participation tend to revolve around the social aspect, affiliation, and being on a team and then developing skills, but for boys the order is reversed.(2)

And as girls mature, sports can play a significant role in helping them achieve their independence in a healthy and empowering manner. In 1997, the President's Council on Physical Fitness and Sport released a report which compiled research information from the disciplines of psychology, sociology, and physiology. The report cites studies showing that girls' participation in sport enhances body image, self-esteem, confidence, and scholastic performance while it decreases school drop-out rates, and reduces the risk of many physiological conditions such as obesity, osteoporosis, and depression.(3) However, anyone who has been a teenage girl or knows a teenage girl can attest to the fact that adolescence can be a challenging time. Add the pressure to excel in sport, and it's not surprising that you find many adolescent female athletes experiencing sports-related problems.

The principles of sports psychology are not gender-specific, and although men and women share many similarities throughout their sports experiences, it has become evident that young female athletes have specific needs because of the different pressures and expectations they face not only in sports but in life.

Research has found that as girls enter adolescence, they begin to restrain the expression of thoughts, feelings, concerns, and questions in order to meet cultural demands of being a nice, good girl.(4,5,6,7) Other studies have pointed to the fact that girls are far more dissatisfied with themselves and with their bodies than are boys. They also experience more distress than boys and much more often direct this distress inward.(8)

As athletes, young women have the tremendous task of negotiating adolescence, a time of uncertainty and change, while simultaneously negotiating sports, a process of uncertainty and change. Although men, too, experience adolescence, the maturation process often enhances their sports performance by bringing new physical strength and confidence. For women, physical maturation may do the same, but very often does not. Women may become confused by their changing bodies, changing needs, and changing responses. Parents and coaches become baffled by the emergence of a new personality. Activities she once took great enjoyment in are suddenly a cause of great stress. She may lose her curiosity and become less inclined to take risks. In the past, situations that she easily bounced back from now seem to be major setbacks. As she changes, society's expectations for her change as do her reactions to situations, and these new attitudes and behaviors effect sports performance.

In the past, young female athletes have been solely responsible for dealing with their ever-changing selves. I have worked with so many athletes who at ten years old would become motivated and determined after a coach yelled at them. By the age of thirteen, those same young women would find themselves in tears, paralyzed by their coach's words. Many of these young women feel out of control. They are confused by their new reactions to familiar situations and assume, as do others, that something is wrong with them. No one seems to understand, and no one seems to have a solution. Coaches and parents tell them to shape up their attitudes, and they want to shape up to feel better, but often the feelings of powerlessness are overwhelming.

These young women search for ways to cope, but are left wondering where they can find control in a body and soul that feels completely out of control. Many resort to disordered eating in an attempt to empower themselves and take control of their lives. Some quit sports in an attempt to rid themselves of what they perceive to be causing them pain and confusion— quitting long before their talent has had a chance to develop or before their minds have had a chance to understand or benefit from the pursuit.

In order to respond to the needs of a young female athlete, we can apply principles and skills from the field of sports psychology to influence the athlete herself as well as her environment. By addressing her specific concerns and simultaneously structuring the environment in a way that helps meet these demands, we can provide a young woman athlete with the best chance of realizing her athletic potential and enjoying the process.

This book doesn't pretend to have all the answers or even most of them. It is a compilation of issues that I've confronted in my work with young female athletes and the ways in which I've tried to help. The names are not real and many times the examples are combinations of several different athletes, families, and sports. Some situations are more common than others; some may seem wildly improbable in regards to your own sports experiences. It is important to look at each scenario and take from it the lesson that is being taught and apply it accordingly. My hope is that you will be able to identify with some of the stories told and the approaches used and be able to help a young woman you know to develop a new way of thinking about herself and her own situation.

The biggest step is realizing how powerful the mind is in athletics and how it can be trained, just like the body, to help maximize the vast benefits sports participation can bring to a young woman's life.

1

First Things First: Getting Her Started

Tomboy. All right, call me a tomboy. Tomboys get medals. Tomboys win championships. Tomboys can fly. Oh, and tomboys aren't boys.

—Julie Foudy, member of the 1999 U. S. World Cup Championship Women's Soccer Team

Signing your daughter up for sports seems simple enough. You decide that you would like her to learn a sport, or she comes to you and expresses the desire to play. You choose a sport, find a coach, drive her to practice and games, and encourage her to have fun. Yet from the very first moment, questions arise that most parents aren't confident about answering. Participation in sports often requires much thought on the part of parents, but keep in mind there is no one magic formula for making the sports experience enjoyable and productive. However, there are some basic guidelines parents can use to address the many concerns with which they may be confronted.

SO, WHICH SPORT?

Five-year-old Molly is quiet and shy. Six-year-old Aida is rambunctious, raucous, and filled with endless energy.

"How do we find the right sport?" their parents wanted to know.

Molly and Aida obviously have vastly different personalities. Yet a girl's personality shouldn't be the only factor used to decide which sport she should try. Although for some sports aggressive play may be beneficial, this is not always the case, just as being a passive player is not always a detriment to sports performance.

I tend to suggest that very young girls, like Molly and Aida, be given the opportunity to have a variety of movement experiences. At young ages, it's important for children to discover the numerous ways their body can move. Youngsters primarily learn through imitation, and by the age of six or seven, most of the basic motor skills will be developed. As children move into preadolescence (six to ten years), sports will provide opportunities for socializing with friends and the development of more complex motor skills. At this stage of maturation, children begin to formulate self-perceptions of physical, social, and cognitive competency. Therefore, it's important to emphasize effort and attitude and provide experiences that she can master effectively.

Often, team sports are recommended in these early years because there is less pressure on individual performance. Success is judged by team effort and team performance, which helps children to feel successful. Girls learn the important lesson that they have a vital role to play on a team and as a result may be less inclined to place too much emphasis on their own shortcomings or abilities.

In individual sports, such as tennis or figure skating, girls learn self-reliance and motivation. Individual sports allow girls the opportunity to develop a set of motor skills with competition being a separate step in the learning process. Therefore, girls can find out if they enjoy the sport enough to pursue it at a competitive level. If they choose not to compete, individual sports typically have tests or markers of improvement which enable girls to perform while competing against themselves. Regardless of competitive involvement, individual sports will help them discover the necessity of finding ways to create success and process failure. Through competition kids will learn that their successes and failures are determined by their own performance. For some young girls, that kind of performance responsibility and pressure can be overwhelming. Most often, I recommend that young girls who want to compete try team sports in the beginning and, if they appear to possess the maturity to accept responsibility for performance successes and failures, then add on an individual sport.

A good gauge for parents is to watch their daughter during a game or practice. If she's someone who is happiest when being "on stage" or the center of attention, an individual or performance sport might be a good choice right away. In sports like figure skating or gymnastics, girls have plenty of opportunities to perform without having to sit on the bench. On the other hand, girls who express fear about being evaluated or judged often enjoy timed sports like track and field or swimming. Although these sports require individual performance, athletes are still part of a team and can experience a sense of belonging and support from the group.

What I like about team sports is that the life skills they teach are easily identifiable, and therefore even a child can be taught that these skills are transferable to other aspects of her life. Team sports especially emphasize cooperation and learning to work with others for a common goal. A small, young girl playing soccer, for example, can learn that by passing the ball to an open teammate, she can give the team a better chance to score. Girls learn to rely on one another, to trust a teammate for the good of the team, and to value the role of each player. Through team sports participation, girls can grasp the important concept that teams are chosen based upon strengths and abilities rather than popularity.

What I like about individual sports is that athletes must be self-motivated and self-reliant, as there are no team goals or team responsibilities to guide them. It's critical for them to develop a personal vision of where they want to go and how they will get there. Athletes learn to trust themselves physically and emotionally. However, many feel the pressure of being judged and valued solely on their physical abilities and competitive outcomes. In team sports, athletes' competencies can be evaluated and roles created to enhance their strengths. There are no such roles in individual sports. Therefore, individual-sport athletes must learn to value short-term goals as a means to achieving their long-term dreams. By placing importance on the small steps that lead to performance improvements, they are able to feel good about themselves regardless of overall outcomes. As a result, individual-sport athletes learn to create their own successes, but at times may find it difficult to separate their worth as people from their performance outcomes.

If shy Molly is to participate in a team sport, it would be helpful to find a sport in which she is equal in ability to the rest of the girls. This may alleviate some of her feelings of self-consciousness regarding her physical abilities. If a team is formed and a few "outsiders" are brought in to participate, those "outsiders" can be left feeling more like "outcasts." It would be an ideal situation if Molly already were friends with another girl on her team rather than being placed in the uncomfortable position of having to make new friends while also being judged on her physical capabilities. However, some leagues have a firm rule that prevents you from making team selection requests. Therefore, Molly may first need to try and socialize and become comfortable with the other girls before exploring the limits of her physical potential.

"Molly needs to learn that it's okay to feel scared about messing up or looking uncoordinated," I told her parents. "One of the reasons she might be shy is that she doesn't want to make a mistake. You need to let her know that in sports, it's okay to make a mistake, that everyone makes mistakes, but that you see her putting forth effort and taking chances as a real sign of success. By doing so, you place emphasis on the necessity of taking risks and putting forth effort, which are two critical life skills that can be acquired through participation in sports."

Soccer is a wonderful sport for girls to learn at Molly and Aida's age. In the beginning, it doesn't require skills other than being able to run and kick, and it teaches many motor skill fundamentals that will help them make the transition to other sports. At the beginning level, scores are rarely kept, and in fact, most often games are played without goalies so that it is easy for girls to score. Some leagues require that younger athletes play on a smaller field. They "shrink" the playing field to make sure each athlete, despite her level of aggressiveness, becomes involved. Once these players reach a certain age they graduate to a regulation-size field.

"If the field is big, sometimes a girl can stand way off on the other side and never even get close to the ball," a coach told me. "We call them the daisy pickers, or hair-twirlers. They're more interested in everything else except the game because the game is too far away. But if the field is small, the ball is bound to cross her path. And even if she just swats at it, she is involved. Eventually, she'll realize it's fun to be included in the action and most likely will start taking more of an interest."

FAST FACTS

➡ **76.3% of girls aged nine to twelve cited "fun" as the primary reason to be physically active.(1)**

Finding a Sport

- Ask questions. Find out if she likes running, throwing, swinging a bat or a racket. Has she seen a sport on television that looks like fun? What do girls in her neighborhood or school play? What sounds exciting to her?
- Try a few out. Take her ice skating, kick a soccer ball around in the front yard, shoot baskets at the local school, teach her somersaults, let her swing a bat as you pitch a whiffle ball to her, get out your old tennis racket—see what she seems to enjoy doing.
- Make phone calls. Check with the local YMCA or Boys and Girls Club, find out what's offered. Try calling friends who have older daughters and check with churches and schools. If there are no organized teams in your area, think about helping to develop one.
- Listen to her. If she hates doing the sport you choose, don't push. Find out why she seems to dislike it. Make sure it's not because she's afraid or shy. She may truly hate softball because it's too slow, or soccer because it's too fast. If that's the case, make sure she follows through on her sports commitment by having her finish the season or her scheduled lessons and then try something else.
- Examine your motivation. Ask yourself why you want your daughter to participate in sports. Make sure your motivations include benefits to your daughter's emotional and physical development, and not to fulfill some void in your own life. Choose a sport for her, not for you. Just because you were a great tennis player doesn't mean she will be. Nor does it mean that because you couldn't turn a cartwheel, she can't as well.
- Think alternative sports. The United State Olympic Committee has set up funding in four cities—San Antonio, Minneapolis, Salt Lake City and Atlanta—to help develop young athletes and en-

courage them to join in sports, such as fencing or diving, that aren't as familiar or accessible as more traditional sports. Your daughter might not be a great basketball player, but maybe she's cut out to kayak or play ice hockey.

A breakdown of what is offered is as follows:

ATLANTA: Targets athletes for canoeing-kayaking, judo, and team handball, and is scheduled to add another one or two sports in the near future.

MINNEAPOLIS: Offers biathlon (skiing and rifle shooting), cross-country skiing, curling, speed skating, team handball, weight lifting, and women's ice hockey.

SALT LAKE CITY: Promotes bobsled, luge, mountain biking, Nordic combined (cross-country skiing and ski jumping), ski jumping, and speed skating.

SAN ANTONIO: Offers badminton, diving, road and mountain biking, gymnastics, volleyball, and swimming; in the near future, may add track and field and soccer.

FAST FACTS

➡ Preschool children were studied to examine how young children interact in the context of learning fundamental motor skills. Findings showed that girls interacted in a cooperative, caring, and sharing manner while boys interacted in a competitive, individualized, and egocentric manner. In addition, both boys and girls tried to maintain their gender style of interaction when dealing with the opposite sex.(2)

HOW DO WE CHOOSE A COACH?

In the early years of sports participation, very often parents do not choose a coach. Instead, they rely on local school or recreation center leagues, which organize teams and activities. Most often, the coach is the mother or father of one of the players. Nevertheless, it is still important to make sure the coach stresses the process of sports participation, not just the results. Yes, winning is certainly more fun than losing and can serve as an outcome goal to motivate players. However, undue emphasis on winning can prevent athletes from seeing the other benefits of sports participation. Young girls need to learn that if they want to win they must spend the majority of their efforts focused not on the win but on how to win.

Before signing your daughter up for instruction or a team, I suggest spending some time observing the coach in practice and game situations. If you are considering an individual sport, you will have much more control over your choice of a coach. When picking a league, watching games allows you to see the various coaching styles within the organization. How does the coach react to failure? When a child cries, how does the coach respond? What kind of feedback is given? Is feedback distributed evenly among all players? There may be certain patterns that emerge with one league's coaches versus another but there is no guarantee that the coach assigned to your child's teams will be better or worse than most.

Throughout her athletic career, a girl will have many kinds of coaches with many kinds of personalities and training methods. Learning how to respond and communicate with the coach is critical to athletic success. Since this is such an important topic, a separate chapter has been devoted to coaching issues as they pertain to athletes moving up the competitive ranks. Yet parents and athletes must begin interacting and building relationships with coaches from the onset of sports participation. In the early years, it is critical that the coach shares the same ideals and values that you, as parents, view as vital to your child's development.

Reflecting back to the case of shy Molly, she may need a coach who will provide positive, nurturing feedback to help her process failure and success. If it appears the coach is someone who is a strict disciplinarian and doesn't interact much with the players other than barking orders, look for someone else. Up to the age of five, girls need a coach who provides fun, shares in that fun, and exposes them to a variety of body movements, activities, and games.

By the time girls enter preadolescence (six to ten), they are able to think about movement and verbalize their thoughts and feelings. At this stage of development, children are capable of viewing a situation from another person's perspective and can selectively attend to what is important while ignoring the unimportant. Preadolescent girls spend a great deal of energy and effort developing and nurturing friendships. Girls may suddenly have one or two best friends.

As the child enters these early school years, she will benefit from a coach who not only explains technique and strategy but actually demonstrates the incorrect and correct way of doing something. Coaches may need to help children develop strategies to remember the elements of a correct movement like counting steps or telling them to pick their leg up as if they were walking up a step. When providing movement feedback, it's critical that coaches provide information that is clear and descriptive. For example, someone who, instead of merely saying, "That was a smart play, Molly," says: "Good job, Molly. You saw that Kyra was open and passed the ball to her instead of panicking and kicking it away. That was really using your head to make a great play."

A detached coach is not going to help Molly. If she doesn't understand, she probably won't ask for help or pose questions and could easily be overlooked. She will follow the rules and the coach's orders, and almost never complain. Since Molly will rarely speak up, the coach will most likely pay her thoughts and feelings little attention. When she does choose to express herself, the coach's response to these words can have a direct impact on future behavior. If she is belittled or told to be quiet, her fear of speaking will only increase. A coach can help build Molly's confidence by asking for her thoughts and opinions about certain situations and events. The coach may find that Molly shies away from answering such questions because she is fearful there is only one right answer. The coach can guide her through this fear by telling her there is no right or wrong answer and asking, "If you had to take a guess, what might your opinion be?"

When choosing a coach for Aida, different needs must be considered. Due to her outgoing and rambunctious nature, she may get bored easily. Aida's parents might want to consider a coach who stresses fundamental skills that can be learned to channel energy, such as cooperation and concentration. A sport that keeps practice randomized, varied, and teaches a wide variety of skills—such as basketball, or gymnastics—probably would be suitable for Aida. A coach who runs efficient, interesting practices with little down time may have a better shot at keeping Aida's interest. The most critical factor in the selection of a coach is considering exactly what gains you as parents want your daughter to reap from participation as well as your daughter's own reasons for involvement. You may hope that she learns how to focus, while she may just want to have fun and make new friends. When it comes time to make decisions regarding which sport and which coach, both of these factors need to be weighed and discussed.

FAST FACTS

➡ According to a study done at the University of Virginia, if a girl does not participate in sports by the time she is ten, there is only a 10% chance she will participate when she is twenty-five.(3)

➡ Half of all girls who participate in some kind of sports experience have higher than average levels of self-esteem and less depression.(4)

Questions to Ask Yourself as She Gets Ready to Play

1. Are you committed to the champion or to the child? Sport is a journey that can teach a young girl valuable life skills. But only as long as parents don't confuse achievement with winning. If you can only commit yourself to supporting her sports participation if she is very talented and wins often, understand that is an unrealistic standard and sends the wrong signals. It is the process of competing, of being an athlete, that will help your daughter learn much more valuable life skills. Hire a coach to meet the needs of your future champion, so you can be sure to meet the needs of your child.

2. What are the reasons you have enrolled or want to enroll your daughter in sports? What do you hope she gets from the experience? Be honest with yourself and try to recognize if it is important to you for reasons other than her physical and emotional development. This awareness will help you to guide and support your daughter through her sports experiences.

3. Why does she want to participate in sports? Understand her goals. Is it to have fun? Make friends? Stay fit? In the beginning, she will probably want to participate to have fun and be with her friends. However, later her goals may change. Your goals for her may not

match her own goals. It is imperative that you understand and respect the benefits your daughter hopes to receive through sports. You can remind her of these goals, especially when she hits obstacles. Having an awareness of your daughter's goals will help you clarify and define your role in her sports participation.

4. Can you accept her victories and defeats in a rational manner? Every athlete fails. It is the one constant in sports. Failure is unavoidable, but the manner in which you react to success and failure teaches your child lifelong lessons. Being able to use sports success and failure as a learning experience is critical to your daughter's emotional and athletic growth. You are the ones she will look for to share her elation and devastation. In this role, you will need to be prepared to put your emotions aside, help your daughter express her own feelings, and try to see sports from her perspective.

5. Can you accept that your daughter will, inevitably, disappoint you? Can you accept your child's disappointment? There will be situations throughout your daughter's sports participation that will bring you great frustration. You may make personal and family sacrifices for sports and find yourself asking, "Is this really worth it?" That is an important question to ask yourself. However, as long as you expect your daughter to keep persevering through tough times, you must do the same. Preparing yourself to cope with frustration and disappointment is critical to sports success.

6. Can you give your daughter the autonomy to make her own decisions? When your daughter competes in sports, she is solely responsible for her play. She needs to feel in control of her athletic career, and you can help by letting her have input into decisions about sports. In the end, you as parents will determine who or what will drive the decisions. Sometimes, your child's wishes and desires will drive the decisions, and sometimes parental wishes and desires will drive the decisions, and sometimes family considerations will drive the decisions. However, sound decision-making regarding sports should include your daughter having a voice in the process.

7. Can you react to her performances in a way that teaches her appropriate coping skills? When children observe adults cheating,

yelling, complaining, and making excuses, sports can be a negative influence. Instead, be a role model and through your own actions teach acceptance of responsibility and proper behavioral skills.

8. Can you be patient and allow your daughter to develop at her own rate? Your child may not progress in the same time frame as her peers. Your daughter will be frustrated and disappointed with such lulls in learning, but plateaus in motor skill development are natural. As skill level increases, children will demonstrate smaller and smaller strides in learning. The improvement will be seen more in refinement and consistency of skills. You need to be patient, recognize the small improvements, and point them out to your daughter. When you avoid dwelling on why she isn't moving ahead and choose instead to emphasize the process of improvement, your daughter benefits.

9. Can you settle for personal improvement rather than wins? There are many steps and building blocks to winning. Your daughter will not always win, but may make huge personal improvements. Your daughter won't like losing. As parents, it is imperative that you help her recognize personal strides in performance and how they relate to her longer term goals. Outcome goals are necessary, but the truly important goals are the ones that tell athletes how to create the outcome. These are small-task goals, like "I need to think about keeping my eye on the ball." Although winning may not happen instantly, you are teaching your child how to give herself the best chance of winning by emphasizing the importance and joy of the small steps that ultimately lead to the realization of a dream.

10. Can you recognize your daughter's interests outside of sports? When you and your daughter are devoting so much time, money, and energy to sports, it can be difficult to remember that she has other facets of her personality. She is not just an athlete, but a sister, friend, daughter, artist, scholar, musician, etc. It is essential to recognize the importance of all these interests in her life. That doesn't mean she has to give equal time to each activity, just that you acknowledge that interests other than sports are a part of who she is and aspires to be.

QUICK QUESTIONS

How does the parents' role change as a girl progresses in sports?

In the beginning, parents are needed for practically everything. They are the main support system. Parents make the decision, provide encouragement, advice, and love. Children at this stage of sport involvement may only participate in a limited number of official practices with a coach and it is common for parents to fill this void by acting as a secondary coach. Parents may actually participate in the sport with their child, give pointers, and teach new skills. As she becomes more committed to sport, parents are needed less for additional coaching, but often more for encouragement and support. In later years, athletes become fairly self-sufficient and begin to accept responsibilities for their sports careers. Parents, however, remain an integral part of the competitive experience. As children become more and more committed to sports, a parent's role may appear to diminish more and more. This adjustment can be quite difficult.

Typically, parent involvement levels fall into three categories: Overinvolved, moderately involved, and underinvolved.(5) As a child's participation and progress in sports increases, parents may move from one category of involvement to another. Overinvolved parents tend to emphasize winning, view athletic success as providing later opportunities in education or career, and have difficulties separating their own wishes from the needs of their children. Very often they communicate to their daughter that love is conditional on performance.

Moderately involved parents tend to provide firm parental direction with flexibility. They allow their daughters to participate in decision-making. Although they are supportive, ultimate decisions about participation and level of achievement are made by the athlete. Parents take an active role in meeting with coaches and setting appropriate goals.

Underinvolved parents appear to have little interest in their child's sport participation. They don't attend games, talk with coaches, provide guidance in goal setting, or volunteer for activities related to the sport. Since little value is placed on participation, it can be difficult for children with underinvolved parents to become confident athletes.

FAST FACTS

➡ 80% of women identified as key leaders in Fortune 500 companies participated in sports during their childhood and identified themselves as having been "tomboys."(6)

Raising children in competitive sports can challenge even the most well-prepared parents. At every turn, families are faced with critical decisions and unique circumstances regarding athletic participation. Healthy parental involvement is an elusive standard that is not easily mastered. We've all heard horror stories of sports parents who place so much importance on their child's athletic performance that it becomes life-debilitating for the youngster. I've been to competitions where parents scream and their daughters cry. I've seen parents cry and daughters scream. I've talked to athletes who want to quit because parental pressure is too great. I've counseled other athletes who want to quit because they think their parents don't care enough.

All parents want the best for their children. But many place so much emphasis on winning, they squelch opportunities for long-term success and health. Often parents ask me, "How do I encourage excellence without becoming the proverbial 'pushy parent'?" "What should my role be when it comes to sports?" It is obvious they want to be supportive, but they also want to avoid unhealthy overinvolvement. Balancing the development of a champion with the development of a child is not an easy task.

When addressing this topic, I encourage parents to **AFFIRM** their children:

A—give AFFECTION regardless of performance outcome. Children need to know their failures and successes don't affect parental support or acceptance. Unconditional parental love gives kids a safe haven from which to launch lofty dreams and ambitions. Conversely, children who believe their worth to Mom or Dad increases with every ribbon and trophy will most likely buckle under the weight of unrealistic expectations. You can express unconditional love by communicating to your children that your love is based on who they are rather than what they accomplish. Avoid criticism after disappointing competitions and emphasize improvements in performance rather than results. Value who your children are as people by asking them for their thoughts and opinions, especially on topics unrelated to sports. Instead of asking, "How was practice today?" try asking, "How do you feel today?" When you show your children affection by sharing experiences and interests beyond sports, you affirm their value and reinforce their self-esteem. The pursuit of excellence is then transformed from a daunting task to a realistic goal.

F—be FOCUSED but don't coach. It is the parents' job to develop the child and the coach's job to develop the champion. So stay away from detailed technical discussions about performance. Instead, encourage your children to establish good goal-setting habits. On the way to practice ask, "What are your goals for today's practice?" "How are you going to work toward those goals?" That preliminary discussion serves as a great springboard for processing practice later. "What went well today?" And "What helped you reach your goals?" Or "What hindered you from reaching some of your goals?" These talks help clarify the goal-setting process, which is a valuable component of competitive success and an effective life skill as well.

F—be FLEXIBLE. At the first sign of success, single-minded parents place their budding athletes on the fast track to the Olympics without taking time to find out their goals and objectives. (And without discussing the time frame with the coach!) Some parents have to "die to their own dream" before their children can truly enjoy sports participation. Learn to set aside your own feelings and take cues from your children. Allow your agenda to be set by what is best for your children's long-term health and well-being, not short-term goals. Sometimes children may not want to talk about sports. Don't make them relive practice on the car ride home if they don't choose to share. Being flexible enables both you and your athlete to enjoy the journey more fully.

I—INTERACT without dominating the conversation. A supportive parent listens more than talks. Parents provide great comfort for children by creating a safe environment in which children know it is acceptable to express true feelings of loss and disappointment. A key element in establishing that safe environment is learning to listen with your ears and not your mouth. Listen for descriptive words that express how your children feel about themselves and their performances. It is natural for your children at times to speak negatively about themselves and their performances. However, when they begin to catastrophize the situation and make their negativity permanent by using such words as "always" and "never" or describing themselves as feeling "hopeless" or "helpless," your children need assistance in developing appropriate coping skills. Once they express their feelings, validate the experience by paraphrasing what you hear. For example, when your child tells you, "I'm so nervous," a typical response is to attempt to dispel the anxiety by saying, "Don't be nervous . . . there is no reason to be nervous." Instead, validate what you hear by saying, "I understand that you might be scared. Those feelings are natural before a competition. Even though you're anxious, I bet you can think your way through a great performance." By listening to your children, you communicate to them that their thoughts and feelings are worthy of expression and you respect their sport experience.

R—REFRAME. It's the parents' role to provide perspective. Remind your children of the bigger picture, which includes long-term goals and other aspects of their life, such as academics, friendships, family, and spirituality. Your guidance and feedback affirms that sport is only one aspect of a multidimensional life. This truth serves as a valuable balance to the pressures of competition. If your athletes are struggling after a difficult workout, try to reshape their view of the situation by asking open-ended questions that elicit positive responses like, "What went well today?" If they respond, "I don't know," try asking, "Well, if you had to take a guess?" Remind your children of the many benefits they receive as a result of their sports participation. As athletes gain perspective, the weight of the challenge lessens and they are more able to enjoy their involvement.

M—MODEL. Parents are some of the most powerful role models for children. Kids learn valuable coping skills watching Mom and Dad deal with difficult situations. Examine how you talk about your own day. Do you come home from work harping on the negatives, focused on the uncontrollable, and blaming others, or do you balance negative with positive and search for solutions to the uncontrollable? Show them it's okay to become frustrated, upset, or even angry while practicing and competing. But exhibit the healthy way to respond to anger and frustration. For example, when you get upset with your children say, "I'm really angry. I need to get my thoughts together before we discuss this any further. I am going to get some water. I'd like you to meet me back here in five minutes so we can discuss this." This lets them know it's okay to be angry and that effective responses and coping mechanisms for your anger exist. Live your own life with integrity by ensuring that your actions correspond with your values and beliefs. When you make mistakes, admit your errors, and explain to your children the more appropriate response. Your personal life experiences can provide powerful learning opportunities for your children.

With circumstances and personalities so varied, there certainly is no one formula for successful parenting of athletes. But by focusing energies on the child, parents can provide support, encouragement, and boundaries without becoming overbearing. Athletes may or may not realize their ultimate dreams in sports. However, when parents maintain a strong commitment to character development, they create an environment that gives their daughters the best chance for becoming a champion while ensuring they enjoy the journey.

FAST FACTS

➡ In a study of highly talented children in swimming, tennis, music, and dance, parents "were all genuinely concerned about their children and wanted to do the best for them at all stages of their development. To a large extent they could be described as child-oriented and willing to devote their time, resources, and energy to giving each of their children the best conditions they could provide for them. . . . To excel, to do one's best, to work hard, and to spend one's time constructively were emphasized over and over again. The athletes were encouraged to participate in sports at an early age, and this involvement was highly valued by parents. The parents strongly encouraged the child in his/her chosen talent field and gave less support to other possible talent fields. The parents were interested in athletics, encouraged participation in more than sport, and felt sports would enhance the child's life. Families played a critical role at every point in their quest for excellence."(7)

Now That She's Playing:
Keeping It Positive

Heroes and cowards feel exactly the same fear. Heroes just react to fear
differently.

—Cus D'Amato, former trainer of Mike Tyson

Once your daughter begins playing sports or taking lessons, it is critical for you to provide the proper emotional and motivational support
to help her get the most out of the participation and develop as an athlete
and young woman. Parents are in a position to transform sports from an
activity that simply develops motor skills to an experience that teaches life
lessons. In order for this to occur, parents must focus their feedback on
their daughter's mental approach to the game rather than simply on game
outcomes. Parents can show their children through their words and actions
that the process of winning is just as important as the winning itself.

In order to introduce young women to the many benefits of sports, it's
critical that parents have an awareness of the factors that affect performance. These factors include internal control, perceptions, and thoughts.
These factors influence performance, training, and the overall enjoyment
an athlete experiences in sports. This chapter provides a brief introduction
to the concepts of each, and throughout the book, you will find real-life examples of the ways in which these factors alter performance and the way an
athlete sees herself and her situation.

In the introduction, I discussed external pressures and internal pressures
that influence performance. Together, external and internal pressures make
up a model that I have termed the "Pressure Loop" (see Figure 1). It's im-

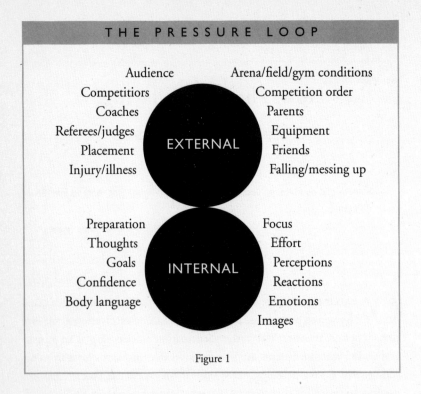

THE PRESSURE LOOP

EXTERNAL

Audience
Competitiors
Coaches
Referees/judges
Placement
Injury/illness

Arena/field/gym conditions
Competition order
Parents
Equipment
Friends
Falling/messing up

INTERNAL

Preparation
Thoughts
Goals
Confidence
Body language

Focus
Effort
Perceptions
Reactions
Emotions
Images

Figure 1

portant to introduce the concept of the Pressure Loop to athletes early in their sports careers. The Pressure Loop illustrates the way in which internal control influences the athletic experience. This internal control creates the foundation from which parents can use sport to teach children life lessons.

The external loop depicts the worries that athletes have identified as being important to them. Worry is produced when attention is directed to aspects of performance that are external or outside of a person's control. For athletes, these pressures come from worry about parents, coaches, media, spectators, officials, judges, placement, injury, competitors, falling, failing, and losing. I've found that many athletes spend the majority of their time thinking and worrying about the externals, which keeps their focus centered on the problem and can lead them to feel out of control and scared. Athletes consumed by worries about the uncontrollable and unpredictable describe themselves as feeling under pressure, helpless, hopeless, and simply "stressed out."

The internal factors can be used by athletes to deal with the external factors. These internals tend to be much more difficult for athletes to identify and therefore not much attention is paid to them. It is much easier for an athlete—particularly a young athlete—to grasp onto external issues because they are easy to define. She understands that she is worried about who is watching, whom she is competing against, or whether she will disappoint her parents or her coach. Yet most likely she cannot tell you how she copes with those worries. And very often, as she searches for solutions to alleviate her concerns, she finds her options very limited.

For example, an ice skater who doesn't like the way the ice feels before a certain performance keeps worrying about the ice conditions and uses that to reinforce her fear that she might not skate well. And yet there is nothing she can do about the condition of the ice. It's important for her to learn how to shift her focus from the ice—what she can't control—to an internal factor—perhaps thinking about what she needs to remember to land a certain jump or breathing deeply to relax herself and tune out the feel of the ice. This allows her to take charge of the situation by changing the way she views and addresses the problem.

Another example I see often comes when a coach tells an athlete something she doesn't like hearing. She then begins to ponder why the coach is in such a bad mood and may even rehearse in her head all the things she would say to her coach if there were no rules or consequences for expressing what she really thought at that very moment. This thought process keeps her focused on the coach (external and uncontrollable) rather than on her response to the coach's words (internal and controllable). If she replaced the thoughts about her coach's bad mood with other thoughts— about implementing the coach's information, or changing her body language to show that she was trying, or visualizing the correction, or using deep breathing to reduce her tension, or anything else under her control— she would be more apt to make progress and feel in control of her performance.

Teaching athletes how to use their thoughts, perceptions, images, body language, focus, and effort to move ahead are the life lessons of sports. Too many disregard the internal circle altogether, instead focusing their attention on performance outcomes. Their approach is to just try and eliminate all of the stressors in their life. However, if you eliminate all of the stressors from life, you end up having no life! Instead, athletes need to develop ways to respond and cope effectively with the various stressors they encounter. That's where the internal loop becomes critical to success and enjoyment. Athletes must learn to use qualities that reside within themselves and are under their control to respond effectively to their challenges.

INTERNAL CONTROL

"She's afraid they'll laugh at her."

One day a woman I know quite well called me to ask about her ten-year-old daughter, Amanda, who was playing on her first soccer team or rather, not playing on her first soccer team.

"She's fine with practice," Amanda's mother said, "but it's so hard to get her to go into the game because she's afraid everyone will laugh at her if she makes a mistake."

"What does her coach say?" I asked.

"Not much," she sighed. "He keeps telling her she should try, but she won't do it."

The orientation among young girls to feel self-conscious and worry about what others will think of them is quite common. Add in an eagerness to please parents, coaches, and teammates, it's not surprising that many young girls lack confidence out on the field. When an athlete has fallen behind in skill level, it can be difficult for her to perform and she often begins to believe that her lack of skill or perceived lack of skill is permanent. In her mind, it is inevitable that she will make mistakes because she has made mistakes in the past. Consequently, she believes that other athletes will make judgments about her athletic ability, and will laugh and ridicule her. It's important to make sure an athlete is given time to work on improving skills rather than just being thrown into performance situations that are simply above her level of play. If you allow her some time to just play in an unstructured environment, she can work on improving her physical skills without being self-conscious. Although this can prove to be a difficult time for your child, it's an ideal time for you to teach her to accept mistakes and lulls in learning as part of the sport process.

. . .

"Amanda, I hear from your mom that you are pretty scared about making a mistake while playing in a game," I said.

"Yeah. I know they want me to play, but I don't want to at all," she said.

"How do you know they want you to play?"

"They keep telling me that I'll be fine when I get out there," she said. "They say that I don't make as many mistakes as anyone else, but I know they are just trying to make me feel good. But I don't want to play."

"It sounds like you really mean it," I said, validating her feelings. "I wonder, though, if you knew there was no way you would make a mistake, I wonder if then you'd want to play?"

"Yeah, I think so," she said. "Because then the other kids wouldn't laugh at me, and I wouldn't look stupid."

"So, it's not that you don't want to play, it's that you want to play, you just don't want to make any mistakes," I said.

"Yeah," she said. "Everyone keeps telling me to think positive, but I can't. I just know I'll mess up."

"Well, I'm not going to try and convince you that you won't mess up," I said. "We can't predict whether or not you will or won't mess up. We can't even know whether or not kids will laugh at you."

"What do you mean?"

"Who controls what those other kids do or say?"

"I don't know. Not me."

"That's right," I said. "You don't control them or their actions or reactions to things. All you can control is yourself."

"Yeah, but I'm just scared," she said.

"I know that you don't want to mess up and thinking about it scares you. That takes a lot of energy, worrying about messing up. What if you tried putting all that energy you use worrying about your teammates and your errors into how hard you run up and back on the field or how much you pay attention to where the ball is or figuring out how you can help the team? Those are things you can control. When you worry about aspects of the game you can't do anything about, like what your friends say or messing up, maybe that's when you start to feel really scared and helpless."

"I might still make a mistake and they'll still laugh," she said.

"Yeah, they might," I said. "But you have a choice as to how you react, that's the key. I wish we could eliminate all the worries you have, but we can't. We all have worries. Worries are normal and natural. I remember I used to be really scared before I had to compete in skating. Sometimes, I felt like I could hardly breathe. Yet, what I came to realize was that even when I felt scared I could control the kinds of things I thought about when I got on the ice to compete. As long as I used my energy to create helpful thoughts, I could skate really well even when I was scared. So, you don't have to eliminate the fear in order to perform well. What you need to do is direct your energy and effort to the things that you can change about your performance. This puts you in charge, not anyone else."

"So, instead of thinking about how I might mess up and be made fun of, I should think about how to play better?" she asked.

"That's right. You may still feel scared about playing, but you give yourself a really good chance of playing well."

Even if Amanda was to make a mistake, if she was concentrating on something she could control, then she would also feel a sense of accomplishment, which just might override the fear.

"Helping Amanda," I told her mother, "means more than just telling her she'll be fine in a game. That places her focus on the wrong thing—the outcome of her performance. And as much time you spend convincing her she will be fine, she will spend just as much time convincing you and herself that she won't be fine. Remind her that soccer is something she wants to do. When you want to do something, you must focus your attention on how to get what you want. Help her identify the internals that could assist her in meeting the goal. At the very least, she will begin to feel more in command of her performance."

HOW CAN I HELP HER DEVELOP INTERNAL THINKING?

The best way is to lead by example. Through your own actions and words, you can place importance on the internal process of sport. When you come home from work, do you harp on the negative and uncontrollable? Or do you talk about how you might make yourself feel better about the situation? Show her there are many ways to choose to think about problems, and share with her events in your own life where you changed the situation by changing the very way you viewed the situation.

For example, say a coworker received a promotion you had hoped to get. Instead of directing anger at your coworker and talking badly about him or her, you choose to focus on yourself. You decide to see the situation as an indicator that the department is ready and willing to give promotions. You examine what actions you can take to improve your chances of receiving a promotion and decide to work on a specific project with more energy and creativity, spending less time complaining and more time enjoying the process of your work. You also decide to speak with your supervisor and get input about ways in which you can improve your chances of meeting the goal. Regardless of whether you receive the promotion or not, you have put yourself in control, and by changing yourself, you have changed the situation. Be sure to discuss with your daughter the actions you took that turned a potentially negative event into a productive learning experience.

Another way to promote the concept of internal control is to show her that you value it. When taking her to sporting events, be sure to point out the athletes you see applying internal skills to raise their level of play. For example, instead of praising the goalie for making a tremendous save, praise the athlete who made a mistake and quickly recovered. Ask your daughter for her opinion on how the athlete was able to do that.

And as your daughter progresses in sports, help her to see how she created her own success. Reassure her that mistakes and failures are only temporary setbacks. Instead of giving technical advice she's already received from the coach, concentrate on how she can change what happened rather than the fact that it happened. The questions you ask can promote internal thinking. So rather than giving advice or providing the answers, try asking a question. For example, if a soccer player made a bad corner kick that went out of bounds, rather than asking her, "What happened on that corner?" ask something like, "I wonder what you can do next time to make sure that corner kick ends up where you want it?" This gets her started in making a change in the way she views, thinks about, and controls her situation.

It's crucial to provide descriptive feedback about the inner strengths that may have affected your daughter's performance. Descriptive feedback focuses on how an athlete created the success rather than the success itself. For example, instead of saying to a skater, "Great performance," say something like, "I saw how you kept your shoulders down and your head up and that showed me you were trying to project confidence." Instead of saying to a basketball player, "Great free throw shooting at the end of the game," say something like, "I saw you take a few seconds to focus in on what you were about to do before you put the ball up. That was great concentration."

Many young athletes worry about making mistakes. Parents need to help them realize that as in success, there, too, is opportunity in failure. I often point out to athletes the choices they have available to them in dealing with failure or loss. They can quit sports. They can feel sorry for themselves and their performance outcome or they can find a lesson to be learned from the loss and use it to motivate them to be better the next time.

You may find that your daughter has difficulty finding a new perspective because she places too much emphasis on the probability of things happening a certain way rather than remembering to look at all the possibilities. Remind her that if she has the opportunity to fail, she also has the opportunity to succeed. All she has to do is acknowledge that success is possible. It doesn't have to be probable, but if she admits it's possible, then she can begin to choose thoughts, feelings, actions and images that will help her transform the possible into the probable.

FAST FACTS

➡ Mary Lou Retton's suggestions for helping put an athlete in control include allowing the athlete to pick her own music; involving the athlete in choreographing of routines; and keeping the lines of communication open with coaches and parents.(1)

THE INTERNAL SKILLS

Once the internal pressures are identified, athletes can begin to learn to apply the skills in practice and competition. When training the mind to handle the rigors of athletic competition, the first two internal factors an athlete needs to understand and strengthen are her perceptions and thoughts.

An athlete's perception is the way in which she chooses to see herself and her situation. It is quite common for an athlete to get stuck in one way of seeing herself, such as when she views mistakes and failures as devastating. I don't know many athletes who say after a poor performance, "Wow, that was a great learning experience." They probably have a conditioned response that doesn't consider looking at errors and failure as opportunities for growth.

If the way she sees herself does *not* match how she acts, performance will be affected. When an athlete's self-perceptions and actions match, she is quite comfortable. For instance, if an athlete believes she is capable of performing well and then performs well, she feels good. However, if an athlete sees herself as incapable of performing well and then performs well, she feels some discomfort, because her self-perceptions and actions do not match.

Most likely, she will explain away this inconsistency between how she sees herself and how she actually performed by attributing the success to luck. It's not that her self-perception was wrong, she simply was lucky enough to perform well this one time. As a result, this athlete can experience success after success and never feel confident. In order to feel confident, she must change her self-perception and take credit for the success. However, it can be extremely difficult to change self-perceptions. Many young women tell me they see themselves as incapable and actually perform terribly only to return after the performance to tell me, "See, I told you I couldn't do it." They actually find support for their negative self-perceptions rather than take the risk of altering the very way they see themselves.

FAST FACTS

➡ Self-efficacy deals with an individual's belief that she can successfully complete a task. Self-efficacy is not concerned with the skills one has but with judgments of what one can do with whatever skills one possesses.(2)

Perceptions

"She's doing well, but thinks it's because of luck."
Sabrina, a thirteen-year-old basketball player, recently joined a new

team. She didn't know any of the girls and was really nervous when she got into a game for the first time. Sabrina played extremely well, however, and took the last shot, which won the game. Later, her mother overheard her tell a new teammate that she must have been lucky to make that shot because she was so nervous and scared about it. Her mother asked me about this.

"Shouldn't she feel proud that she played well?" she asked.

I explained to Sabrina's mother that many of the young women I work with are afraid that if they attribute success to themselves, they will be seen as arrogant and stuck-up. And some are afraid that if they believe in their abilities and skills and then can't follow through, they will have failed. To them it is safer to pretend that they really don't expect or seek success. That way, if it doesn't happen, others won't think badly of them, because they never really sought success in the first place.

When you listen to boys talk about their play, you will often hear them discussing the great play they made or how they have really improved in their speed or strength. The other boys nod their heads and acknowledge these improvements. "Yeah, that play was so awesome. I've never seen anything like it." When you sit around and listen to young girls talk, the dialogue is quite different. It is usually about something they don't have or something they dislike about themselves. "I'm so fat," or "My skin is so broken out," or "Coach hates me," or "My backhand is so bad." They don't ever want to appear that they are bragging. For girls, it is acceptable to talk about all the qualities they don't like about themselves, not the attributes they do like. When something goes wrong, girls quickly attribute it to themselves—"I'm stupid" or "I'm not talented"—whereas boys tend to attribute it to something outside of themselves—"That ref gives such bad calls" or "That pitcher is so quick." Boys tend to see reasons other than themselves for their failure. This can help them maintain their confidence and keep them motivated to try again, knowing they have a chance to get it right next time.

Sabrina needs to be taught how to process her success. Her mother said that in the past, with her old team, she was quick to take responsibility for her failures. This was because she could easily identify what went wrong in a play. But when she encountered success, she had a harder time figuring out how she contributed to the good play. Many times this difficulty in taking credit for success is related to the fact that adults don't teach kids how to process success, only how to process failure. When kids are successful, adults say, "Good job." They don't say, "Good job. You squared your feet up just right and took a deep breath. That made it easier for you to make that shot."

This is essential descriptive feedback because it tells Sabrina how she contributed to her own positive outcome rather than just acknowledging the outcome itself. By processing her success in this way, Sabrina is given something to think about that she had not already considered. The descriptive feedback points out that she plays a vital role in her performance outcomes.

When I spoke with Sabrina, I asked her why she thought she was just lucky to have hit the winning shot.

"Because I was so nervous," she said, "it must have been luck."

"Well, let's say that you are right," I said. "But how many times have you practiced and hit shots like that, maybe not game-winning shots, but that shot in particular?"

She laughed.

"All the time—we practice that all the time."

"Do you think that maybe your hard work at practicing the shot might have been stronger than the nervousness you felt?" I asked.

"Could be," she said and smiled.

"I think it was an even greater accomplishment because you did it despite your nervousness," I said. "That was instinct and hard work paying off."

She beamed.

"Maybe you're right," she said. "I have worked hard."

It's meaningful when parents assist their daughter in taking credit and responsibility for her successes. It is not success itself that builds athletic confidence in a young woman, rather attributing the success back to herself. When children are encouraged to talk about how they created the outcome, this places value on the process of sports achievement, not just the result. Try having family discussions that revolve around successes rather than errors. This teaches children to think about and take pride in the good moments. When failure hits, alleviate some of the pressure. Parents don't have to find all the answers, rather, they should show their daughter that they trust she can figure it out for herself.

Parents can promote the idea of trust by valuing their daughter's opinion on a broad range of topics. Ask her for advice about personal situations, thereby sending the message that her thoughts and feelings are important. When she reports what a teacher, coach, or friend did or said, ask her how she feels about that comment or event. When she knows her feelings, thoughts, and opinions are accepted and viewed as important, she develops self-esteem. This self-esteem will provide her with great strength as she meets the demands and challenges of her many pursuits.

Perceptions can be powerful shapers of behavior, especially when they are paired with thoughts. Athletes' perceptions affect performance through their thoughts. The way athletes see a situation or see themselves directly affects what they choose to think about, which in turn affects how they perform.

Athletes have the power to choose to think in ways that give themselves the best chance of success. Many athletes believe that the way they feel about something is the same as the way they think about it. However, what one feels is separate from what one thinks. For instance, athletes can feel doubtful and scared before an event and manage to think their way through a great performance. Feelings and thoughts are separate internal factors.

When it comes to thoughts, athletes tend to have conversations in their heads called "self-talk." It is a technique that even the youngest of athletes can use as a springboard to the more advanced ways of using her mind to improve her performance. There are three different types of self-talk.

Most athletes are familiar with negative self-talk. Everybody, at times, thinks negatively. It's normal and natural. But when overused and without balancing it with the two other types of self-talk—positive and effective—the impact can be devastating to performance and enjoyment of sports.

Most athletes will tell you that to overcome negative thinking they try to think positively. They will also tell you that positive thinking doesn't always work, especially when they have a difficult time "buying it." When an athlete is really frustrated, the last action she wants to take is to say, "I can do it." At that moment, she doesn't believe she can do it, so the statement has little impact.

In this case, positive thinking doesn't help her through the situation because it keeps her focused on the outcome. Whether she is thinking positively or negatively, in both instances she is trying to convince herself that she will produce a certain outcome. This doesn't help her to figure out what to do to produce the desired result.

The key to working through frustration is applying effective thinking, which provides information to the body about how to change the situation. Effective thinking takes an athlete's focus off of whether she will or won't do it and instead places her attention on figuring out how to do it. It's a simple concept that is difficult to apply during times of frustration, but when done well has a tremendous impact on performance, training, and the way in which the athlete feels about herself. If she can train that "little voice" in her head to think positively and effectively rather than negatively, then she gives herself the best possible chance to succeed physically.

Take for example, a runner whose perception about her training is that it's too hard. As she runs, her self-talk will include statements to support how hard it is, such as, "This is so hard. I'm really tired today and don't feel like being here. I'm running such lousy times nothing is going to help. I wish I could just go home and go to bed." She could change her self-talk by first accepting that training feels hard and choose to think her way through a productive practice session. Her self-talk might include statements such as, "It feels really hard to train today so no matter what times I run, I will be learning to push myself when I feel lousy. I need to think about my stride and when I start to feel fatigued, work on my abdominal breathing. If I complete those two tasks, I will consider this a productive workout."

After a game or a practice, ask a young woman what she was saying to herself as she shot jumpers or hit a backhand. It's interesting to hear her responses, that is, if she can remember. Many athletes tell me they don't pay attention to what they are thinking. Even more tell me they were saying, "Don't miss it, don't miss it." I encourage athletes to direct that "little voice" in their head to provide the body with useful information. Effective thinking involves telling the body how to do a skill, like "arch it lightly," or "racket-head level," or whatever statements have helped them produce success in the past. Some athletes think up phrases or rhymes to help them get through difficult training routines or performances, such as "Stay tight to keep it light," or "Run to fun."

FAST FACTS

➡ Athletes who are predominantly task-oriented determine their success by effort and skill improvement. When focused on task goals, athletes are more likely to behave in a motivated manner.(3)

Thoughts

"I'm afraid she's not very athletic."

Sandra is an eleven-year-old softball player who rarely gets into the game. She can't hit, can't throw very far, and is afraid of ground balls. Still, she wants to be part of the team. Her best friends are on the team, and they have great pizza parties after every game. However, Sandra is becoming more and more upset because she doesn't play much and when she does, she usually makes a mistake. Her parents try to be supportive and positive, but are afraid of what damage this might be doing to her confidence.

This is a very common situation. Not every player on the team can be the superstar. It is important that Sandra's parents continue to remind Sandra why she's on the team—friendship, camaraderie, being part of something fun. If Sandra can feel that she has a role to play on the team, then she can be a great addition even if her skills aren't at the same level as the other girls.

Hitting better and throwing farther are great goals, but very broad, general goals that take a long time to accomplish. I suggested to Sandra's parents that they help her break those goals down into smaller components.

"What is one specific task she can do to hit better?" I asked her father.

"Well, for one, she needs to learn to keep her eye on the ball," he said.

"Then that's what she should think about," I replied.

I met with Sandra one day after school, and told her about my plan to have her think about one specific goal each day in practice for a week.

"Today," I told her, "I want you only to think about keeping your eye on the ball. Just that. I don't want you to think about your swing or stance or anything other than watching that ball. I want you to actually swing, but you are only to think about keeping your eye on the ball."

Sandra seemed a little perplexed.

"Just that?" she asked.

"Just that."

At the end of the week, I met with Sandra again.

"Did you think about keeping your eye on the ball?" I asked.

"Every day," she answered. "I did what you said. I thought only about watching the ball, watching the ball, and I tried hard, but it didn't—"

I cut her off.

"It doesn't matter what the result was," I said. "You accomplished the task I gave you. It's not easy to think about only one part of the swing. In fact, it's really difficult. But all the great athletes teach themselves to control their thoughts. By succeeding at that task, you just took one step in improving your game and your skills as an athlete."

Sandra smiled at the realization.

"I guess I did," she said.

I met with her parents after that week and told them to assist Sandra in picking a new technical focus point each week. Sandra was already realizing that by improving her mental skills, she was placing herself in a better position to improve her physical skills. I told them to continue to praise her for making those strides. I also suggested they call her coach and let him know about the program so that he could reinforce Sandra's progress in her effort, concentration, and self-talk.

If Sandra continued to be surpassed in ability level, she would probably at some point be cut from the softball team. I told her parents to make sure that she had other activities in her life at which she was progressing. She could always transfer the skills she learned in softball to another sport or activity where her strengths would be better used.

"Always remind her," I told them, "that what she is learning from softball—even if it's how to control her thoughts—is something that will last forever."

QUICK QUESTIONS

How can I help build her confidence?

Parents can teach children about confidence by helping them to take credit for their successes. It's important to communicate to a young woman that confidence is a private belief in herself and doesn't require that she outwardly express this belief to others. Let her know it's appropriate to discuss and take pride in accomplishment by having family discussions that revolve around the good behaviors of family members. Parents can talk openly about their own successes and explain how they feel they created them. Be sure to publicly praise children not just for the result but for the behavior that produced the result. Every once in a while catch your daughter doing something right.

When failure occurs, let it go. Help her accept it, figure out what to do differently, and move on. Even after a dismal performance, find something positive about it, like, "You played your heart out," or "I know how hard you were trying." Parents can help rechannel bad feelings by pointing out something under her control that she accomplished, such as, "You really maintained focus even when you missed that spike," or, "I know missing that jump made you mad, but you went on to skate wonderfully. That's tough to do."

Try to ask open-ended questions that elicit a positive response, like, "What do you think you can do this week to help correct things that went wrong?" instead of, "Why did you do that?" It can be helpful to place a great deal of emphasis on her opinion of her performance instead of zeroing in on the comments of others. Ask how she felt and what she thought and pay close attention to the feelings expressed so you can reflect back to her what you heard. For example, your daughter tells you, "I'm so angry at the coach. She yelled at me today and I really didn't deserve it. Sometimes I do, but today I was giving one hundred percent effort." You respond, "It sounds like you were really giving it your all today at practice. I can hear that you are frustrated with your coach for not recognizing your tremendous effort. I can understand that you might be angry for not getting the positive feedback you had expected."

Guide her to acknowledge all of the factors that may have affected performance, even ones that aren't directly about her. For instance, when she plays great basketball but gets beaten, does that mean she is part of a lousy team or that the other team had an awesome day? Point out the specific tasks you think helped her to succeed and value those aspects of her performance more than the outcome. No matter what, help her to take responsibility for her success. If you find that she is only willing to be accountable for failure, building her confidence will be a daunting task.

FAST FACTS

➡ Exercise and sports participation can be used to enhance mental health of adolescent females by offering them positive feelings about body image, improved self-esteem, tangible experiences of competency and success and increased self-confidence.(4)

SHE'S GOOD, BUT HER TEAM ISN'T

Amber, twelve, is by far the best player on her lacrosse team. She plays every minute of every game and is often the star. Her team, however, is not very good, and more often than not, they lose. Amber's mother worries that her daughter is getting discouraged and not really trying anymore. Amber is increasingly frustrated when someone makes a mistake or a bad decision, especially when those errors have cost them an easy win. "She knows she's the best on the team, but she can't understand why nobody else is stepping up to help win games."

"Amber needs to take a long look at how she got to where she is and realize that her teammates allow her the forum to be a great player," I said. "Those same teammates are just as important to the team as she is just in different ways."

I told her mother to try watching a game and identify a role for each player on the team. She could point out to Amber the various contributions players make. Amber's mother would need to emphasize that there are many ways for Amber herself to improve as a player, even in a situation where the other girls are a level behind.

"What weaknesses does Amber have, do you think?" I asked.

"Well, patience for one," her mother said and laughed.

"And patience, believe it or not, is an important part of becoming a really great and self-confident athlete," I said. "If you stress the long-term goals to her, rather than the shorter term outcomes, she might be able to see that she can improve in the current situation."

"Amber," I asked her one day. "What upsets you most about your team?"

"Well, we're not very good. I do okay, but nobody else seems to know what they're doing. They're making dumb decisions, nobody plays hard and we lose."

"If you could help them become better," I said, "what would you do?"

"Well, I'd probably go back and have them learn the basic things, like passing and positioning."

"Have you suggested this to your coach?" I asked.

"Yeah, he says I'm probably right and sometimes we work on those things, but it doesn't seem to help."

"Do you think you can improve your game?"

"Yes, I know I need to do that, but I can't on this team," she said.

I asked her whether there might be a way for her to improve her own skills while still being a part of the team. Perhaps she could find some older players to work out with from time to time. On off days, she could organize workouts with some of her teammates and work on the fundamentals that need improvement.

"What are your strengths?" I asked.

"Well, I'm good with the stick and I score a lot of goals because I'm quick," she said.

"What are your weaknesses?" I asked.

"I think I need to get better at my passes and defense," she said.

I suggested that at practice and during games she concentrate on beefing up those skills rather than thinking about how everyone else was playing and whether they were winning or losing. Once she looked for solutions, her focus would no longer be on the problem. Then, maybe her role on the team would change from star to leader.

"By working on your game, working to make yourself better, you'll challenge yourself and stay motivated and interested," I told her. "Think about taking your own game to the next level. It's okay to feel down about losing.

Yet, losing in and of itself can't prevent you from making yourself a better player."

Winning is a wonderful part of a young woman's sports experience. But if the focus is solely on winning, she is bound to end up frustrated and disappointed because, more often than not, she won't win. Processing losses—even a lot of losses—is an important skill for parents to teach. Being able to deal with success often comes naturally, while knowing how to take failure and use it as a stepping stone to success requires much more work.

In Chapter 6, I talk more thoroughly about ways parents can help their daughters to identify and grasp the concepts of internal control, perceptions, and thoughts. But it is important to introduce these skills early as a way to deal with the immediate problems and pressures that face even the youngest athletes. These skills can produce changes in the way an athlete feels, thinks, acts, and ultimately performs. Gaining an awareness of internal control, perceptions, and thoughts and learning how to apply these principles to the sports arena will help her deal not only with sports performance, but with life challenges as well. Even if an athlete is never capable of reaching her ultimate goal, helping her learn to take charge and find ways to meet her challenges is truly a lifelong gift.

FAST FACTS

➡ 208 high school students identified as having the promise of exceptional talent in the areas of art, music, athletics, mathematics, and science were studied to identify ways in which they differed from students with more ordinary talents. Talented teens had skills that were considered useful, had personalities conducive to both hard work and openness to experience, had economized their attention and diverted more of their energy into their talents, had more conservative orientations toward sex and the opposite-sex peer relations, reported that home environments provided both support and challenge, were most influenced by teachers who created an environment in which they felt supported and stimulated, and found their involvement to be both satisfying at the moment and promising of long-term rewards.(5)

3

Coaching the Coaches: Making Sure She Gets What's Right for Her

Always remember the tremendous power you have as a coach to help another human being maximize their potential; pursue this awesome responsibility daily with intensity and integrity.

—Dr. Harvey Schiller, CEO and chairman of YankeeNets and former executive director, U.S. Olympic Committee

Many top athletes tell me that their coaches along the way were a greater source of influence on their lives than their teachers, their peers, and at times even their parents.

"I learned how to focus, how to stick with something until I got it right, how to work and push myself harder than I ever thought possible because of one coach I had," an athlete told me recently. "His influence on my life was immeasurable."

Because of their significance in your daughter's life, choosing coaches and monitoring their coaching methods, techniques, and strategies is extremely important. It's vital that coaches understand how substantial their role is in shaping the way an athlete feels about herself as a sportswoman and as a person. How she is coached will have an impact on her life both on and off of the playing field.

When choosing a coach, parents must first attempt to find out how the coach approaches and deals with different situations. Investigate before deciding. Find out how much emphasis the coach places on winning. Yes, winning is important, but it is not the sole reason your daughter is playing sports. Make sure to remind yourself and your daughter's coach of this point.

Ask the coach how decisions are made with regards to scheduling, time commitments, and expectations about attendance at practice. Find out how the coach handles disciplinary issues. Has he ever thrown an athlete out of a game? Out of practice? For what reasons?

Make sure you understand how playing time is decided. Is it based on attendance and attitude? Is every player given the opportunity to participate? Does the decision involve a player's skill or the team's needs? Coaches have different ideas on how to decide playing time, and often the criteria used depend upon the level of athletes being coached. It's important that both you and your daughter understand the standards being applied and hold the coach accountable to these policies. Most of all, make sure the coach's guidelines correspond with your idea of what your daughter's sports experience should entail.

Choosing a coach who is also able to structure a healthy training environment for your daughter is critical. Parents create a safe and open environment for their children at home. The coach must create one at practice. It is a delicate balance.

Healthy environments are structured to meet an athlete's many needs. Just as parents must recognize all dimensions of their daughter's personality, a coach needs to recognize all the reasons why an athlete participates in sports. For example, competitive ice skaters are generally required to train up to three hours a day, not including off-ice strength training and lessons in dance. With that rigorous schedule, it is important that a skater also has fun and is able to enjoy the companionship and camaraderie of other skaters. By being aware of the need for fun, coaches can structure the environment in a way that combines rigorous training with some alternative activities that are useful yet amusing as well—for example, allowing athletes to work with one another or providing rewards such as ringing a bell when athletes show good effort. The result of that mixture is improved motivation and enhanced performance. Remember, children are supposed to play sports, not work sports.

Effective coaches also know how to adapt to the individual. It is a difficult task to adjust coaching to different personalities, but it is warranted at times. For example, a gymnast who is extremely hard on herself will not benefit from long and extended periods of yelling and negative motivation. Her own negativity coupled with the stinging words of the coach leave this athlete with little resources to fight back and turn the situation into a challenge. Instead, she disintegrates, using the coach's negative words to reinforce her own negative self-perceptions. It would be more effective for the coach to teach her ways to refocus negative thoughts in order to get back on track. This is not to say that coaches don't need to set limits and demands. They do. It's the coach's job to push an athlete to raise her own expectations. Yet coaches are most effective in that role when they find a method that suits each child. What motivates one athlete may not motivate another.

HOW CAN I TELL IF A COACH IS RIGHT FOR MY DAUGHTER?

To answer that question, parents can begin by analyzing their own values. For example, what are you looking for in a coach? Do you want someone who values just the champion or the child, too? Do you want someone who is going to befriend your child and spend a lot of time instilling values of sportsmanship and good behavior? Do you want someone who is going to provide technical information and expertise? Do you prefer a coach who will interact with your daughter a lot? Do you want a coach who uses a support team of people as a complement to his or her program? Is it important how a coach reacts to and deals with an athlete's disappointment and failure? Is it important to know what kind of goals the coach has for your daughter and for his or her own career? What type of plan and time frame does the coach have for meeting those goals? What does the coach see as your role? How does the coach like to resolve conflict?

It's important to address such questions and ask them up front before commitments to the coach or league are finalized. This way all of the expectations for coach, parent, and athlete are out on the table. You know what you are getting, and differences in expectations can be negotiated. You can choose to accept those qualities about the coach that you don't like or train somewhere else.

Too many people look to one coach to meet all of their daughter's needs. In reality, coaches have different roles. One coach may be really tough, a motivator, the person for whom the athlete learns how to perform. Although this coach may not provide a lot of support in terms of listening to athlete and parent concerns, there may be someone else on the training team who does play such a role. In other words, you may not be able to find everything you are looking for in one person. Look at the coach's strengths and figure out if those strengths match some of your daughter's needs. Then you can address whether or not you can find other people or other ways to meet the needs that this coach won't be able to satisfy.

If you know that as a parent you would like weekly contact with the coach, ask if this can be arranged or suggest something more manageable, such as biweekly or monthly meetings. Be clear about how you would like to see a coach deal with your daughter's anger and frustration. Find out how the coach deals with difficult situations, like an unmotivated athlete or an overmotivated athlete. If your child is negative, ask the coach how she might respond. Watch the coach in action and be sure to determine whether the coach treats every athlete exactly the same or accounts for individual differences and trains athletes accordingly. Take your daughter for a trial run before making any quick decisions. Watch the coach-athlete interaction and see how your daughter responds to different coaching styles. Above all else, once you are getting ready to select a coach, make sure your daughter is informed about how the coach will treat her in various situations. Your daughter may decide not to train with a certain coach because of the motivational style used, but at least you haven't had to endure seven months of displeasure to find this out.

When looking for the right coach keep in mind that recent research has shown that training environments do affect an athlete's sports experience. One study found that female gymnasts who trained in environments they perceived to be task oriented—those that rewarded hard work and personal improvement and promoted cooperative learning—had higher self-esteem, better body images, less stress, and more enjoyment of their sport than did those athletes who trained in environments they perceived to be ego oriented—those that encouraged rivalry among athletes and winning at all costs and in which greater attention was paid to the most talented athletes.(1) Remember, motivation and performance are affected by a combination of both personal factors and the environments within which children train.

FAST FACTS

➡ Amanda Borden, 1996 Olympic gold medalist in gymnastics, attributed much of her athletic success to her coach, Mary Lee Tracy. Factors she identified as being important included feeling that her coach was her best friend; that her coach cared about her as a person first and a gymnast second; and being able to communicate with her coach.(2)

QUICK QUESTIONS

Are female coaches better for female athletes?

I can't answer this with a definitive yes or no. Every athlete has specific needs, and one athlete may respond better to a male coach while another does better with a female coach. I don't necessarily believe it's a male coach versus female coach issue, because it is important for both male and female coaches to understand the female sports perspective. Coaches and research groups have identified some consistent themes in the female sport experience. Coaches, whether male or female, should be aware that female athletes tend to want to develop personal relationships with them and prefer coaches who communicate openly and are empathetic. Female athletes value friendship and like to focus on team unity. This team unity often results from their sensitivity to the thoughts and feelings of their teammates. They place a high value on personal improvement and prefer not to have their confidence attacked. When it comes to disclosure of feelings, they may be more comfortable talking with a female coach than a male.(3)

Athletes I've spoken to at all levels have not expressed a uniform opinion on this issue. To them, it is most important to have a competent coach who cares about them as people and as athletes. There is some feeling that males are used to coaching predominantly male sports and therefore are not in tune with a woman's experience in sports. However, an inexperienced female coach can be just as out of touch with the female sport experience as a man.

FAST FACTS

➡ Val Ackerman, president of the WNBA, states, "I think our teams are less concerned about whether [the coaches] are men or women than what their job qualifications are."(4)

In order to maintain a productive coach-parent relationship, it's critical to have an awareness not only of how a coach intends to handle certain situations but of the manner in which a coach actually implements training philosophies. The way in which a coach structures practice, uses discipline, prepares for games, and interacts with individual athletes is critical to shaping the sports experience for your daughter. When looking for a coach, typically you will see one of these three types of coaches:

Do As I Say—This coach treats athletes like robots. The coach holds all of the control. The coach directs practices and controls communication. The athletes are expected to show up and do as they are told. Decisions are to be accepted because the coach says they were made in the best interest of the athlete or team. The outcome is the primary focus, and mistakes are punished. Very often, rivalry among athletes is promoted and encouraged.

It's Your Sport—Athletes hold the majority of the power; they are required and expected to self-motivate. The coach acts as a technician and source of information for skill development.

The Complete Champion—This coach values athletes' opinions and looks for their guidance in decision-making. The coach adjusts training style to athletes' needs and develops goals and action plans with their input. The athletes and their coach work as a team to find ways to help meet their stated goals. The coach maintains respect and authority by providing clear expectations and discipline in a caring manner. This coach helps athletes learn to take control of their own performances by valuing self-improvement and cooperative learning.

Remember, your daughter will have many different types of coaches throughout her athletic career, and adjusting and adapting will be a key challenge for her. As a parent, you can encourage her to incorporate mental skills into practice and use internal control, perception, and thoughts to

help her deal with different situations that arise concerning the relationship she has with her coach.

HOW TOUGH SHOULD A COACH BE?

Karen is the coach of a twelve- and thirteen-year-old soccer team. She
has coached girls for ten years and has always believed in positive coaching.
Several of the parents, however, would like to see her crack down, be tougher
on the girls, provide more discipline and rigid training standards. She admitted to the parents that she'd "like to give these girls a big, swift verbal
kick in their rears" but was worried that it might do more harm than good.

So who's right? What style of coaching works best?

It's an interesting question. Throughout sports history there have been
differing views on how to coach and motivate young athletes. There are
many who believe that humiliation and fear tactics are effective methods.
However, I have never believed that you get much in the long term by
stripping athletes of their dignity, which undermines their ability to feel
good about themselves and to take the physical and emotional risks required to be successful. As girls mature and go through adolescence, they
may lose their optimism, self-confidence, and resiliency. Therefore, encouragement from adults can be particularly empowering for adolescent women.
A little inspiration may get her started on the path to trusting what she
thinks and feels.

A few years ago a young and upcoming gymnastics coach came to me for
advice, torn as he was searching to define his own coaching philosophy. His
training as a coach had occurred in a system that instilled fear in gymnasts
and one that had been extremely successful in terms of producing champion after champion. Unfortunately, these seemingly effective coaching
techniques had contributed to producing young women who were scared,
were stressed-out, lacked enjoyment in their sport, and had low self-esteem.

"I just am not sure what to do," he told me. "Everyone looks out for the
whole athlete here, but I wonder if it will produce champions? I feel like
I'm looked down upon when I yell at the kids, but sometimes they need
that. Some athletes really respond to it."

"Well, I agree that some athletes do respond to being yelled at and having very clear expectations set," I said. "However, others don't. It's a challenge

to know how to motivate each individual. The most important concept to remember is that the yelling itself doesn't change performance. What happens is that when you yell, you inspire the athlete to change herself and her approach in some way. So, she changes. It is the changes within her that affects performance, not the fact that you yelled. That is why yelling will work for some and not for others."

"But do you think that you can be nice and still get the most out of athletes?" he asked.

"I think there are a variety of coaching styles that produce top performers," I said. "You can be consistent, clear and firm about your expectations without ridiculing or tearing a child apart. There is a big difference between stating your expectations and getting a child to push past her limitations and attacking her as a person for mistakes and failures. I haven't seen that threats and intimidation work very well for the long term. They tend to have short-term effects, but kids can't tolerate that kind of pressure and stress day in and day out. They get emotionally burned out from striving to avoid the wrath of the coach. Eventually, they lose their enjoyment of the sport and their stress increases to an intolerable level. Then I get a phone call that they want to quit."

"So, you wouldn't use fear at all?" he asked.

"I try and get coaches to eliminate threatening in their coaching," I said. "I'd rather have them explain their rationale behind a coaching technique or philosophy."

I gave this example. A gymnast doesn't complete her series on beam. Instead of threatening to throw her out of the gym and telling her she can never come back, I suggest that her coach first choose to attack her behavior by changing the purpose of the practice. Say something like, "I can see you haven't committed fully to this skill and that you are getting frustrated. When you commit to your series you do it beautifully. It's much easier to do your series when you don't have any fear. However, today you have some fear, which makes this skill ten times harder. You already know how to do this skill when you don't have any fear, now you need to teach your body to do it when you feel scared. In order to do this, we need to break the skill down and focus on each technical element. I want you to pad the beam and then think only about keeping your shoulders blocked. I need you to do five in a row with the correct technique. You'll have to stay on this rotation until you complete the assignment. I don't care if you hit them, just get your shoulders in the right position." This way, I explained, the coach would be setting clear boundaries and guidelines but also changing the purpose of the practice, thereby making it more worthwhile for the gymnast to at least attempt the skill. He attaches a consequence to the behavior without phrasing it in a threatening way. He provides her with a reason to take the risk of doing the skill even if it isn't perfect. This type of language is not belittling and yet can be stated strongly without the athlete feeling dumb or stupid about her fear and mistakes. In turn, the coach makes it more likely that she will take the risk of doing the skill because she is no longer assuming that to complete the skill she must be free of fear. Instead the task is to work productively with the fear.

When athletes are younger, they may respond to temper and outbursts of anger. If a coach gets angry and they perform well, typically both athlete and coach attribute the success back to the coach's behavior rather than to an internal change and response in the athlete. This only leads athletes to feel powerless about their performance. It's critical to discuss with the athlete her own response to the demands and figure out how it positively affected performance. This empowers her to take responsibility for the success.

"If you do happen to get really angry and lose your temper, process it with the athlete after it's blown over," I told him. "Ask her, 'When I got mad, something in you changed. What was that? How did you get yourself to perform knowing I was so angry?' Throw the ball back into her court and help her figure out how she changed her own performance."

It's important that parents remember that a tough coach doesn't have to yell and scream and intimidate. A tough coach is consistent about setting clear, challenging expectations and requiring athletes to give 100 percent in trying to meet those expectations. A coach does need to push an athlete beyond what she thinks she is capable of accomplishing. Effective coaches use what I call "perform on demand" coaching. The coach might ask the athlete to perform three release moves in a row and if she misses one she must begin over again. The coach is testing the athlete and placing pressure on her similar to the pressure she will feel at a competition. These drills help teach her how to perform. Athletes who learn how to perform for the coach gain valuable experience for performing under pressure. However, I don't recommend requiring "perform on demand" exercises on a daily basis. It is easy for athletes to get emotionally and physically exhausted from the constant pressure of having to perform. Instead, specific times during practice need to be set aside for these performance tests, and the coach should take time to explain the benefits the athlete will receive from completing the exercise. These drills can also be used to work on mental training. When an athlete devises key thoughts to focus on, her chances of dealing with the pressure and completing the task successfully improve. A key thought, phrase or image provides the athlete with some internal control over her performance. It's the coach's job to point out errors, give corrections, discipline lack of effort, and be demanding—but coaches can be demanding without resorting to ridicule or humiliation. If you see a coach resorting to that, check out whether it's a pattern of behavior or just a one-time event. If it appears to be a pattern of destructive behavior, it is up to the parents to step in and have a discussion with the coach.

FAST FACTS

➡ Higher player ability and more frequent praise and information from coaches (in response to good performances/effort) was related to higher perceived competence in adolescent female hockey players.(5)

HER COACH DOESN'T KNOW WHAT HE'S DOING

Sandra and Bill are the parents of Debbie, an eleven-year-old basketball player. Bill played college basketball and has coached Debbie since she was five. Now she's playing for another coach, who Bill feels doesn't know what he's doing. Away from practice and games, Bill continually bad-mouths the coach, and his daughter has begun to bad-mouth him, too. Bill is considering taking his daughter off the team because he doesn't think she'll learn anything. Sandra, on the other hand, believes her daughter will have many different kinds of coaches if she continues to play sports and needs to learn how to adjust. Debbie doesn't know whom to believe.

This is a very serious situation, because as soon as parents criticize the coach in front of their daughter, the coach is immediately demoted in the athlete's mind. One of the greatest compliments I have ever received came from a young athlete who told her mom that I could explain the rationale of a coach without putting down or criticizing the coach. Yet by exploring the coach's rationale, I was able to help the athlete feel better about her situation and choose appropriate coping skills. Coaches are certainly wrong sometimes. But rather than criticizing them behind their backs, parents would be better served to deal directly with the coaches. By pointing his finger at the coach, Bill does not affect the situation positively and actually helps to further break down the relationship between coach and athlete.

Instead of making accusations, Bill might better help Debbie by engaging the coach in a discussion about tactics and strategy. Bill will want to avoid attacking the coach because doing so will only lead the coach to defend his position and stance. By sticking to tactics and strategy, which are truly the issues, the coach will be more likely to open up and have a discussion with Bill. This exchange of dialogue might give Bill an understanding of the coach's rationale for certain decisions and these explanations may change Bill's perspective.

With Debbie, Bill needs to remind himself that he doesn't coach her anymore. Although her new coach's style may be quite different from what she is accustomed to, that doesn't necessarily mean it is bad. Bill should find a way to point out the positive behaviors of the coach, which would, in turn, help Debbie build trust in the coach. If her father highlights only the negatives, Debbie isn't going to listen to any good information the coach most likely possesses. Bill can always supplement certain skills and drills at home without undermining his daughter's trust in an authority figure.

Bill needs to remember that Debbie's coach has an entire team of athletes to worry about while Bill has only one worry—Debbie. So each of these men will make decisions differently because they have different responsibilities. Bill could point this out to Debbie by saying, "Coach Hinzlar has lots of duties. He needs to get the team playing better defense. Yet I think you are a very good defensive player. Since the team needs the majority of its work on defense, maybe we can get you some more work on your shooting by practicing at home." This statement explains the coach's rationale for certain training practices without degrading him.

I encouraged Debbie to ask the coach questions when she is confused by his decisions. Bad-mouthing does nothing to help her or the situation. She could try saying, "Hey, Coach, I'm a little worried. I know I need lots of work on my shooting and we as a team are focusing on defense right now. Can you help me?" This type of unthreatening remark tells the coach that she has different needs, yet it doesn't put him on the spot to defend his coaching style. It also clearly and honestly expresses what Debbie feels.

THE COACH PICKS ON HER

Celia, a thirteen-year-old swimmer, comes home in tears after nearly every practice because her coach yells. Her mother spoke with the coach, telling him that the way he coaches is wrong.

The coach explained simply that if she didn't like it, Celia could quit.

One of the struggles that parents and coaches run into is that they often have differing concerns. The primary concern of this coach seems to be performance. He is trying to motivate and get the most out of his swimmers, which he feels can best be done by yelling and instilling some fear. Celia's mom is more concerned with her daughter's well-being than with performance, and would prefer that fear and negative reinforcement be eliminated. She doesn't want her daughter to be a great swimmer at the expense of her health and self-esteem. But Celia's coach has performance as his main concern and may not be aware of the toll it's taking on Celia. He is doing what he feels necessary to produce a champion. Perhaps there is a balance.

Typically, when a child is yelled at and comes home in tears every day, she will eventually burn out. The stress of trying to avoid the humiliation of negative reinforcement combined with the loss of enjoyment will push her to quit the sport. But Celia's mom didn't help the situation by attacking the coach's style. Naturally he was going to defend his actions.

Instead, she might have tried approaching the coach by stating her concerns about her daughter and highlighting her worries that Celia might be losing interest in the sport. In this way, she opens the door for the coach to talk about what might be upsetting Celia.

If he says Celia is merely being a baby and a wimp and she just has to get used to it, then her mother should state her concerns about Celia as a person, not just an athlete.

"Tell him that you are concerned that Celia is not handling the intense pressure of practice very well and that she comes home with a negative attitude," I said. "Let him know how you see practice affecting her mood at home and ask him if he sees any changes in her performance. This way you are connecting to what he thinks is important—performance. Ask if there is anything you can do to help at home. If he seems receptive, throw out some suggestions—like you think she needs a break or some strategies to build her confidence.

"Start there and try to leave the meeting with an agreed-upon environmental change, be it at home or training. Eventually, if the situation seems to continue to deteriorate, you'll have to begin talking with the coach about whether or not this program is the most suitable match for Celia," I said.

How to Talk with a Coach

Before entering a discussion with a coach:

- Remember there are a variety of purposes for coach-parent meetings; don't wait for a crisis to occur to set a meeting with the coach.
- Consider your own views. What do you really think? Do you want to reprimand the coach or find solutions? Do you want to question a decision or understand the rationale behind the decision?
- Make sure you've thought about solutions, including changes that will benefit the coach as well. For example, "If you could inform me when Jane isn't following through on your instructions I can better support you at home."
- Remind yourself to tell the coach that you are interested in his or her viewpoint.
- Remind yourself to give the coach the opportunity to correct any false perceptions.
- Check your emotions at the door.

FAST FACTS

➡ A group of high school coaches cited their responsibilities to be stressing academics, presenting high school and college requirements, setting a positive example, developing communication skills with parents and athletes, and informing students about life after athletics.(6)

SHE'S BETTER THAN THE OTHERS, BUT HE WON'T PLAY HER

Lori is a fourteen-year-old soccer player who has a lot of talent but not much drive. She didn't always start but was given a great deal of playing time. But after the team played miserably in one game, losing to a less talented team, the coach announced that he was only going to play "the warriors, the people who want to work hard out there." Lori wasn't one of them and rode the bench for most of the next two games, leaving the second game in tears. Her father called the coach, angry that Lori wasn't being used. The coach tried to explain his reasoning, that he needed Lori to give 100 percent effort on the field, but her dad wasn't satisfied with the answer. "She should be playing, that's all there is to it," he said. "I just don't think he likes her."

Coaches tell me that when they hear parents say, "You don't like my daughter," their immediate response is, "We have nothing to talk about." They believe that getting into discussions along those lines is unproductive. Most coaches will tell you that liking and disliking athletes does not figure into how they coach or make decisions.

In talking to a coach, parents need to remember that they must avoid being accusatory. All that does is aggravate an already tough situation. Parents (and their daughters) are better served by asking for explanations and expressing true feelings.

For example, Lori's parents might say: "We think Lori is being treated unfairly, because she clearly is one of the best players, and we think you just don't like her." However, it would be more productive for them to state the facts and not assume they know what the coach is thinking: "We see that Lori is not starting this year. We know she didn't start last year because of her size. Yet this year she has grown and she spent all summer working on her shooting. She really looked strong in the summer leagues to us, and we thought she might start. We're a little confused as to why she has been benched the last few games."

These statements open up a discussion in which the coach can respond with his rationale for the starting lineup. The best action parents can take is to state that they respect the coach's decision but want to understand how those decisions are made. Sometimes there aren't any easy guidelines, just a judgment by the coach. Then a parent can ask how or what their daughter needs to do to eventually earn a starting position. This enables the coach to set clear expectations, and parents come away from the conversation knowing what is expected, too. Finally, even if parents don't agree with the decision, they need to help their daughter feel good about her role on the team. Find out from the coach what he or she sees as the athlete's role. This helps your daughter get used to her role as a substitute, reliever and, perhaps, a team motivator. Then, you can positively reinforce your daughter for successfully carrying out her role on the team.

QUICK QUESTIONS

What if a coach plays favorites?

Even when coaches are sure they aren't playing favorites, parents often think they are showing favoritism. Essentially, this is because coaches have many concerns, whereas parents really have only one priority—their child. This, I've seen, can lead to conflict.

However, when a team has a star player, a coach may indeed favor her or appear to favor her because she contributes in a way to gain the coach's focus. And even though a coach never intends to play favorites, it may seem to others that some athletes get more attention and playing time. Very often, for the good of the team, coaches need to adapt their coaching style to best meet the needs of individual athletes. During these times, it may look to observers that special treatment is being given to certain players. However, there may be a sound reason for the coach's actions.

One question I like parents to ask themselves is whether this favoritism affects their daughter's attention from the coach or her level of play. Very often more attention given to one athlete does not mean that the attention another athlete gets is not sufficient. Sometimes, certain athletes need more of something from a coach. This is not always constant and can change from day to day. So, the critical question becomes, Does the coach's showing favoritism negatively influence your own daughter? If not, it really shouldn't be an issue as long as your daughter is getting what she needs. If favoritism does bother your daughter, she needs to remind herself of the internal control factor. She can't control the coach. Ask her why she is play-ing—for the coach's attention or for skill attainment? Revisit her personal goals and discuss the reasons for her participation in the sport. Remind her that a coach's attention is not a measure of his or her confidence in her ath-letic abilities.

If she feels she needs extra help, then encourage her to address that with the coach. If she is too shy, you can speak with the coach, but it is usually more well received coming directly from the athlete. If you decide to meet with the coach, instead of attacking his favoritism, attack the real problem, which is that your daughter is missing out on important coaching time.

Be sure to find out what the coach's lack of concern means. Perhaps the coach feels your daughter is progressing nicely. Very often coaches make the mistake of giving the problem child the most attention instead of rein-forcing the child who does it right. For instance, the child who keeps talk-ing as the coach is trying to address the team is often told, "Be quiet, hush." A more effective response might be for the coach to thank all of the other children for their undivided attention. Often, in my role, I am able to point this type of praise out to a coach and make sure the coach rein-forces behavior that he or she would like to see more often rather than less often.

I DON'T KNOW WHAT HER COACH IS TRYING TO DO!

A mother called me about her daughter, Mary, who was complaining about her coach. Mary loved to skate, practiced daily, and set yearly goals of trying to get new jumps and improve her skating. She competed a few times a year and was usually pleased with her outcomes. Mary's mom said to me, "I respect her coach, but I tend to wonder what is happening. I know Mary isn't a disobedient child, and yet her coach keeps ending her lessons early because Mary isn't doing the jumps. I don't know if I like the coach handling things this way, yet I don't want to interfere. Maybe I'm not getting the whole story from Mary. What should I do?"

Parents have a right to know the rationale for a coach's actions, espe-cially when those actions are teaching athletes how to deal with anger and frustration. Many parents take no action with coaches for fear that they might be labeled meddling or pushy sports parents. It's essential for both parties to try and work as a team to help the child. Many parent-coach conflicts arise because the coach's main priority is the child's physical skill, while a parent's main priority may have nothing to do with sports skills. In this case, Mary's mom really did need a clarification on what was happening. She was interpreting the coach's action as an indicator that something was wrong or bad about Mary's attitude. This may or may not have been the case. It turned out that I had a meeting scheduled with Mary the next day, so I would investigate what was causing the breakdown in communication between athlete and coach. This was a relief for her mom, who really wanted Mary and her coach to work through this on their own.

I arrived at the rink and first talked with Mary's coach.

"She just doesn't listen to me. She has to do certain things in order to be competitive and I feel like I'm always pulling teeth to get her to do anything. I get so frustrated that I just can't take another minute of her moping around with her head down and her arms by her side."

I had seen this behavior in Mary, so I could identify with what the coach was describing.

"Yes," I said. "I can understand your frustration. I have seen her act out like that, yet I'd like to focus on what happened yesterday."

"Oh, she always has an excuse," she said. "'I'm too tired' or 'I can't right now' or 'It's too crowded' or 'I need a drink of water.' She doesn't get what it takes to meet her goals. So, yesterday, I asked her to do her program again after she missed five elements, and she told me she was too tired. I knew she was tired. That is why she missed so many elements and that's why I wanted her to do the program again. My temper flared. Her lesson was almost over, so I just ended it."

My next task was to find out how Mary was interpreting her coach's actions.

"Mary, I heard you and your coach have been having some disagreements. Can you tell me about that?"

"Yeah. She keeps kicking me off my lessons," she said.

"Do you understand why?"

"No," she said. "Like yesterday, I was just too tired to do the program again so I told her that and she got all mad."

"Well, you are right that your coach is very frustrated with you right now and she would really prefer not to end your lessons. Do you understand why she asked you to do your program again? It's called skating a double run-through of your program."

A puzzled Mary said, "Well, she was mad that I missed my jumps. Right?"

"I understand how you felt as though this exercise was directly related to the missed jumps in your program. The rationale for the exercise wasn't made clear to you. However, your coach asked you to do the program again in order to improve your stamina. The purpose for a double run-through is to do the program while your body is fatigued. The rationale is that if you can do two programs in a row in practice, it will seem really easy to do only one in competition."

"It's punishment," she said.

"I can see how you might think that," I said. "Your coach wants to prepare you physically so that you can meet your goals. That's her job. She knows that in order for you to perform to your expectations, you must prepare properly. She gets frustrated because she feels you are resistant to training. You told me that you would like to skate a clean program in this competition. What does your training need to entail to help you meet that goal?"

"I definitely need to do the program every day, which I do. But I guess I also need to improve my stamina and speed. There are lots of different ways I can work on that stuff."

"That's right, and Mary, if you decide that you don't want to carry out the necessary training tasks to meet your goals, that's okay. However, you will probably want to adjust your goals accordingly. You can't expect to meet the goal if you aren't willing to put in the required work. Your coach has reviewed your goals with you and set the training plan. It's her job to get you trained and prepared so that you can meet your goals. It sounds like you agree with the training plan, but maybe need a clarification of how the plan relates to your goals."

"I want to do it," she said. "But she pushes me to do it."

"It sounds to me like you practice. Yet maybe you don't push yourself in practice," I said. "In other words, once you feel tired or sore or like you don't want to do something, instead of pushing through that and seeing how much more you can do, you give in to yourself. This way you never find out how really good you could be. You just stay at the same level, because you don't ever test your capabilities. If I were to ask you to do five double axels in a row and you completed five, you would have set a standard for yourself that you were capable of hitting five. The next day if I asked you to do six but you felt tired, my guess is that you would back off totally. Obviously, when you feel tired, hitting five in a row will be much harder to do than when you feel rested and strong. But, instead of giving in to yourself totally, you could reset the goal and attempt to do three. Then, you have pushed yourself to know that when you are tired you can hit three. Next time, you can push a little more and see if when you are tired you can hit four. Eventually, being tired will not affect your daily accomplishments at all because you will have trained yourself to push through it.

"I suggest you use a feeling scale. Before each practice, rate how you feel on a scale of one to ten, with one being the worst and ten being the best. If you feel a one, you need to set different standards for yourself than if you feel a ten. If you feel a five, that doesn't mean you just give up and go home rather than set some realistic yet challenging goals. After the session, rate how well you think you skated using the same scale. You will quickly see that even when you don't feel all that great, you can still be productive."

Once Mary understood the rationale for her coach's actions, we could get started on developing a clear action plan that gave her daily tasks. I reiterated to the coach the necessity of explaining the purposes behind the requests she made of Mary. For example, if she asked Mary to do five in a row of a jump, she should tell Mary that this exercise is to increase jump consistency. When Mary understood why she was being required to do certain drills, she wouldn't assume it was punishment, rather, she could view it as a way to help meet her goals. This outlook changed the very way she approached her practices. The coach made sure to take the extra time to spell out the purposes of her requests—in her own words, she would "explain to Mary how to get it."

FAST FACTS

➡ Giving information frequently after good performances and encouragement combined with information after poorer performances is associated with effectiveness, competence, and enjoyment.(7)

CAN COACH-PARENT DISCUSSIONS
ACTUALLY BE PRODUCTIVE?

Yes. Coaches and parents can work together. However, both parties need to consider the different agendas and preconceived notions each brings to the table. Parents often feel anxious about talking with coaches because they feel as though the coach blames them for a lack of performance or bad attitude on the part of their child. They believe that others see them as deficient in the parenting department. Parents can often leave coaching meetings feeling bewildered by a coach's criticisms of their child and find themselves wondering if it's all their child's fault. Parents very often complain to me that they worry they may say something to upset the coach and the coach will take it out on the child.

Coaches, on the other hand, have questions being shot at them by every parent and feel criticized and undervalued. They may view certain questions on the part of parents to be attacks on their decision-making or coaching strategies. Coaches often feel a great deal of pressure to produce winning teams and athletes. They may feel this pressure from parents as well as outside sources, as coaches' jobs and reputations are built on the successes of their athletes. Remember, a coach's number one priority may not be the well-being of your child, but your child's performance. Coaches are in the business of producing success, and very often coaching philosophies and strategies are determined by how the coach defines success. If a coach appears to be controlling to you, he or she probably feels that complete control will ensure success. Effective coaches do develop a coaching philosophy, and it's important for parents to understand and respect it. At the same time, coaches must possess the courage to evaluate and adjust their coaching patterns in order to best meet the needs of the athlete.

Despite such differences, parents and coaches do share some common interests. It's helpful for parents to be informed by coaches of potential concerns early before a crisis occurs. The same holds true for parents; they should inform coaches of potential pitfalls—both emotional and physical. Parents have important information about their children, and so do coaches. An open exchange of this unique knowledge can prove to be helpful to all involved.

Many parents feel their daughters and the coaches push them out of the sports process. In fact, parents have a great deal to contribute, and coaches often need parental support and reinforcement. Exchanges of information without blaming and finger-pointing can lead to productive problem-solving. Instead of having coaches tell parents what to do and parents tell coaches what to do, both parties can let the other know what they are doing right. A little positive reinforcement can go a long way in maintaining a high level of coaching and parenting.

It's critical for parents to leave a conference feeling good about their child, so feedback should remain balanced; parents can always try pointing out something about their daughter that the coach may have overlooked. Parents can contribute positively to the sports experience by letting the coach know they are willing to reinforce at home the athletic principles being taught on the field.

When Should I Ask for a Coach-Parent Meeting?

1. When you want to find out the goals and game plan for the next few months so that you can provide appropriate feedback. Prior to the meeting, let the coach know you are asking about the game plan, not questioning or refuting the plan. This meeting is to help ensure that you provide effective and accurate feedback to your child. For instance, if the coach is working on changing technique or game strategy, you can provide positive feedback to your daughter that relates specifically to these issues. This will help you to avoid giving feedback about something unrelated to the monthly goals. The coach will be overjoyed to meet with you for this purpose.

2. When you want to get information on the risks of the sport, rules, regulations, and procedures.

3. When you want to have a dialogue about your role and what is expected of you and your child.
4. When you want to get acquainted with the coach and share positive feedback as well as voice any concerns. Also, when you'd like to gain understanding of rationale for certain decisions.
5. When you want to negotiate or come to terms with any expectations you see as unreasonable or unclear.

Five Steps to Use in Coach-Parent Meetings

1. Start with what is going well.
2. Stick to a discussion about the child's behavior that is of concern.
3. Remember to avoid telling the coach what to do.
4. Describe what you think the child needs.
5. Suggest a plan that includes your own role in helping.

Communication between parents and coaches is of critical importance as is the communication between coach and athlete. Sports performance is affected not only by the personality of the athlete but by the environment in which she trains. Athletes need to learn to adapt to their coach's style and coaches need to learn to shape the environment in a way that suits the athlete. When this mutual understanding occurs, the sport experience can be enhanced at many levels.

ALL HE SEEMS TO DO IS YELL AT HER

Jenny is a fourteen-year-old figure skater I'd known for a while through other skaters. One day after practice she said to me, "My coach yells at me all the time. Today he started screaming that I wasn't trying and then told me I couldn't leave the ice until I landed ten combination jumps in a row," she said. "I am so mad at him, it's so unfair."

"What was your response when he told you that?" I asked.

"I tried to do ten, but I couldn't do it. I was too mad at him. Why is he taking everything out on me just because he's in a bad mood?"

It was clear that Jenny, while attempting the jumps, was focusing on her coach rather than on her response to her coach. She had many choices available to her, but she chose to rehearse in her head everything she would say to her coach so she wouldn't get in trouble for saying it. Obviously, this wasn't going to help Jenny land ten jumps in a row.

Jenny seemed to interpret that having to hit ten in a row was punishment. And yet her coach viewed it as a valid exercise that would strengthen her physical capabilities and provide her with the ability to "perform on demand" as is so essential in competition. If her coach had taken a minute to explain the purpose of the assignment, Jenny may have been more likely to take a positive approach to the task. At the very least, her focus may have shifted from analyzing her coach's mood to finding a way to complete what he had asked of her.

Many coaches, however, don't understand this concept and believe that their tough demeanor and words in and of themselves are effective coaching tools. However, even when coaches are frustrated, they tend to provide information that can be useful to the athlete. Parents can ease the situation by helping their daughters learn how to "tune out" the coach's tone of voice, pick out the important information, and put that information to use. It's hard to get athletes to do this, however, because of the importance many place on being accepted and approved of by their coaches.

Jenny truly liked her coach, and her parents believed he was a good coach—demanding, firm, and effective. What Jenny needed to learn was that her coach's demeanor wasn't important in this situation and she needed to get past her anger to a point where she could do what he wanted her to do.

Many coaches say things that don't sit well with athletes, such as, "Why can't you do this?" This leaves an athlete to come up with all the reasons why she can't and gets her focused on her coach's disapproval. It's a tough task, but the question needs to be reframed into something that will elicit a positive response. For example, the coach could restate the question "Why can't you do this?" as "What can you do to make this better?" This will help her to find a solution, rather than simply highlight the problem.

I asked Jenny about being angry at her coach.

"How is being mad going to help you do what it is he wants you to do?" I asked.

"I don't know," she said.

"You've got to do the ten jumps, right?"

"If I want to get out of here tonight."

"So being mad isn't going to help," I said. "What would? What did he tell you about how to land that jump? Think of what he was saying during the lesson, before he yelled and you got so mad."

"He kept talking about my leg going through," she said.

"That's right. Thinking about something that relates to how to do the jump puts you in better control of the situation. If you don't land them, make sure you give yourself feedback about whether or not you made the correction. If you continue to miss the jump, you'll have to break it down until you can make all of the technical corrections. Try and stay focused on the corrections—and see what happens," I said.

She said she'd give it a try.

The coach could have helped the situation by giving Jenny specific technical information to think about (controllable). This would shift her attention from outcome (whether or not she lands the jump) to process (how to land the jump). Once Jenny completed the exercise, the coach could provide process feedback, "You really did keep your arm in front on those ten," versus outcome feedback, "Yep, you missed all ten again." The former type of feedback reinforces to Jenny that it is worthwhile and necessary to focus on the process.

In order to assist Jenny in improving her attitude, the coach needed to be more specific about what he saw in Jenny that led him to believe she was not trying. Since Jenny was frustrated, it was likely that her shoulders were raised to her ears and pushed forward, her head was drooping, and her eyes were down or darting all around. The coach could have asked Jenny to change her body language (controllable). The idea is to give athletes something specific to do that is under their control. One of the best ways for Jenny to control landing ten jumps in a row is through her thoughts, body language, effort, focus, etc. By giving Jenny something specific to do that is under her control, the coach sends a strong message that focusing on the controllable is just as important as landing the jump. He is providing her with a way to seize control and give herself the best shot at being successful.

Finally, Jenny needed some help in changing her outlook. Jenny seemed to interpret the ten in a row request as punishment. Yet the coach viewed it as a valid exercise that would strengthen Jenny's physical capabilities and provide her with the opportunity to "perform on demand" as is required in competition. If the coach had taken a second to explain the purpose of the assignment, Jenny may have been more likely to take a positive approach to the task. At the very least, her focus may have shifted from analyzing the coach's mood and blaming him for her situation to finding a way to complete the assignment.

In the future, the coach should be sure to require "perform on demand" training at a variety of intervals during practice, not just when Jenny is practicing inconsistently. Then she would be more likely to perceive the exercise as a benefit to her skating rather than a punishment. By changing himself, the coach changes the environment and assists Jenny in changing her own response to the situation. He empowers her to take charge.

FAST FACTS

➡ Learning a positive approach to coaching results in lower player dropout rates (5%, compared to 26% with untrained coaches).(8)

Tips for Coaches:

1. Ask Better Questions: In order to help athletes focus on the controllable, ask better questions. Questions should help them focus on internals. "Why can't you do this?" is a bad question, because athletes are left with no choice but to come up with all the reasons why they can't. Instead, ask, "What can you do to make this better?" You may get the response, "I don't know." Try replying with, "Well, if you had to take a guess?" This lets athletes off the hook from having to find the right answer. It lets them know it's okay to be wrong. After all, it's just their best guess.

2. Be a Good Role Model: Coaches' reactions to situations are a model to children of how to deal with strong emotions. How often have we seen the sideline rants and raves? That reaction is clearly not beneficial to anyone, but often it's all an athlete has to go by when dealing with reactions to tough situations. Share with

young women some personal, effective coping strategies, like counting to one hundred, taking a deep breath, or immediately focusing on something else.

3. Turn Failure into Learning: Most often discussion about expectations, goals, and strategies take place after poor performances. Make sure to use both success and failure in a positive way. After good and poor outcomes, performances need to be evaluated, corrections need to be addressed, and controllable goals set. Use failure as a lesson rather than a punishment. Assist athletes in feeling good about themselves. For example, "We both know that you didn't perform your best today. Yet your speed really improved. Once you get used to skating aggressively like today, you'll be unstoppable."

4. Make Expectations Reasonable: Expectations should be appropriate and in agreement with athletes' own performance expectations. Provide athletes with expectations that are under their control (specific thoughts, focus, precompetition routine). If an athlete has clear outcome expectations, be sure to encourage her to set goals related to the actual performance as well as task-oriented goals, which are the internal skills she can use during a game or competition to help create the desired performance. The idea is that if the athlete carries out the task goals, she will most likely meet her performance goals, which in turn will give her a good chance of achieving the desired result.

5. Focus on Corrections: Find opportunities to praise good behavior and point out progress. Make sure athletes are given chances to come up with ways to change their own behavior. Assist athletes by giving them a specific correction (e.g. straighten left arm) and keep them focused on that one correction rather than the outcome. This shows athletes that the small stepping stones are important. If you remain focused on giving feedback about the correction, athletes' focus will shift from "why can't I land it?" (outcome) to "I need to keep my left arm straight" (process).

4

Parenting: When Mom and Dad Need Guidance

I didn't play for my folks; my passion came from within not from some external source. I believe that's the reason why I'm still playing after 20 years—because I play for me.

—Julie Foudy, member of the 1999 U.S. World Cup
Championship Women's Soccer Team

Y ou blew it," comes the cry from the stands. "How can you make such a bonehead play like that? You'll never win anything making mistakes like that. What's wrong with you anyway?"

We've all heard the horror stories of the stereotypical "Little League parents," the mother and father who become so overly involved and obsessed with their child's athletic performance that they destroy their daughter's passion to play. Screaming parents and crying children or crying parents and screaming children have become part of the fabric of youth sport. I've spent time with athletes who want to quit because of parental pressure to excel and I've talked with athletes who want to quit because they believe their parents don't care enough.

Parenting a young athlete and dealing with parents as a young athlete is not always easy.

"I get so scared to play sometimes, to take a chance because I'm afraid my dad will yell at me," one eleven-year-old volleyball player told me. "If he's going to be mad, I'd rather not play."

"I try to do what she says I should do," a thirteen-year-old skater told me about her mom, "but she never skated and what she tells me is different from what my coach wants. I don't know what to do. I need to listen to my coach but I can't stand arguing with my mom."

People often underestimate the importance of the parent's role in an athlete's development, especially in that of a young girl, who may be more prone than a boy to take a parent's overbearing behavior personally, interpreting it to be an indicator of her own weakness. The actions of parents directly affect whether the sports experience enhances or impairs a young woman's development not only as an athlete, but as a person. Most often parents have good intentions and attempt to show support and help their children believe in their capabilities. But sometimes in their attempts to be supportive parents go overboard and increase expectations to a level that is unmanageable and sometimes even damaging to the athlete.

SHE DREADS THE CAR RIDE HOME

Ashley, a thirteen-year-old basketball player, came home after a game extremely upset.

"What happened? Did you lose?" her mother asked.

"No, we won," she said. "And I thought I played pretty good. But Dad didn't think so. He thinks I stink, that I'm out of shape, that I have no heart."

It turns out that whenever Ashley's father took her to a game, he would use the car ride home to give his daughter pointers and his opinion of how she played.

"I just gave her a few pointers," he told his wife. "I only want her to be the best she can, and she could be a lot better if she'd pay more attention to conditioning—she had no legs in the fourth quarter. None. So I told her she should work out more. And she made some terrible passes. There was one where it almost cost them the game. So I told her about that, too."

Unwittingly, Ashley's father was committing perhaps the most common mistake in youth sports—using the car ride home to offer feedback, whether well-intentioned or not. It may seem natural and convenient for parents to want to discuss the game immediately, but parents need to understand that the period following practice and competition is a crucial time for a young athlete. It's important she be given the freedom to process it on her own.

The car ride home can appear to be the perfect time to discuss recent sporting developments, especially for busy families who find it difficult to squeeze one more activity into their child's day. However, your child is physically and mentally exhausted, and the last thing she wants to do is relive every moment of her practice or game. If parents receive one-word answers or silence, they can be sure that their child feels trapped with no way out. One athlete told me, "When I leave the gym, I get in the car and have to answer in detail questions about my workout. I can't get out of the car and if we hit traffic I have to talk for a whole hour. I feel trapped." You may find your daughter's aversion to reliving practice especially strong when she has performed poorly or made mistakes. More often than not, she knows exactly what she did wrong and is feeling bad about herself. This is not the time to criticize or evaluate what happened—give her time to sort things out for herself. If parents feel they must talk about the meet or game or the coaching, there are ways to do it so that a young athlete feels good about herself and learns from the experience.

I encouraged Ashley to talk with her father about how she felt. She told me, "I can't. He'll just get angry at me." Although Ashley was resistant to speaking with her father about this issue, I felt it was critical to address. I decided to help open discussions about the topic by first formulating with Ashley a pregame and postgame routine. The pregame routine would be a series of physical and mental exercises used to prepare Ashley for the upcoming game. The postgame routine would be used to give Ashley time to deal with her elation or disappointment over the game by herself.

Ashley and I spoke with her father and told him what we'd come up with and that she'd need his help.

"Ashley needs to prepare herself mentally and physically for the game," I told him. "She would like to know where you will be in case she needs something. But it is critical that you let her do what she feels necessary to get ready to play."

"How about after the game?" he asked.

"She wants to see you after the game, but she needs time to process the results for herself. She spends time with the coaches and her teammates and then jumps in the car with you. She hasn't had a second to review her own performance. I suggest you give her a chance to analyze it for herself and set a time later that day to discuss it together."

"Well, that's okay, but if I don't say anything at all I know she'll get upset," he said.

"That's a good point. Your immediate feedback can focus on Ashley's mental approach to basketball. Remember, the coach is teaching physical skills and strategies of success. You, as a parent, teach the rest. Find something positive in her performance that she might not see or consider, such as her focus or persistence. Although you may be providing her with great information, it's not being heard. Immediately following the game, give her the pats on the back that no one else does. Praise her effort and the things that created the success, not just the outcome. Make a deal with her that you won't analyze the game if she gives you five or ten minutes of time to discuss it later that evening or the next day. If she knows the discussion has a specific start and end time, she will be more likely to participate in the conversation. You can guide the discussion and let her come up with the answers. Help her to review her goals, identify potential or current obstacles in meeting those goals, and brainstorm ways to improve her chances for success. Remember, let her figure it out. When it comes to sports performance, let Ashley be the expert."

In the beginning years of sports, athletes will very much look forward to sharing the details of practice with you in and out of the car. However, as skill level increases, so do expectations. Athletes practice skills and plays they are expected to know how to execute, and months may go by before something new and unexpected is accomplished. Of course, those moments of utter satisfaction will be freely expressed and shared in and out of the car. It can be difficult for athletes to relive a day that was all about completing or not completing skills they were supposed to know how to do. They may leave practice wanting to forget about it or scared that they are letting the team down or worried about starting time or wondering what the coach thinks. The last reaction they want from a parent on their ride home is one of disappointment. Provide children with what they don't get anywhere else: a new perspective.

FAST FACTS

➡ Parents of six-to-twelve-year-olds were monitored for comments
they made on the sidelines of 147 games/matches; about 47% of
their comments were found to be positive, while almost 35%
were classified as negative.(1)

ONE OF OUR MOTHERS YELLED
AT ANOTHER PLAYER

Recently I heard about a situation at a basketball game where two girls
came off the court arguing and then grabbed their bags and left for their
respective cars. One of the girls passed by a teammate, who asked what had
happened.

"Oh, I don't know," she said. "Sheryl was just yelling at me about something for no reason. I don't know why she was so mad at me."

Sheryl's mother overheard these comments and jumped into the conversation.

"I'll tell you why she's yelling. It's because you don't pass the ball," she
said angrily. "You shoot too much. That would be fine if you could make
all your shots, but you don't, do you? You are a selfish player and you think
you're great. You know what? You're not. You're lucky to be on this team."

The girl burst into tears.

Before intruding into a conflict among teammates, it's critical for parents to identify exactly what they are hoping to accomplish. This parent
was frustrated by a player's attitude and performance during games. The
frustration both she and her daughter felt may have been quite valid, but
her verbal assault on the young player did not help alleviate the frustration
or resolve the situation. In fact, it made it worse for all involved.

It is not a parent's place to point out weaknesses in other players' mental or physical abilities. If this is to be done, it is a job for the coach. Young
women need to learn to resolve conflict on their own, especially when they
are part of a team. Loyalty to teammates is a critical component of success, and player's strengths need to be promoted while weaknesses are addressed within the team itself.

If the goal in this situation was to change the player's attitude, the approach used was not only unsuccessful but destructive. Instead of attacking the player, this mother might have tried focusing attention on her own daughter by encouraging her to confront this issue. "I overheard your teammate saying that she didn't understand why you were upset with her. The two of you are part of a team and working toward the same goal. I would encourage you to hear each other out and try to understand each others' perspective. You both have great strengths and contribute to this team. It would be a shame to let your differences tear apart team unity. I would advocate that you initiate a conversation with her, and I would be happy to find a third party to guide the discussion."

If you witness a parent verbally attacking another person's child, report it to that child's parents immediately as well as to the coach. The coach and parents can then decide whether or not to report it to a higher authority. It is one thing for a child to ask for another parent's opinion. It is entirely unacceptable for a parent to criticize, belittle, and berate players. When parents are concerned with other children's behavior, a call directly to the child's parents may be warranted, but only if the call is placed with the goal being to work together to find a solution. Calling parents to point the finger at their child will not be productive. Sheryl's mother might have called the other girl's mother and said, "I am concerned that our daughters have been having some conflict during games. I would like to talk with you about trying to help them resolve this in a productive manner." The coach and school counselor can be good resources for helping settle team conflicts. Remember, parental actions are a model of appropriate behavior for young women.

FAST FACTS

➡ On "Silent Sunday," parents and coaches in the Northern Ohio Girls Soccer League are mum: no cheering, clapping, griping, or chattering pointers. League president Al Soper states, "Bring your child, sit in your lawn chair and watch."(2)

➡ In September of 1999, a father in Eastlake, Ohio was charged with misdemeanor assault after he allegedly punched a player on an opposing team at a high school soccer match. His son had just tangled with the player.(3)

HER FATHER EMBARRASSES HER

Olivia, a fourteen-year-old volleyball player, is ready to quit the sport, even though she is highly talented and really enjoys the camaraderie of playing with her teammates. But her father has put so much pressure on her that it is literally making her sick. Before games she is so nervous that she often vomits. She is afraid to make a mistake and have to endure her father's disapproval and criticism. He is extremely vocal at games and demonstrative with his disgust, throwing his baseball cap to the ground when someone on Olivia's team does something wrong. In the car on the way home, he is full of questions for Olivia about why she did something one way and not another. He's even questioned her heart. "Are you sure you're trying your hardest?" he asked after one game. He attends almost every practice and travels to all the games.

Part of the problem is that Olivia's father and mother are divorced and her mother has custody. Her father desperately wants to be a part of Olivia's life and he thinks that by coaching and critiquing her, he is helping Olivia as an athlete and forming a closer father-daughter relationship. In reality, however, it's just the opposite. Lately, Olivia has been trying to invent reasons why she can't see her dad and has talked about quitting volleyball so that he won't come to her games or practices.

"Olivia, how does your dad affect the way you play?" I asked her one afternoon.

"I know he means well, but I can't concentrate when he's at the games, and I get scared that I'm going to do something wrong," she said. "And then I'll get yelled at on the way home."

"Are you a different player when he's not there?" I asked.

"Yeah, it's more fun. It's like I can just play, take more chances," she said. "It's like, you know, a big weight is lifted off me when I step out onto the court."

Olivia told me she had never really spoken of her feelings to her father. She tried to bring it up once, but her dad told her she needed to stop being so sensitive, to toughen up. She never mentioned it again, afraid he'd become angry. Her mother was aware of how she felt, however, but didn't know what to tell her other than, "Just don't pay attention to him."

"But it's hard," Olivia said. "I can't just tune him out."

I met with Olivia for several weeks before I asked to meet with her father. He was reluctant to see me, but when Olivia told him she'd really like it if he would talk to me, he agreed. We talked for a while about his relationship with Olivia.

"How do you feel about your relationship with Olivia?" I asked.

"It's pretty good," he said. "It's hard not living with her and it's been an adjustment trying to coordinate our schedules in order to be together. She's got school, sports, friends, her mom. She's busier than I am."

"I can understand what a time of transition this must be for both of you. How about sports? What do you think your role is in her life when it comes to volleyball?" I asked.

"Well, I think it's a little of everything. I try to help her by coming to all the games and as many practices as I can and offer my suggestions," he said. "Her mother isn't very athletic, so I think I fill that need for her."

"It sounds as if you are trying to be positive and supportive when it comes to Olivia's sports involvement," I said. "Sometimes the manner in which we phrase criticism and support can have an impact on children."

"Yeah. I tend to ask her why she did certain things in the game, mistakes, you know," he said.

"What kind of emotions do you express during these conversations?"

"Sometimes I'm angry, I guess. It really bothers me to see the breakdowns on that team," he admitted. "Olivia is very talented, and when she screws up it hurts the team and vice versa."

Olivia had told me that her father often compares her play with that of others on the team and tells her how she should be doing things on the court. This is critical feedback. It sends a subtle message to Olivia that there is a right way, which is his way. This limits her from exploring strategies that she thinks might work best.

"I'm wondering if you find your feedback to be effective in changing the way Olivia plays or improving her performance."

"Well, she listens, I know that," he said. "But I'm not really seeing any difference in her play, no."

I told him in my experience with athletes and parents, I've found the most effective way for parents to help their teenage daughters is by asking questions rather than giving answers, providing unconditional support and allowing their daughters to find solutions on their own.

"I don't know how to talk to Olivia like that," he said. "I'd be lying. I think it's better for me to tell her what I think and then she can digest it and learn from it."

Parents often use the statement, "I don't know how to talk to her" to justify their negativism. They believe they should be able to say what they think without concerning themselves with how they say what they think. However, it is important to keep in mind that the goal is to be heard. Many times in order to guide children in behavioral change, parents will need to change the very way they communicate information to their daughters.

"You need to tell the truth to Olivia," I said. "Yet you also need to try and communicate in a way that allows Olivia not only to hear you, but to act on your words. Olivia values your opinions so much that when they are expressed in a negative manner and as declarations of truths, she closes up because she feels attacked as a person. It would be helpful if you could give Olivia the opportunity to share with you what is true and meaningful to her."

He was quiet.

"Let me ask you this. How would you feel at work if someone hung over your desk asking you questions like, 'Why are you doing it this way? Don't you think you could do it like Bob? What's wrong with you, aren't you trying? Bob always gets his work done on time and now he's gone home and you're still here? What's wrong with you? Don't you realize you are letting down your coworkers?' "

The questions were extreme, but I got my point across. Parents often give well-meaning advice that is even quite accurate. But the mistake they make is stressing errors and getting caught up in the technical details. The coach has already provided such advice. It is much more helpful to give athletes feedback about something they haven't evaluated rather than something they already know. Be especially careful to avoid pinpointing mistakes that might have caused embarrassment or feelings of guilt. In these situations, parents want to talk about the athlete's feelings and reactions to the mistake rather than the mistake itself.

"There are ways for you to help Olivia and really be heard rather than having her simply dismiss your advice," I said. "For example, try expressing to Olivia thoughts you want her to focus on while playing. Instead of saying, 'You are barely swinging through when you spike that ball,' say, 'It looks like you are working on following through longer when you swing on a spike.' That puts her focus on the follow-through rather than on the mistake. It communicates to her that you understand what she is trying to improve without her feeling attacked for poor technique."

He looked confused.

"You help her by phrasing things in a positive manner, helping her concentrate on how to get the outcome she desires. Ask her how she would increase the distance on the ball. This question allows her the opportunity to teach you something. Meanwhile, you have taught Olivia the process of how to get focused on the correction," I told him. "Give it a try—I think you'll notice a difference in Olivia's reaction to you.

"And remember," I said, "Olivia's at the age and experience level where you need to begin to trust her ability to evaluate her play and make changes accordingly. You want to try and help her become her own coach. When she's in a game, it's her responsibility to think effectively and raise her performance level. Give her some space on a daily basis to direct herself."

He agreed to try it.

A few weeks later I went to one of Olivia's games. Her dad was sitting up in the stands and didn't see me slip in the door. I watched Olivia play and her father's reaction. She made several beautiful plays, which her father applauded, saying quietly, "Way to go." When she missed a dig because she was out of position, he was silent as Olivia shook her head in dismay. After the game I sought them both out.

"How's the training going?" I asked her father.

"It's like I have a new dad," Olivia chimed in. "We had a long talk about the way he talks to me and how I talk back. We agreed that if he wouldn't say negative things or dwell on my screw-ups, I'd talk more about what happened from my end of things. He asks me questions now and helps point out how I can turn a mistake into a correction. If it's no big deal, he reminds me not to sweat it. I don't have to analyze everything."

I think they're on their way to a stronger relationship on many fronts.

How to Talk to Her

- Try to stick with corrections rather than mistakes—"I can tell you're working to get the footwork down," instead of, "Your footwork is still messing you up."
- Let her know you understand what she might be feeling—"It must be really frustrating for you" or "I know you feel badly about to-day's game."
- Add a positive observation. "You really look like you're concentrating out there."
- Provide hope for the future. "I know when you get it, your kicks are going to send the ball a tremendous distance."
- Allow her to find her own answers, but pose the questions. "I wonder what you could do to get that crossover dribble down?"
- Avoid comparisons to other athletes.
- Validate what she feels rather than belittling what she says is happening. "I see that fall you took really scared you. It's okay to be scared, but you need to see that you're healthy and safe," rather than, "Why are you so scared? It was just a fall."
- Avoid sarcastic comments. Don't say, "Are you going to cry again?" Understand what she feels is very real. You may not agree with it, but that doesn't mean it isn't important. Let her know you understand her thoughts and feelings rather than judging them. Say, "I understand that you are very frustrated right now and need to cry. But I bet if we think about it, we can come up with some ways to make you feel better about things."
- Focus her attention on the mental aspects of her game. "I saw you really trying to project confidence today. After you double-faulted, I saw you put your shoulders down and it looked as if you were trying to collect your thoughts. Good job."

FAST FACTS

➡ A study of elite figure skaters found that when parental support and involvement were absent or excessive, skaters experienced stress, and when it was moderate they experienced enjoyment.

The former skaters identified conflict, criticism, expectations, and lack of autonomy as stress creators, while family closeness was associated with enjoyment.(4)

OUR TEAMMATE'S FATHER BETRAYED US

Robin has been a member of a twelve-and-under club soccer team, the Toros, near her home for the past two years. In the middle of Robin's second season, her father abruptly pulled her from the Toros and signed her up for the team's biggest rival, the Pride.

Her father had been upset with the poor showing of the Toros, his daughter's playing time, and what he believed was lousy coaching. Quietly, he had tried to start a mutiny, attempting to garner support from other parents to bring in a third coach to work with the girls. However, his attempts were thwarted when at a team meeting, the coaches were given a vote of confidence by the rest of the parents. The following week, he pulled Robin from the team to join the Pride.

The Toros' coaches and parents, and moreover, Robin's teammates, felt betrayed. When the two teams met several weeks later, Robin told her parents she was scared to play, fearing that someone on her old team would try to "take her out." The coach of the Toros refused to shake Robin's father's hand before the match. Tension was high. Robin played and scored her team's first goal—her best friend from the Toros, Rebecca, had been guarding her and let her by. The Toros, however, got a late goal to tie the game.

Rebecca was devastated that she had let Robin score. Robin felt confused because her father didn't understand why the coach had chosen not to shake his hand. Both Rebecca's and Robin's mothers called me to help sort out the situation and restore peace.

My first thought was for both families to meet together with me, but tension was still high and I decided it was not the right time for a summit. Instead, I met with each girl separately.

I saw Robin first.

"Robin, how did you feel about leaving the Toros?" I asked.

"Well, I knew I'd miss my friends," she said, "but I thought I'd do better and would be used right if I changed teams. I didn't like leaving, but I liked it, which might not make sense."

"No, I understand. It actually makes a lot of sense," I said. "If I'm hearing you right, it sounds like you were looking forward to some new opportunities but at the same time felt some loss about leaving. You can be excited about moving forward and still feel a loss about what you are leaving."

"I don't know. Now they're probably glad," she said.

"But in the beginning, how do you think they felt?"

"Maybe a little sad or betrayed," she said.

"Were you sad in the beginning, too?" I asked.

"Yeah."

"Sounds like when you left the Toros it was a loss for both you and Rebecca," I said.

I asked her whether she had felt involved in the decision to switch teams, or if it was strictly her father's decision. She said she was involved, but her body language suggested that she wasn't comfortable with the move. It was important to talk to Robin about focusing on what she could control. It was clear that her father thought switching teams was the best move for his daughter. Many people would argue that he was not teaching her the importance of honoring commitments, instead suggesting to her that if she finds herself in an unfavorable situation, there is always a way out.

But the decision had been made, and Robin, whether she liked the decision or not, was going to have to adjust.

And Rebecca and the Toros had to adjust to the change and realize that Robin's departure was not something they could control. However, their feelings about her were controllable. Rebecca felt betrayed because she assumed that Robin had had a strong voice in the decision to switch teams. Perhaps, by identifying reasons to be angry with Robin, Rebecca could distance herself from some of the hurt. However, such a response only served to cover her true feelings and didn't allow her to attack the real issue, which was her response to the unfortunate chain of events.

I talked about this with Rebecca.

"Robin hasn't changed as a person just because she changed teams," I told her. "And the fact that she left your team doesn't mean she thinks any less of you. It was a situation her father felt was best for her. Sometimes people disagree."

"But her dad lied to our coach about whether he was switching Robin," Rebecca protested.

"If that's so, then your coach and Rebecca's father need to talk things out," I said, "but that doesn't affect you or the team. You need to focus on your own game plan and how to beat the Pride. Robin is just one player. Winning the game means concentrating on your play as a team against their team.

"Next time you play, acknowledge and accept that you might experience some strong feelings when it comes to playing the Pride, yet you don't have to let those feelings rule your game. You can think your way through a great game," I said. "Think about the Toros. Even if you have to guard Robin, focus on guarding a player rather than your former teammate, and then your focus will be on what is required of you to perform well."

"That's going to be hard," Rebecca said. "For her, too. She actually thought we might try to hurt her."

"Yes, it will be hard for both of you," I told her. "But you cannot be responsible for Robin's thoughts and feelings. Take charge of what you can control, and that is you."

I spoke separately on the phone with Robin's father and the Toros coach. Both needed to realize that their actions directly affected the way the girls felt about one another and the game. Both agreed that they had set poor examples and had let their own frustrations rise above team goals. I suggested that they explain to the girls how they wished they had handled the situation, which would turn an unfortunate situation into a learning experience for the team.

"If you want the Toros to forget about all this and move on, you need to do so, too," I told the coach.

I also recommended that the coach communicate to the team his wishes for Robin's continued success and let them know it is possible to be friends with Robin even if she does play on another team. And even though they may not have liked to lose Robin to the Pride, they can't change it.

"Ask the girls, too, how they would solve the problem," I said. "Let them feel they are part of the solution. This is a way to teach these girls how to respond to difficult situations and remain in control of their performance."

When the opportunity arises, it's important for parents to encourage their daughters to accept other people's decisions and focus attention back to their own goals. Robin and Rebecca shared the same goals, they just chose different paths to get there. Not everyone achieves their goals with the same plan. It is important to accept in others the ways that might work for them.

QUICK QUESTIONS

Should I watch practice?

Obviously, parents have a right to watch and see how their daughters are progressing. But make sure she knows that you are there because it is fun for you to watch her participate, not because you want to criticize. That will help take the pressure off her. And even if you know what's happening during practice, ask her to explain different aspects of the training session. Make her the expert. This is her activity, not yours. Give her confidence that she is smart and in control of her sport and that she knows some things Mom and Dad don't. Let her know how proud you are that she is learning new skills and making a strong effort.

THE DOMINEERING MOTHER

Susan is an eleven-year-old swimmer. Her mother, Pam, divorced her father when she was very young and she has little contact with him. Her mother works in a low-paying job and is counting on Susan to get a swimming scholarship to college and dreams that she will make the Olympic team someday. Any extra money Pam earns goes for extra training or a camp somewhere. Susan swims year-round, often for two leagues. In the summer of 1996, Pam borrowed money from the bank to take Susan to the Olympics in Atlanta, where they attended every swimming session.

"Someday you'll be here, too," she told Susan.

Susan's coach called and told me about Pam's obsession with her daughter's swimming.

"For now, Susan seems okay," the coach said, "but I really worry about the pressure her mom's putting on her. It's so obvious. I've asked the mother to call you."

When Pam called, she spoke about the coach's concerns and said, "I just want the best for my daughter. Why is that so bad?"

I told Pam that as long as she was aware of her own goals for Susan, she would have a better chance of keeping everything in perspective. When the Olympics starts to become more of a goal for Pam than for her daughter, that's when Pam would need to take a long look at her commitment and motives. It's fine to have dreams—even big dreams—but for sports to remain beneficial to Susan, Mom needs to understand that her daughter's hard work is worthwhile even if those dreams aren't realized.

"Susan needs to shoot high," I told her mother. "But in order to get there, it's vital she focus on the process: how to get there instead of will I or won't I get there?"

One of the most difficult challenges parents face is trying to motivate without pushing. It takes careful analysis of the athlete's desire, ability, and dedication. The most important message to convey to a young athlete is that parental love and acceptance is not determined by her success in sports.

I asked Pam whether she would make the same sacrifices for Susan if she were a gifted math student instead of a gifted swimmer.

"Of course," she said. "If that's what she wanted to spend time doing, I'd be very supportive."

"Does Susan realize how much you are sacrificing to help her excel in swimming?"

"She knows that I spend a lot of time and I told her about the loan I got to pay for the trip to Atlanta."

"Make sure that Susan doesn't take responsibility for those sacrifices," I said. "It's important for her to hear from you that these are your choices, not her burden. And it's something you may want to rethink, depending on how Susan progresses in the sport."

I've had parents pull their daughters out of a certain sport because they just didn't want to make the family sacrifices anymore. And I've had parents say, "How can I pull her back when she's having so much success?"

Parents need to decide who is driving the decision—themselves or their children. By weighing the relative importance of their own values and commitments, they can usually reach a good, if often difficult, understanding of what is right and what is excessive.

FAST FACTS

➡ National champion figure skaters who held their titles between the years 1985 and 1990 (ten females and seven males) identified family relationships as a source of stress throughout their competitive careers. Stresses included expectations of others, difficult family relationships, and mother's reaction to having less input. The skater's coping strategies included receiving family support, surrounding self with supportive people, and talking to others for reassurance and support.(5)

I DON'T WANT TO LET MY MOM DOWN

Betsy is a sixteen-year-old figure skater. In a competition in which she was expected to win easily and qualify for the national championships, she missed the combination jump in the technical program, taking herself out of contention to qualify. She was devastated, feeling like she let her parents and coaches down, and she talked about quitting skating.

"They have sacrificed so much for me to skate," she said in tears. "It costs so much, and I can't even get to nationals. I'm always choking. Everyone says I have so much potential, but I can't do it when it counts."

"I know you feel badly right now, and it sounds like you have allowed this competition to change the very way you see yourself as a competitor," I said. "You didn't skate your best today, and we need to figure out what happened so you can be sure to fix it next time. Betsy, you did skate very well at a number of competitions this year, including the one that qualified you here. Do a few bad performances make you a total choker under pressure? I don't think so. You skated well at Pippenberg competition, what helped you to do well there?"

"I was really focused there," she said. "I was really nervous there too, but I knew how well I had been training."

"So even though you were nervous, you were able to skate great," I said.

"You kept your focus on your preparation and that helped create a great performance. Just because you had a bad performance doesn't mean those qualities that enabled you to skate well disappear. Those qualities reside within you. You control them. Did you use them today?"

"No," she said, thinking back. "I kept thinking about missing the combo. All I did was worry. I could tell my parents were really nervous for me, and that worried me even more."

"So it's not that you don't possess the qualities necessary to skate great under pressure; maybe you just let other factors get in your way of applying what has worked for you in the past," I said.

But just as Betsy needed to take responsibility for her own skating and her own reactions to things, she needed to let her parents and coaches do the same. It was clear that she was trying to take responsibility for their choices. I talked with her mother.

"Betsy is really worried that she has disappointed you," I said.

"Of course not. We love her no matter what she does in skating," her mother answered.

"I know you love her, yet you may be slightly disappointed," I said. "You have sacrificed a lot to help her excel in skating. It would not be wrong to want her to advance to the next level."

"Well, yes, I guess we were disappointed," she said. "Everyone told us she was the best and we believed it. We still do. I just don't get it. How could she make that kind of mistake? She never does that. I know I shouldn't have said anything to her, but it just didn't make sense to me."

"Did you say anything to her about the burden her skating places on you?" I asked warily.

"Well, I did kind of moan and groan about all the money and told her that we just didn't know how much longer we could keep this all up without her making nationals," she said. "You see, once she gets there we can get some financial help. We were relying on that this year and Betsy knew it."

"I don't know if you see this or not, but it seems to me that Betsy spends a lot of time trying not to disappoint you. It's almost as if she has forgotten what she is striving to achieve."

"I can see that. She does try to please other people. What has caused that? Are we doing something wrong? We try and be really supportive and positive with her."

"It's not about doing something wrong. It's about finding a way to meet Betsy's emotional needs," I said. "She was really upset about the financial burden she has placed on the family. She seems to think that if she doesn't make nationals, all the time and money have been a waste. I'm wondering how you see it. What do you hope she gets from skating?"

"I don't know. I think skating has been a great activity for Betsy," she said. "She has learned so much about herself through the sport and had opportunities to travel and all that. But sometimes I get all wrapped up in worrying about her making nationals, like that will make all the money and time worth it. I don't know if it will, but sometimes I don't know if what she is getting from the sport is worth all the sacrifice."

"Your concerns are totally understandable," I said. "The sport does require a great deal of time, effort, and financial backing. And although you may be confused as to whether those sacrifices are worth it, you have made a choice to support Betsy's efforts in this sport. Those are your choices. I'm wondering if you could point this out to Betsy and relieve her of the burden of taking responsibility for your choices."

"I could try. It's so hard to remember why you do this sport, especially when you are disappointed," she said. "I just started thinking about how we could spend that money and I couldn't hold my tongue."

"I know it's sometimes hard to remember there are other reasons besides making a national team for Betsy's participation in skating," I said. "If you struggle with remembering the benefits of her sport, think about Betsy. Betsy knows you spend lots of money, time, and emotional resources on her sport. By reminding her of these facts after a disappointing performance, you send the message that you are only willing to provide those resources if Betsy gets the desired outcome—making nationals. So when you see Betsy trying to please you, she is desperately trying to do what she can to keep getting the support and resources she needs. She may blame herself for being a burden and view her lack of success as the main problem. It's possible she's thinking that if she could just win, she wouldn't have these worries. However, by thinking solely about getting to nationals and all the bad consequences of not getting there, she loses sight of her original reason for participating in skating. The sole focus becomes the outcome, and all the other benefits Betsy could derive from the sport are forgotten."

"I don't want her to know I feel disappointed," she said.

"Actually," I said. "It's okay to let her know that you are disappointed. Show her that it doesn't change your love for her or your belief in her ability to reach her goals. An important lesson for her to learn is that it's okay to disappoint people. Point out to her that you have probably disappointed her in the past. Once she is relieved of the burden of having to avoid disappointing you, she can get on with trying to figure out how to meet her goals. Sometimes the more you talk about her capabilities, the more pressure she feels. I know you are trying to encourage her by telling her she could be a top finisher at nationals, but Betsy isn't so sure she can meet that challenge. The more you remind her of her potential, the more scared she becomes of not living up to your expectations."

"So what do I say when she starts telling me how awful she feels?"

"Respond by letting her know you understand where she is coming from," I said. "This is the time to listen and respond to her feelings, not express and process your own feelings. You can do that later. Try saying something like, 'Wow, it sounds like this competition has really changed the way you see yourself as a competitor.' This statement brings meaning to the words Betsy is saying. You also want to let her know that you would like to make it all better for her. Try saying, 'I wish I could have willed you to land that combination.'

"I don't have to tell her she isn't a loser," she said. "We always seem to get into these discussions where she is trying to convince me what a loser she is, and I'm trying to convince her she is a winner no matter what."

"You really want to avoid getting into a 'yes I am' 'no you're not' discussion," I said. "Instead, let her know you hear her feelings. I might add something like, 'I guess it must have been really hard for you to mess up when you wanted to do so well.' That statement will get Betsy thinking in a productive way about the situation. She is already questioning herself; she doesn't need more questions."

"Well, sometimes I try and tell her, 'I understand,' and she says, 'No you don't.' What do I do then?" she asked.

"Let her know exactly what you understand," I said. "You may guess wrong, but then she will correct you. Be clear about what you think she is saying."

Communicating clearly with your daughter after disappointment involves making sure that her feelings and thoughts are the focus of attention rather than your own feelings and thoughts. Pointing out those tasks she is accountable for is critical. Do not allow her to take responsibility for your adult choices. When she is expressing negative feelings, let her know you hear her by assigning meaning to what you think she is telling you. Avoid asking questions that she can't possibly answer and don't give advice she isn't ready to accept. Simply use your listening skills.

FAST FACTS

➡ Adolescent athletes (149 female, 130 male, mean age fourteen) who played team sports and perceived their parents to create a task-oriented motivational climate (emphasis on effort and skill mastery) were less likely to experience precompetitive anxiety.(6)

WE'VE GOT THE NEXT MARY LOU RETTON

Elizabeth was a thirteen-year-old gymnast and was having some problems performing to the best of her ability under pressure. Her father called to ask me to work with her and stated, "I need you to understand that we have the next Mary Lou Retton on our hands." I smiled to myself, knowing immediately what issue needed to be attacked.

I met with Elizabeth and her coaches and found out that indeed she was a talented and gifted athlete. She was on her way to making a national team but in the past had some minor setbacks. This was her year to make it to the next level, and her father believed that she would win. Elizabeth had confidence in her ability to make a national team and hoped that she would accomplish this goal. I wondered how Elizabeth felt about the expectations of her father.

"He always says stuff like that and I just kind of laugh to myself. It's kind of annoying, but I've learned to just block it out. Before a competition he tells me how great I am and that I can do it, but then if I don't he yells at me and tells me that there's something wrong with me."

Elizabeth was dealing with a situation that happens frequently. Her father had good intentions. He was supportive of his daughter's talent and ability. However, his expectations for her were so high that even if Elizabeth made a national team, a huge accomplishment, it would not seem like much of an achievement to Elizabeth because she was supposed to do it. After all, in her father's eyes she had the potential to be the next Olympic champion; therefore, making a national team was supposed to happen. The expectation was extreme, and as a result the stepping-stones had become insignificant. The more Elizabeth's father talked about how great she was, the more pressure Elizabeth felt and the more unmotivated she became to reach what seemed like insignificant goals. Elizabeth didn't know what the limits of her capabilities were, but with someone telling her she would be the next Olympic champion, every time she made a mistake she felt like a failure. It was important to focus on what she was achieving now rather than what she should be achieving.

I spoke with Elizabeth's father, and he was very receptive to my feedback. It had never dawned on him that his support and encouragement had become overwhelming pressure. Her father agreed to place his energy on helping her achieve the small stepping-stones and reward her accordingly, even if it was a simple task like hitting her series on beam at the next meet. He quickly changed his behavior and within weeks Elizabeth responded with an improved attitude and performance.

Tips for Parents

1. Get Past the Loss: Try to keep your daughter from venturing into the "coulda, woulda, shoulda, if-only" syndrome. This only slows down the process of learning from mistakes. It keeps her focused on what went wrong and what she wishes would have happened. After a poor performance, help her shift focus by promoting discussions that revolve around immediate changes that will make things better. Allow her to do the work by looking for specifics and devising a plan. Offer your help, and when asking questions, make sure they are ones that focus her attention on solutions. If she isn't responsive, don't push it; she'll come to you when she is ready. Find success in her failure and then let it go.

2. Ask Open-Ended Questions: "What did you do well today?" "How did you feel today?" "What went right?" "How was your self-talk

today?" "What did you learn today?" "What can you do to make things better?" Invite her to share what she wants to with you. Listen to her rather than judge. Avoid telling her that her feelings are right or wrong. You want her to be comfortable and accepting of whatever it is she feels. This will encourage her to share more with you. Her reactions may not match yours, but how she is experiencing sport is what needs to be highlighted.

3. Focus on Corrections: Often, if you're worried over a mistake your daughter has made, she's worried about it, too. The fact that you mention it again after she has lived it, the coach has mentioned it, and her teammates have called her on it reinforces and brings up all of the self-doubt she is struggling to temper. Give her a chance to figure it out on her own so she can say, "This was a problem and I thought about it and committed myself to fixing it." By you pointing it out again, it seems she fixed it only because you told her to, not because she was independent enough to rely on herself and do it on her own. Instead try to give descriptive feedback that doesn't focus on the technical aspects of the sport. For example, say, "That was a great day. You really maintained your focus after you fell off beam. You bounced back more motivated than I've ever seen you." Through your own words, you can encourage positive self-talk and images.

4. Have Family Discussions When Life Is Going Great: The tendency is for families to have discussions and set goals when something has gone wrong. Let your children know it is appropriate and necessary to talk about life when everything is great. Sit around the dinner table and have each family member talk about how well everybody is doing and why.

5. Relive Games or Performances When She's Ready: You may want information, but remember, your daughter was first given feedback from her coach and then probably from her friends and teammates. Most likely she has had little time to process the game and decide what she thinks and feels about it. Give her some time and space to process the event on her own. Make an agreement with your daughter about when to discuss the game. Generally,

avoid doing so on the car ride home. It's too soon. Give her time to think things through and then try to listen.

6. Give Positive Feedback: When trying to be proactive by helping her feel positive and competent, support the goals she accomplished and the skills she performed well, and be sure to praise her effort, persistence, and focus. Help her see the things she did well. Let her know that your support of her and sports is not just determined by the outcome. Praise the mental aspects of her game and those things she controls. Even if the ultimate goal has yet to be achieved, make sure you praise the small improvements and corrections she makes. If these small progressions are important to you, they will be more likely to be important to her. Assist her in feeling good about herself, even when faced with defeat. Try saying something like, "You didn't play your best today and I know you are disappointed, but your speed really improved today, and once you get the hard jumps more consistent, you'll be unstoppable."

7. Be a Good Role Model: Your daughter will learn from you how to deal with difficult situations. If you get out of control, you model this ineffective response to your daughter. If you find yourself angry at your daughter or her coach or the referee or another player or parent, make sure you think about your actions before you respond. The way you deal with strong emotions is a key learning tool for kids. Share effective coping strategies. For example, when you get upset with your child, say, "I'm really angry with your behavior. I need to get my thoughts together and then we will discuss this further. I am going into the kitchen to get some water. Be back here in five minutes so we can discuss this." This lets kids know it's okay to be angry, but you can have effective responses and coping mechanisms for your anger. Remember, be aware of the way in which you talk about your own day. Do you come home from work harping on the negatives, focused on the uncontrollable, and blaming others, or do you balance negative with positive and search for solutions to the uncontrollable? These are powerful messages you send to your children.

8. Be a Parent, Not a Game-Day Coach: Before a game or competition, don't remind her to think about technical skills or remind her of corrections she's made. Don't tell her where to be on the field or court; don't give advice on shooting techniques or passing methods, either. Show her that you trust her to get focused and ready for competition. When it comes time to compete, it's vital for athletes to trust their trained bodies. It is time to execute, not overthink and analyze. Show your daughter that you trust her too. The more you fidget with her and tell her what to do to get ready, the more you send the message that you don't trust her. Let her know that you are there to support her and that you believe in her ability. Back away and show that you believe in her.

9. Provide Her with Choices: Providing your daughter with choices gives her a feeling of being in control. Allow her to process defeats and develop strategies to improve the situation. Acknowledge your daughter's feelings of anger, disappointment, and frustration without trying to talk her out of them or fix them. Avoid judging her feelings. Instead, simply acknowledge that all of her feelings are acceptable. Once she embraces her feelings, she can learn to cope with them.

10. Stay Focused: Make sure you talk to your child about herself and her own personal improvement. Avoid comparisons to others, as she cannot control them. The more she thinks about competitors, the more she helps them and hurts herself. Typically, she raises the standard of another person's play in her head. As a result, she is focused on their proficiencies, not their weaknesses. Your daughter ends up thinking about her competitor rather than herself and begins to feel out of control. Watch your own talk. Do you place great emphasis on how others evaluate you? If so, your daughter may pick up on this and become more concerned about what others think than her own standards. If someone is unaware of your daughter's personal daily and monthly goals, their opinions should not be as important as those of the people intimately involved in her sports experience. However, even the evaluations of those people intimately involved need to be balanced with emphasis on your daughter's own opinions and thoughts. For instance, a mother of a gymnast would pick her daughter up

from practice and immediately ask what the coaches thought of the practice and whether they had doled out any praise. Processing practice revolved solely around the opinions of the coaches. Although it is natural and helpful for parents to understand how the coaches think their daughter is progressing, it is also essential to gain an awareness of the child's opinion of herself and her training sessions. By asking questions such as, "How did you feel today?" "What went well at practice?" and "How are you feeling about your progress?" parents express to their daughter that her self-evaluations are of great value.

5

Effective Training: How to Help Her Get the Most Out of Practice

Natural talent only determines the limits of your athletic potential. It's dedication, a willingness to learn, and discipline in your life that makes you great.

—Billie Jean King

- A competitive figure skater spends 650 hours per year practicing to compete for 42 minutes—about seven competitions per year.
- A soccer player practices 208 hours per year to play for 40 hours—about 30 games per year.

By those sheer numbers alone, it is very clear that training and practice significantly shape the experience a young woman has in sports. It is at practice that she will spend the bulk of her time as an athlete. Competing is exhilarating, but when a competition or game is over, within twenty-four hours the athlete finds herself back at practice, preparing for the next game or meet. And because it takes so much preparation to be successful, it is essential that an athlete not only learn from her training sessions but enjoy them as well. To ensure training productivity and enjoyment, she must understand the important role practice plays in skill development. It is the biggest part of the process that moves her toward achieving goals.

Most of us associate training and practice with physical skills and strategy. And to a large degree, that is true. But what many athletes don't understand is that mental training is equally important, because what the body does is dictated by the mind. During practice, as in games or performances, an athlete must constantly deal with the emotions that surface as she goes through the process. There are many occasions an athlete finds herself frustrated, angry and confused, afraid, and even bored. How she handles those emotions and feelings are directly responsible for not only how she performs and competes, but for her overall enjoyment and growth gained by participating in sports.

PURPOSES OF PRACTICE

To get the most out of practices, an athlete needs to be encouraged to see that there are many different reasons why she trains. Too many athletes believe that practice is merely a measure of improvement, and that outlook doesn't equip them to deal with the many distinct emotions that arise in both practice and competition.

For example, a sprinter who believes that practice is only worthwhile if she performs to her best will feel wonderful when she runs her best time in practice. Elated because of the time, she then sets an unrealistic standard for the next day's practice. "I'll never run slower than that again. As a matter of fact, I want to run even faster tomorrow."

By viewing practice as worthwhile only if the highest standard of performance is met, this athlete sets herself up for disappointment. It is unrealistic to think she'll run a personal best every single time she practices. She denies herself the opportunity to become even better because, once she does run slower, she will feel as if she has failed. She will label her practice "good" only if she comes close to or meets her personal best time. This eliminates all other purposes for practice and makes it difficult for her to make the technical changes that may be necessary to improve her speed and consistency.

The better thought process would be, "I ran my best time ever today because I was able to keep my head down on my start. If I concentrate on that every day, I'll continue to improve." By identifying how she ran better and attaching a different purpose to practice, in this case working on technique, she sets reasonable standards for herself and remains open to seeing the small improvements that in time will create the desired outcome.

Of course, that doesn't mean that an athlete won't struggle as she finds different purposes for practice. A tennis player trying to increase the power of her serve, for example, might lose accuracy for a few days while making the adjustments. It is important that athletes and parents remain calm through these periods of relearning or improving and resist the urge to panic or assume that the skill is lost forever.

SELF-TALK

There are many ways to teach an athlete to use her mind as a practice tool. One of the most effective methods I've seen is self-talk, the conversations we all have with ourselves every minute of our lives. Have you ever tried to not think, even for just five seconds? It's impossible. You think about not thinking or shutting off your mind or the noises you hear. We constantly have conversations with ourselves. An athlete needs to learn to pay attention to these important dialogues within her head.

I've found that most athletes tend to hear two voices: the critic and the acceptor. The critic reminds her that no matter what she does, it can always be better. The critic is the negative thinker that tells her she can't do it and comes up with all the reasons to support why she can't or won't. The acceptor is the more positive voice, telling her she can do it and creating all the reasons to support why she can or will do it.

During practice, an athlete tends to vacillate between these two types of thought processes. The critic convinces her she won't do it and the acceptor tells her she will do it. The problem with this type of self-talk can be seen when an athlete has a frustrating day and the critic's voice becomes extremely loud. In order to combat this powerful negative voice, the athlete often tries to talk to herself in a more positive and accepting manner. The obstacle occurs when the athlete just can't believe the positive voice, and she finds that she can only be accepting and positive about herself up to a point. The acceptor is silenced by severe mistakes or mistakes she perceives to be unacceptable.

In order for skill improvement to occur, the athlete must learn how to switch on another voice—a voice that focuses her attention on how to improve rather than on whether she does improve. This type of self-talk is called effective thinking. For example, a gymnast working on a release move thinks positively when she completes the move successfully, but as soon as she misses a few, she begins to think negatively. She tries to be positive but continues to miss skills and reverts to being negative. Then, she remembers that some sports psychology lady told her to think positively, so she tries it, misses another skill, and ends up back at the negative. Throughout her workout she is saying to herself, "I can. Oh, no I can't. Yes, I can. Oh, no I can't. I can—I can't—I can—I can't—I can—I can't."

She gets stuck because her self-talk is entirely related to the outcome of the task. She cannot possibly make improvements until she shifts her attention to how to do the skill. As soon as an athlete begins to think effectively, her frustration becomes much more controllable.

APPLICATION OF EFFECTIVE THINKING

Once athletes learn that effective thinking exists, the next step is application of it during practices. As athletes develop, they tend to become proficient at identifying their technical errors. Very often they will be able to explain in great detail the mechanics or lack thereof in their skills. However, very few are as good at turning those mistakes into corrections. Instead of struggling to create a correction, an athlete will choose to tell her body what she doesn't want it to do instead of what she wants it to do. When an athlete tells herself, "Don't bend over," she must first see herself doing the skill bent over, so she can then instruct her body not to do it that way. It would be much simpler and clearer for her to instruct her body, "Stand up straight."

The information an athlete gives to her body is most useful when it is clear and specific. For instance, a skater told me, "I need to jump higher." I asked, "How do you do that?" She responded, "What do you mean? You just jump." There are many ways to jump higher, and I wanted the skater to clearly tell her body what to do. Thus, "jump higher" becomes "bend your left knee" or "take your right leg through." Many athletes understand technique so well they could write a lengthy paper describing the biomechanics of the motor skill. However, it saves a great deal of time to provide simple and clear information that instructs the body exactly how to make the desired movement.

EFFECTIVE THINKING FEEDBACK

Once an athlete identifies a mistake and turns that mistake into a correction, she has one last step to complete the effective thinking process. The last step involves the feedback she gives herself after completing a skill or drill attempt. Many times I see an athlete try to make a correction but not get the desired outcome. For instance, a skater who tries to make a technical correction on the jump and then falls down will often provide feedback to herself about the outcome. She says, "That wasn't good. I fell down. That correction doesn't work." Although the feedback about the outcome is accurate—she did indeed fall down—the feedback is unhelpful. By giving herself feedback about the outcome she wastes time stating the obvious and doesn't teach her body anything. It is clear by the fall or missed attempt that the skill wasn't good enough. However, what is truly important and missing from the feedback is information about the correction.

Effective feedback needs to be related to the correction. The athlete should ask, "Did I or didn't I make the correction?" At this point, it's critical for the athlete to move beyond the undesirable skill outcome and focus her attention on the small steps that when put together make the skill work correctly. When an athlete places emphasis on skill correction, she can take satisfaction in her progress and reduce the level of frustration considerably. She continues to make progress by fixing parts of the skill. Finally, when all steps are corrected, the skill will be executed successfully. The athlete may not get the hoped-for outcome immediately, but she can certainly leave practice having improved one part of the skill and thus managed her frustration.

It is vital for athletes to understand that effective practice is not about eliminating but truly managing frustration. Too many athletes believe that if they do everything correctly every day, they won't get frustrated and they won't have setbacks. This is unrealistic. Practice is about correcting errors and improving consistency, so by nature it is frustrating. Effective practice is learning to react to frustration in a manner that allows progress to continue.

SHE'S SO NEGATIVE WHEN SHE TRAINS

Jane is a fourteen-year-old competitive ice skater who found that two days before an important competition, she couldn't land her most difficult jump, the double axel, with any consistency. I arrived at the rink and found her at the barrier in tears.

"I can't do it," she sobbed. "I could but now I can't. What's wrong with me?"

I told her to take a deep breath and to concentrate on what I was about to say.

"I understand you are very frustrated," I said softly. "I really wish I could make your double axel come back right now. Unfortunately, I can't. So, we need to figure out how to react to this situation."

"What do you mean, react?" she asked a little warily.

"Let's think now. What are your options in how you deal with this problem?" I asked her.

She paused and began thinking.

I was trying to stop Jane from focusing on the external problem (not landing) and to start thinking about the internal solution (her reaction to not landing). I wanted her to understand that she had a choice in how to respond to a difficult, uncomfortable, and frightening situation. First, I acknowledged what she was feeling and told her I wished I could make it better. Next, I said "I can't make it better," which gave the power for change back to her. And then I challenged Jane to think of ways to handle the situation.

"What do you mean by options?" she asked.

"Well, let's think," I said. "You can go home and beat yourself up and make yourself miserable like you are now over this jump. And you can think about how awful you'll do in competition, but you will still end up having to come in here tomorrow and work on the jump."

"That's what I usually do," she admitted. "I don't like that option."

"Well, then," I said, "What are the others?"

"I could think about landing the jump," she began, "all the times I've done it before and think really positively."

"Yes, you could," I said. "Is that what you would like to do?"

"No, I don't really believe that right now. I feel like I can't do it. I already tried to think positively and it didn't work."

"Do you have any other options?" I asked.

Jane thought and adamantly stated, *"No."*

"Okay, then what will it be?"

"Well, I guess I do have another option. I could just wait and it will come back. That's how it's been in the past. I just wait and the jump comes back to me."

"Okay, so you will just wait?"

"No, I can't wait right now because it always takes me two weeks to get the jump back and the competition is in two days."

"Wait a second," I said. "If your plan is to just wait for the jump to come back, why couldn't it come back the day of the competition? It's entirely possible. You can't have it both ways. If you wait, you have to be open to the possibility that the jump could come back as easily tomorrow as in two weeks. If you wait, it could come back at any time."

I had pointed out a different way for Jane to see her situation, and she quickly realized that I had caught her trying to rationalize her negativity and she laughed. "Okay. That makes sense. I guess I'll wait and hope it happens in the next two days."

"Okay," I said. "Now before you go I just want to let you know that you've forgotten a very important option."

She looked puzzled. "I have? What?"

"In the past, you haven't just waited," I said. "You have accepted the fact that the jump is not as good as you want it to be, and you focused your attention on how to improve it. You stopped dwelling on the outcome and instead directed all of your energies to correcting the jump. You thought about your corrections and made small improvements each day. You made the jump better through your thoughts and perceptions of the situation, not by waiting. Sometimes you even chose not to think about anything too specific in the jump. You just thought of your lucky number, thirteen, or thought about your favorite ice cream flavors, and this helped you let it happen instead of forcing it. The bottom line is in the past you spent no time beating yourself up or asking unhelpful questions like, 'Why can't I land it?' You spent all of your time focused on fixing the jump."

"I did?" she asked. "I guess I forgot all that."

Jane had a choice to make in her thinking. If she wanted to be self-defeating, I was going to let her, but not until she understood that type of thinking was by choice. Parents and coaches can help break the cycle of negative thinking by giving an athlete information she may have overlooked. Too often, however, they try to process the situation for the athlete and figure it out for her by asking the same questions she is asking herself. What she needs is help to get beyond all the reasons something isn't working and focus on how to make it work.

Once Jane was reintroduced to the process that had brought success, she was able to dismiss the negative thoughts and rechannel her mind in a positive direction. By putting herself in control of the situation, Jane came back to practice the very next day and landed the jump without a problem. In competition two days later, Jane hit the jump once and missed it once, but refused to let herself be more than momentarily frustrated.

Jane had used her thought process to take action and change the situation. A simple way for Jane to remember how to switch to effective thinking was to use a three-step process to gaining focus: **ACT**.

A—Acknowledge that a change in thought and attitude must occur.

C—Choose to concentrate on one thought related to the situation at hand—what is happening right now in the present.

T—Toughen body language to set the framework for success—head up, shoulders down, chest out.

An Ineffective-Thinking Athlete:

- Asks herself questions that have useless answers, such as, "Why am I so bad?"
- Is unaware that her thoughts are based on the past or the future.
- Concentrates on why she CAN'T do something correctly.
- Uses body language that says, "I'm terrible"; her head and eyes are down, shoulders hunched.

An Effective-Thinking Athlete:

- Acknowledges that she needs to concentrate on what is happening right now.
- Asks herself open-ended, positive-minded questions, such as, "What can I think about to make this better? What one thing can I focus on next time that might help?"
- Concentrates on how to do it.
- Uses body language that says, "I'm confident that I'm giving it my best shot"; her head is up, shoulders back, chest out.

FAST FACTS

➡ Twenty-four junior tennis players were observed during tournament matches and their observable self-talk, gestures, and match scores were recorded. Players also described their positive, negative, and other thoughts on a postmatch questionnaire. Findings indicated that negative self-talk was associated with losing and that players who reported believing in the utility of self-talk won more points than players who did not.(1)

ALL SHE CAN THINK ABOUT IS THE FALL

Laticia is a fifteen-year-old gymnast who was a level 10 working her way up to elite when she suffered a really hard fall on balance beam. Her injuries were minor and she recovered physically very quickly. However, her performance level remained well below her capabilities. She would not do anything on beam that required her to go backward. Slowly, her balking (stopping herself before full rotation was completed) began to be carried over to vault. If she didn't start rotating, she couldn't compete. She admitted to me, when she called, that she couldn't get the fall out of her mind.

"Every time I step up on beam, it's all I can think about, no matter how hard I try not to remember it," she said. "I don't know how to get it out of my head."

"I can understand how scary it must be to keep seeing that fall in your head," I said.

"Yeah. I keep trying to block it out," she said. "It gets really tiring trying to motivate myself to get through the fear. I'm so sick of trying to convince myself to do things that I used to do without any thought."

"You mentioned that you have a lot of fear," I said. "If you had to take a guess at what is scary about going backward, what would it be?"

"Oh, I know exactly what I'm scared of," she said. "I feel like I was lucky not getting hurt on that fall. All the same, for a minute, I thought I was really hurt. I don't want to ever have that scary feeling of wondering if I'm okay or not. I just don't want to hurt myself anymore."

"When you start to feel scared, do you feel it in your body somewhere?" I asked.

"Yeah, I feel queasy and my stomach feels like it's in knots. My heart starts pounding pretty quickly, too."

"That's good, actually," I said. "It's important for you to pay attention to what your body is telling you. When you feel queasy and your stomach knots up, what do you start to think about?"

"As soon as my stomach gets like that, I know I'm scared," she said. "I pretty much dread the rest of the day because I know it's going to revolve around me trying to battle my fear. I think about blocking out my fear and trying to make my stomach unknot. But the more I think about that the worse my fear seems to get. It's like I know once I get scared I'm not going to do anything."

"Sounds like when your body feels the fear, you start to try and make the fear go away," I said.

"Of course. I'm trying to get back to how I used to feel before my series. I never felt scared or thought about anything. I try to clear my mind and get rid of the fear so I can do something," she said.

"I wonder if you really have to get rid of the fear to do the series?" I asked.

"What do you mean?" she asked, puzzled, "Are you saying that I could do it with the fear?"

"Well," I said, "It makes sense to me that you would have some fear and doubt about certain skills right now. Does it seem normal to you that you might be scared before your series or worry about falling again?"

"Sure."

"Okay," I started, "Have you ever done anything else when you felt scared? Let's think about walking across the balance beam. You can do that very easily. Now, if I raised that balance beam one hundred feet in the air, could you walk across it?"

"Sure, but it's not the same."

"Right. What changes?"

"It's one hundred feet in the air! I'd worry about falling off."

"So, the physical skill doesn't change just because the situation changes. What changes is you. The physical requirements remain the same, but your thoughts about the skill are drastically different. You might worry about falling off and getting hurt and not getting across. These thoughts intensify those signs of fear you feel in your body, making you even more scared, which leads you to think about even worse outcomes, which may eventually paralyze you from even trying."

"So it's okay to be scared? I can do the skills even when I feel so awful?"

"Absolutely," I said. "Fear makes it seem harder to do the skills, but just because you feel scared doesn't mean you are going to get hurt. It sounds like when you feel scared you try to eliminate the fear, and when you can't make it stop, you get even more scared, and convince yourself that the skills are impossible to do. You absolutely need to separate what you feel from what you think. When you separate what you feel from what you think, you can feel scared, yet still think your way through your routine."

What sets athletes apart is not that one is scared and the other isn't. It's that some athletes are able to learn to react to their fear and work through it. If Laticia could learn to do some skills when she was scared, she would develop the necessary mental skills to get herself through this phase of her training.

"It makes sense, but I know how scared I am. I just get tired of trying," she said.

"I know how frustrating it must be to have to think about something that used to come so easily," I told her. "But it is really good training for you. It's pretty easy to do skills that you feel good about. The quality that sets athletes apart is not that one athlete has fear and another doesn't have fear. It's that some athletes are able to learn to react to their fear and work through it while others don't know how to do that. So if you can learn how to do some skills when you are scared, you don't have to worry about being so perfect all the time. You can get injured and feel scared and doubtful, but have the mental skills to get yourself through those tough times."

"Yeah. I'd like to be able to do that," she said. "Are you saying that this fear thing isn't permanent?"

"I don't think it has to be permanent. However, you need to think about this as a new skill. It feels different to do a series on beam when you are feeling scared. Yet I bet your fear isn't the same intensity everyday."

"That's true. Sometimes I'm petrified and other days I feel like I might actually do it, but I haven't."

"My guess is that as soon as you get scared you assume you can't do the skill. Yet one day you might be only slightly fearful, while on another day much more fearful. Fear isn't fear. There are different degrees and depending upon the intensity you can work through the fear," I said.

I suggested Laticia change her expectation for her series on beam.

"I'd like you to keep track of how scared you are on a scale of one to ten, with one being not scared at all and ten being petrified. When you feel a ten, the best use of your time is to do simple exercises or use a spot or go on the low beam. When you feel a one, little thought will be needed for you to complete the skill. When you feel about a five, that is when you need to use your effective thinking to work your way through the skill. When you are a five, don't expect to do a perfect series, rather try and get it going by taking the small steps. You might try a few with a spot and then pad the beam and finally remove the mats. During each step, be sure to pick helpful thoughts that are separate from what you feel."

Laticia and I approached working on reacting better to her fear by differentiating various intensity levels of fear and separating her thoughts and images from the feelings. Her coach worked with us and was willing to start at the beginning steps of the skill by padding the beam and spotting. This gave Laticia an opportunity to work on her mental approach and do the skill without so much fear. She gained confidence knowing that she hadn't lost the feel for the skill, and developed an effective way to think about it while being successful.

I also had her begin to learn how to visualize the skills in her mind. In addition to the visualization training, I had her watch old videotape of herself doing the skill correctly. As she watched her series on beam, she would say a key word, "Square," right before throwing the skill. When she went back into the gym, she would use this key word while actually trying the skill. When her body signaled her that she was scared, she would take a deep breath and tell herself, "It's okay to be scared." Next, she would choose the key word from the videotape sessions, "Square." Finally, she would take another deep breath and toughen her body to appear confident. She would count to three and say "Square." If she didn't go on three, she would start the routine again. She had three shots to do the skill, and if she didn't go, she could repad the beam and try again or move on to another event. This structured time gave her a beginning and end point to prevent mental exhaustion. She began doing the skill, and although she had setbacks, she now had some coping skills to deal with them.

FAST FACTS

➡ Even elite athletes experience fear. Here are some of Michelle Kwan's comments about the fear she experienced before the 1997 National Championships. "I totally forgot how to have fun before nationals. It was a dreadful time for me because it was like I focused on the wrong thing. I was thinking of winning and just, 'Okay, I've got to do this' and 'You know, if this doesn't happen things are going to go really badly.' It seemed like I had something to lose and when I was in nationals I didn't have the guts and of course there's no glory. No doubt about it. I was afraid of something like I had a monster on the other side. . . ."(2)

THEY'RE A MESS

Many times I am called to help young women athletes deal with the mistakes they make during a game or competition and resulting failure they feel. Usually it is because their coaches or parents are worried about the toll the bad experience may have on the athlete. Sometimes they want to help the athlete correct the mistake through mental training. Often, it is both.

A coach I know called me one fall afternoon with a frustrated plea for help. He had been the coach of a twelve-year-old girls' soccer team for the past two seasons. The previous weekend they had advanced to the finals of a prestigious tournament. It was the first time they made the finals, and he told me the girls were excited to be playing for the gold medal.

"We talked about staying composed for this game," he said.

"They played with a lot of poise and really knocked themselves out. Nobody came off that field at the end of regulation play with an ounce of energy left."

The problem was, as he explained it, that the game ended in a 1-1 tie, which meant they had to participate in a five-player shootout to decide who would go home with the gold and who would go home with the silver. Only one of the girls on his team made her penalty kick (a free shot at the opposing team's goalie), and they lost the championship. The girls who missed the kicks were sobbing. He had praised his team profusely in front of all the other parents and participants but told me privately, "I'm going to have to find other girls to take those kicks, because these girls aren't mentally tough enough. They're a mess."

He asked me to talk to the team. I eagerly agreed.

The girls were actively involved in soccer drills when I arrived. He blew his whistle and called them over and told them to sit down. He introduced me as "someone who's going to help us understand why we do what we do, bad and good." It was a pretty good introduction.

"Let me ask you a question." I began with the assembled group staring up intensely. "Who here knows what got you girls to the finals of the tournament last week?"

A bunch of hands shot up. I pointed at one little girl with brown hair and big eyes.

"We won all of our games," she answered, followed by a chorus of giggles.

"Yes, that's true," I said, "but what did you do to win those games—and don't tell me you scored more goals than the other team."

More hands shot up.

"We played really hard, especially in the game we were down by a goal, and we didn't let up and we ended up scoring in the last minute to win."

"And we played as a team," another player interjected. "Sometimes that doesn't always happen, but we were passing the ball really well and getting it up to our forwards."

"We played a good defense, too," someone else said.

This was going to be easy. Obviously, the coach had stressed to the team that the journey was just as important as the result. In order to effectively deal with the loss, it was necessary for the team to focus on the positive aspects of their game and acknowledge that their success throughout the tournament was not based solely on the final game.

"That's right," I said. "What enabled you to be successful, to get to that final game, was a combination of effort and focus—not on the other team, but on your own team. You persisted even when you felt tired and down. All of these efforts need to be congratulated. You created wins and the fact that you lost the final game on penalty kicks, well, that does not make you bad players or a bad team."

What I was doing was getting them to reframe their thinking, pointing out that there is always another way to look at a situation. In loss, I was telling them, you must find opportunity so that you can continue to move ahead. I wanted them to have a clear understanding of what produced their success and see that those internal factors that created the desired outcome resided within each of them. Often, loss and disappointment prevent athletes from acknowledging and using their inherent strengths. This team needed a reminder that no matter what the outcome, they could rely on and apply those internal factors to create future successes. Even with that said, I didn't want to just ignore what had gone wrong.

"What *did* go wrong in that final game?" I asked.

"We missed our kicks," someone shouted out. More giggles.

"No," someone else insisted. "We should have never let the game get to the point where we had to *make* penalty kicks." It was obvious someone had been talking with that young lady.

"Great point," I said. "What you need to think about now is how to learn from this experience. The questions you don't want to ask yourself are, 'Why do I always miss pressure shots?' or 'Why didn't I score before we got to the PK situation?' Or any other question that forces you to provide answers related to everything you did incorrectly."

Focusing on the negative is an easy way out for athletes, especially young girls. Many think that if they beat themselves up about mistakes and losses, it will motivate them to be better. But if they only focus on the result, regardless of whether it is negative or positive, they really can't move ahead. In order to move ahead, they must focus on the process. The how-to-get-it-done versus whether or not they did it right or wrong.

In talking with the coach and his team, I learned that indeed, they do practice penalty kicks at every practice, emphasizing the physical skill itself. When the coach gave the girls feedback, it was about their mental toughness—their ability to kick it under pressure, "when it counts." Yet he had never worked on teaching them how to kick under this kind of pressure—the finals of a big tournament that was important to everyone on the team. So for him to say that his players were a "mental mess" was certainly extreme. It wasn't that these girls were poor pressure players, they just didn't know how to control their play under pressure. They couldn't be bad at something they didn't know how to do. The team needed some extra mental preparation for this particular situation.

I told the team that they were no different today than they were before the finals, when they had won every game. One loss didn't eliminate a major accomplishment. However, I also told them it was necessary to better prepare themselves to make shots when the whole game rested on it.

"Kicking under pressure is a skill just like any of the physical skills you learn," I said. "Making the final shot to win a game is probably one of the toughest pressures you'll face as athletes."

I talked with them about how they could better prepare. I asked one of the girls who missed her kick what thoughts she had prior to kicking, how her body felt, and what kinds of distracting thoughts or images were going through her head.

"I don't remember," she answered, "I just wanted to make it bad."

None of the other players could remember how they felt, either. They hadn't been trained to examine their thoughts and feelings in those situations. Their entire focus was on the outcome.

"How many of you believe you're doomed when you have to kick under pressure?" I asked.

About half raised their hands.

"How many of you believe if you make the kick, it's because you got lucky?"

Again, about half raised their hands.

"How can you possibly know whether or not you will make the kick? How many of you are psychic?"

Everyone laughed.

"Unless some of you are psychic, you can't possibly know whether you will make the kick until you actually do it. If you ask yourself the question, 'Will I or won't I make the kick?' you are forcing yourself to predict the future. You can't do this. None of us particularly like unanswered questions, so your brain tries to answer the question. To find an answer, your brain sifts through past experiences. If you have missed in the past, you are going to predict that you will most likely miss again. If you have made the kicks in the past, but simply attributed your success to luck, once again you will predict that you will miss the kick. What do you think would happen if you started believing it wasn't luck, but skill and mental strength that made that ball go in? Do you think it would make a difference?"

Every head nodded.

Once athletes acknowledge that they contribute to their own successful outcomes, they can stop focusing on the outcome and begin thinking about how to reproduce that same type of success. If an athlete wants to make the kicks, she needs to stop trying to convince herself that she will (positive thinking) or won't (negative thinking), and instead accept that she can't predict the outcome and choose to think about how to do it (effective thinking).

Changing perceptions and thoughts is always difficult. With young girls, it's even more difficult. They tend to resist changes in their self-perceptions and most often will explain the inconsistency between how they see themselves ("I can't do it") and how they actually perform ("I did it") away through luck. The other problem is that they will start to think they are bad kickers. In practice, you'll hear them say, "I can't." They then go and intentionally miss their kicks so they can come back with evidence to support and reinforce the self-perception that they cannot do it. They will say to you, "See, I told you I couldn't do it. Before, I just gave you my word, now I gave you proof of my inabilities."

I told the coach that it's important that his players understand that there is always another way to look at the situation. They could choose to look at all the reasons why they missed those kicks, or they could choose to focus on how to give themselves the best chance of making the critical shots.

Once they learned to focus on how to do it, the coach could implement this effective thinking style into workout drills.

QUICK QUESTIONS

How do you practice performing under pressure?

One of the most effective ways is to simulate, as much as possible, pressure situations. The athlete is told to believe a certain set of facts exists, such as, "It's overtime, we're down by a point with two seconds left on the clock and you're at the line. Hit these free throws and we will win the world championship."

Soccer coaches will often tire the athletes out with a difficult physical drill and then make them go right to the ball in order to teach them how to maintain their focus while being tired. It's critical that athletes are told to identify key thoughts or feelings that help them perform well in these challenging situations.

Another idea is to play a game within the game. At the end of practice, for example, tell a soccer team that whoever makes their penalty kicks become members of the all-galactic team, which is afforded special privileges at the next practice. But add a twist, inviting all of the parents to stand around and watch making distracting noises and cheers.

As each player kicks, the coach tries to help her focus as the noise erupts around her. The coach and athlete develop a key word or phrase to concentrate on, like "nice and easy" or "be aggressive" or "follow through." That way the coach is not just telling her to get focused, but showing her how to use effective thinking in order to get focused on how to make the kicks.

Practice drills can also be used to simulate pressurelike situations. For instance, skills can be repeated three, five, or ten times in a row. If the athlete misses one of the five, she must begin again at number one until she completes five skills back to back.

Coaches can be the providers of pressure by asking athletes to "perform on demand." A figure skating coach might tell an athlete, "We are going to work on performing. I want you to go out right now before you have warmed up and do your program with every jump. If you land everything, you are free to work on whatever you choose for the rest of the session. If you miss one element, you will do the program again right away." A key factor here is that the coach has explained the purpose behind the exercise.

There really isn't anything better than experience itself. So provide opportunities for athletes to think in practice like you want them to think in a game. This way, regardless of the pressure situation, they have a planned and practiced pattern of thinking. It's an easy formula. When the situation changes, the athletes' thinking should remain the same. If using key words helps a gymnast hit her routines daily, then when the pressure is intense, she should rely on what has worked for her in training. Each time she does full routines in practice, she can use her key words and talk herself through the skills just as she would in a meet. She can increase the pressure by making certain routines count as if they were the actual competition. Instead of eliminating the pressure by saying, "It's just practice," she thinks about it as if it were her one and only chance to get it right.

It's helpful to specify times during workouts where the idea is to practice performing. When using actual meets or games as warm-ups to more important competitions, make sure athletes take these seriously by attaching importance to them. Adding mental drills to physical drills helps athletes to deal with pressure situations. There is an old adage that says, "Play like you practice." When it comes to learning to compete, the adage needs to be restated as, "Practice like you play."

FAST FACTS

➡ Prior to the 1999 women's World Cup, nine countries spent upwards of $40,000 to allow their teams to train in the United States well before the opening of the games. Countries spent the money to ensure that athletes recovered from jet lag and to have players come together as a team while adjusting to the U.S. environment.(3)

SHE DOESN'T LIKE GOING TO
PRACTICE ANYMORE

"It's just not any fun anymore," Julie, a seventeen-year-old volleyball player, told me one day. "We do the same things over and over and the coach yells, and there are times I really don't want to go at all, even though I love the games."

I hear "It's not fun anymore" far too often from athletes. Usually, as athletes progress and expectations for their performance rise, they have periods of time where they just don't want to play sports. Much of the reason is the pressure an athlete feels to achieve. When she first started in sports, she learned something new every day and was praised for her effort and skill level. At the more advanced level, she is expected to perform to her ability daily without a lot of recognition for doing so. This can be draining, especially if success is measured by reaching outcome goals. As athletes progress it may take them months before they achieve a new goal, and they may even find themselves becoming worse at some skills that used to come so easily. The learning curve changes. Expectations are raised, and pressure mounts. Now, athletes need to call upon their mental strengths.

I asked Julie, "What do you really like about volleyball and sports?"

Julie thought for a few moments, "Well, I really like to play in games. I love to compete. It's fun to be with my teammates."

"Is there anything you enjoy about practice?" I asked.

"Not really anymore. I'm so sick of getting yelled at all the time."

"I can understand how you wouldn't like being yelled at. Can you remember a time when you did like things about practice?"

"Yeah. I used to really like it when we learned different things," she said. "We were constantly learning new plays and skills. It was fun to try out different positions and see what I was good at. I liked trying to make myself stronger in certain areas of my game."

"So it sounds like having a goal to work toward is pretty important in terms of how much you enjoy practice," I said.

"Yes and no. It is important, but it's the coach. I can't stand it anymore. It seems I'm always doing something wrong," she said. "No matter how hard I try it's not good enough. And when I do something well, nobody says anything because I was supposed to do it that way."

Most athletes go through periods when they want to quit or they question their commitment to sports. Very often this process makes them better athletes because they reach back to rediscover why they actually participate in sports. This new way of thinking about their sport may lead to increases in motivation and intensity.

"In the past, the fun was provided for you by your coaches," I said. "Now it sounds like you are going to have to find ways to put some fun back into your sport. It's hard to do something for fifteen hours every week, and the part you love about it you only get to do for two hours a week. That requires you to find things to appreciate about practice so you can enjoy the games and participate at your highest level."

"Okay, but I can't think of anything I like about practice."

"Well, let's start this way," I suggested. "What is your goal for the next six months in volleyball?"

"I want to be a starter."

"What do you need to do to become a starter?" I asked.

"I need to improve the power of my serve, for one thing," she said. "If I do that, I think the coach will start me, but I'm not sure because she doesn't like me much."

"Let's start with the serve first," I said. "How do you improve the power?"

"Extra practice, I guess, but I don't know if I want to do that," she said. "I practice a lot now."

"Well, if you want to be a starter, that is going to require a certain commitment and level of play. If you aren't able to commit yourself to following through on what you know it will take to be a starter, then simply change the goal so that you can enjoy the process."

"I do want to be a starter and I guess I could practice more, but I'm still worried that even if I do, she won't make me one because she doesn't like me," she said.

"Do you think it would be worthwhile to talk to your coach and let her know what your goal is and how you plan to achieve it?" I asked. "You could ask her advice, too, about what she thinks you need to do to become a starter."

"Yeah, maybe."

"Your coach could give you some clear guidelines. You may or may not agree with your coach and you may or may not like what she says, but at least you will have an understanding of the steps necessary to improve your game," I said. "Once you have a clear idea of the steps, you can give yourself daily tasks that you think are going to help you achieve those steps."

"Like a plan?"

"Right, but you will have input into the plan and the goals. Sometimes in practice you will be limited by the demands of the coach. Yet if you know you are working for a goal that you want, the process will make sense. You can always ask the coach for extra time to work on a specific skill as long as you can show her how your request relates to improving your game."

Coaches are the experts in terms of defining action plans for meeting goals. However, sometimes athletes will not trust the plan, especially when their input has not been solicited. Therefore, some of the responsibility for developing an action plan can be shifted to the athlete. This is especially helpful for coaches who are in charge of a team or large group of athletes and cannot be expected to meet one athlete's needs every single day. Once Julie took ownership of the process, she could see how practice fit into her own action plan.

Good coaches know they must vary practice to keep everyone's interest level and motivation high. They understand that when an athlete does something well, she should be encouraged and praised for the way in which she created the desired outcome. This type of descriptive feedback provides the athlete with information about how she created the positive result rather than just reinforcing the result. This lets athletes know that the coach values the process and the internal factors that contribute to success. Even monotonous drills can be used to praise athletes for exhibiting qualities the coach would like to see more often. Good coaches don't assume that athletes know why they performed to expectations, rather, they identify these qualities and place great value on them.

FAST FACTS

➡ A study examining the various aspects of goal setting among youth tennis players showed that improving overall performance, fun/enjoyment, and winning were the three most important goals and that they most preferred setting moderately difficult goals. The most effective type of goals for players were physical conditioning, practice, and skill/technique, whereas the top reasons for setting goals were focusing attention, problem-solving, and increasing effort.(4)

QUICK QUESTIONS

How can I help her stay interested in practice?

There are many ways to keep a young athlete interested in practice. Try having her set mini-goals, for example, making twenty straight free throws before finishing. Challenge her to compete against herself: "See how many laps you can swim under a minute today." Reward her effort instead of results, "You missed that last spike, but you ran harder than anyone else out there today." Help her to remember why she participates in sports. Let her brainstorm some ways she could make practice more fun for herself, like working on something new or working with a friend instead of on her own, or bringing some kind of healthy snack treat for the team before practice. And mix up routines at home; for example, take her for frozen yogurt after practice even if it is before dinner.

FAST FACTS

➡ High training demands are associated with negative mood states.(5)

SHE'S WORKING TOO HARD

Marissa is a seventeen-year-old swimmer who spends three and four hours a day in the pool, sometimes twice a day. All her life she's been told that if she works her hardest, she'll become successful at whatever she pursues. But I got a phone call one day from Marissa's mother, who was concerned that her daughter was working too hard, spending too much time and energy on swimming.

"She's like a zombie at night," her mother said. "She can barely get the energy to eat. I admire her dedication and work ethic, but how can I judge whether this is the right way to go about being in the sport?"

The term "working hard" is one that needs to be defined by athletes, their parents and their coaches on a case-by-case basis. For some athletes, working hard is measured by effort. I worked with one athlete who kept track of her effort level daily by rating herself on a scale from one to ten, one being little effort and ten being great effort. At the end of the week, she was able to tally her effort level on various parts of her practice and conditioning. She had selected a weekly effort level that she needed to maintain to improve in her sport at the pace she desired. The weekly effort level gave her a clear guideline about how much effort she needed to put forth on a daily basis.

But working harder doesn't always mean putting forth more effort or putting in more time. Often, it can mean dealing better with frustration and distraction. Many seemingly hardworking athletes waste time in practice fighting themselves. They get so aggravated over doing something incorrectly that they use up energy battling themselves. Yet they believe they are working hard because they are acknowledging their mistakes, which is a critical part of the training process. However, athletes who think more is better tend to dwell on their mistakes and frustrations mount. Practice then becomes unproductive.

I met with Marissa one weekend morning.

"Your mom says you're really tired at night," I said. "She's worried that you're exhausting yourself."

"Yeah, I do get tired, but my coach says that I need to keep training more and more if I'm ever to get any faster," she said. "Sometimes I can barely drag myself out of the pool after a workout. I don't know what else to do, though."

One of the first things I thought of was that Marissa might be overtrained.

"How have you been performing?" I asked.

"Lately, my times have gotten worse and worse. It's really getting depressing to even go to practice," she said.

A decrease in performance is a classic trait of an overtrained athlete. Simply stated, it means she is training at a level that is too intense and the duration too long for what she can handle. Today, most coaches implement a training schedule using the concept of periodization. In other words, they provide short durations of very high-intensity workouts followed by less intense workouts which allow the athlete to recover physically and mentally. In this way, the athlete can once again be refueled and ready to train at high intensity. Coaches have to take great care in understanding what intensity levels each athlete can handle. Obviously, Marissa was exhausted from high-intensity training every day. However, she indicated that other athletes on her team seemed to be just fine with this same intensity level. So, with Marissa's permission, I called her coach.

"I've spoken with Marissa, and I'm concerned about her energy level," I said.

"Well, she's doing fine," he said. "She just needs to keep pushing and she'll get stronger. The more she can endure these high-intensity training sessions, the better swimmer she will become."

It was clear to me that he believed one training regime was right for every athlete. It was my hope to try to assist the coach in making some environmental changes that might positively affect Marissa's motivation level.

"She will definitely get stronger by pushing through the workouts. Yet I'm somewhat concerned about how much longer she will be able to push herself. The training may be having some emotional effects. Have you noticed anything different about Marissa in practice?"

"Well, she doesn't seem as happy. I figured she was just really worn out," he said. "I keep telling her she's giving great effort, so I figured that would make her feel better. But now that you mention it, she does seem to be kind of dragging herself around."

"That's what I wondered," I said. "Typically, when an athlete gets physically exhausted and doesn't have time to refuel, she starts to feel it mentally. I'm worried that Marissa is going to start to withdraw from swimming because the demands are just too much for her."

"Well," he said, "we are going to start tapering in a week or so. I thought this rest would be good for her and then she would see how all the training pays off in the actual meet."

"That makes sense. Yet when I talked with Marissa I sensed that she is really losing motivation and interest in swimming. It seems hard for her to even think about a meet. She can barely see herself getting through workouts."

"So are you suggesting that I cut back her workouts now?"

"Well, let's weigh the options. If you cut back, will she lose anything?"

"Sure," he said. "She could be training hard for another week, which will eventually make her faster and stronger. But I don't want her to drop out of the sport because I pushed her too hard. Maybe I should ease up for a few days to let her recharge her batteries, and then I can get one or two more hard days in and then taper her."

"That sounds like a really good plan," I said. "Maybe you can let Marissa know what you plan for her so mentally we can prepare her for the next two weeks. I think it would really help her to know exactly what is going to be expected of her."

"Sure. That's not a problem. I think I'll do that for the whole team."

Once he could see that the physical plan of action was not necessarily getting Marissa to where he wanted her to be, he could easily find ways to alter her training. Once the training environment was adjusted it was time to try and help Marissa make some changes.

"Marissa, I know you are feeling really physically tired. How about emotionally?" I asked.

"I just can't think anymore," she said. "All I try to do is hope that I can get through another day of practice. I get home and all I want to do is go to sleep, but I can't even do that because I worry about getting through practice the next day. I love swimming, but I'm not so sure it's worth it," she said.

"Very often when athletes get physically exhausted, they start to feel emotional effects. It sounds like you aren't sure that you really have the resources to meet the practice demands. When that happens, people tend to experience a lot of stress. I've talked to your coach, and he is going to alter your training for the next few weeks. But I wonder what kinds of things you could focus on to help you get through your workouts?"

"Really, he's going to cut back, he thinks that's okay?" she asked with excitement.

"He is going to explain his rationale to you personally. My understanding is that he thinks you can still be as effective and strong, maybe even more so if he eases up on things a bit," I said. "He doesn't want a burned-out swimmer."

"That helps just knowing it's not going to be so hard," she said.

"How about yourself? What can you do during the workout that will help?"

"You mean what should I think about?"

"When practice is going very well, where are your thoughts?"

"Sometimes, I'm thinking about something technical or sometimes I just let my mind take me somewhere else. I just begin thinking about vacation or something fun, but then I don't think I'm concentrating the right way."

"Well," I said. "When you get really exhausted, why don't you try the sixty percent–forty percent rule."

"What's that?"

"That's when you make sure during your workout that you give sixty percent effort to concentrating on technical things and forty percent on thinking about fun things. Very often, when you remember to have fun, you can push yourself beyond what you thought. When you just try to give one hundred percent all the time, and you don't have one hundred percent to give, you may back off completely. When you make it more realistic you can push yourself beyond your imagination. So, if you don't have one hundred percent left, just give what you think you can. In other words, give one hundred percent of sixty percent. It's still making progress."

"I like that. I always think I have to give it all and I just run out of steam," she said. "I'll try it."

I told Marissa to talk to her coach and then chart her exact practice plan for the next two weeks. Knowing what was expected of her and that she could meet the demands would help significantly. This made her not only a hard worker, but an effective worker.

Characteristics of an Effective Worker

- Sets and accomplishes specific goals.
- Comes to practice on time.
- Follows through on assignments.
- Focuses on how to improve.
- Analyzes mistakes, turning them into corrections.

- Gives herself feedback about the corrections rather than the overall results.
- Listens to coach.
- Filters information, devises extra practice plans accordingly.
- Maintains high effort mentally and physically throughout practice.
- Lets go of mistakes.
- Changes purposes for practice as needed, and can switch easily.
- Starts each day fresh.

FAST FACTS

➡ A 1990 survey of college varsity athletes from the Atlantic Coast Conference revealed that 66% of them felt they had experienced overtraining, with almost 50% of those who overtrained indicating it was a bad experience.(6)

SHE CAN'T CONTROL HER ANGER

Sally is a thirteen-year-old tennis player who is a perfectionist—so much so that whenever she misses a shot, even in practice, she works herself into a rage.

"I can't take her anymore," her mother said one day. "Even when I go out and hit balls with her and she misses a few, she wants to quit. Her attitude is driving me crazy. She's so competitive, but all she seems to do lately is beat herself up."

"What kind of feedback do you give to Sally about her play?" I asked.

"I always tell her when she makes a good shot, and tell her not to worry so much about the misses," she said. "I don't put any pressure on her to excel at tennis. I just want her to enjoy the game."

"Although you don't put pressure on her, Sally obviously puts pressure on herself," I said. "Her focus is solely on the outcome of what she does. It sounds as if you have gotten sucked into this a little bit. You tell her that a shot is good, yet what she really needs to hear is what was good about the shot. She needs your help in redirecting her attention from the outcome to the process. You can do this by giving descriptive feedback."

"So instead of telling her what a great game she played, what should I say?" she asked.

"Stick to things that are under Sally's control. Tell her something about how she created the great play, and try not to get too technical," I said. "For instance, 'Those were some great backhands you hit today. It looked like you really kept your eye on the ball and got in position in plenty of time to hit.' If you find her resistant to your comments about her play, all you have to do is help her provide her own descriptive feedback. For instance, you might say, 'Those were some great backhands you hit today. I wonder what you did to help yourself hit like that?' She won't have an answer, but you've got her thinking about the process. By setting the example of how to process her play, eventually she will model this in her self-evaluation."

"What do I do when she comes home and says, 'I had a great day, I got in every serve I tried' or, 'Everything stunk today?'"

"When things go well, don't just stop with the outcome. Ask, 'That's great. I wonder what helped you do that today?' This gets her thinking about how she made her serve work and forces her to attribute the success back to herself. This will help build confidence. When she tells you everything was awful, ask 'Everything? What specifically didn't go well today? Was there anything you could have done to make things better?' Help her to find something that went well. For instance, when she is having a really bad day, it is much harder to make easy shots and maintain focus. Point out how she was able to still make shots being frustrated and upset, even if they were her easier shots. This is an important area of her game that she will need to rely on, especially when she has made a critical error in a match."

Perfectionists tend to only find their best plays acceptable. Everything in the middle is just plain rotten. In fact, the plays that are just mediocre are the ones that will best help perfectionists increase their consistency. If Sally is technically great, she will hit every shot she needs. If she is technically terrible, there is not much she can do. However, it's those days when her technique isn't quite there but shots are still makeable that she really needs to raise her level of play. If she can hit fairly ugly-looking shots, she will become a stronger player. But perfectionists often get angry when they hit ugly shots. They can't see that it is much harder to make something out of a really awful shot than a great shot. And they don't see this because their perception is that only the perfect outcome is worthwhile and acceptable. Often parents reinforce this thinking by only taking notice of the great plays while criticizing the mediocre ones. So, perfectionistic athletes just try to be perfect or close to perfect all the time, because they don't teach themselves how to work through frustration brought on by poor performance. This leads them to want to be error-free all the time. Yet knowing they could be off technically and still get the job done would certainly make them much more confident players.

Sally needs to take a look at her work ethic.

"Do you consider yourself a hard worker?" I asked Sally.

"Oh, yes. My mother and coach always tell me what a good worker I am," she said.

"How about, when you get so angry at yourself that you have to take a break? Are you still working hard?" I asked.

"I don't know," she said, wavering.

"It seems you are spending a lot of energy being angry, yet it doesn't sound like you are getting where you want to go. What kind of play is acceptable to you on a daily basis?" I asked.

"I *should* be able to make all of my easy shots and make the corrections that my coach is asking for. I shouldn't make a whole lot of errors and should avoid any silly mistakes," she said.

"That's a lot of 'shoulds.' It sounds like you want to play your best or close to your best every day?" I asked.

"Pretty much. I'll accept a few minor errors but if I keep missing something I should make, I can't take it," she admitted.

"So you have the same purpose for practice every day. To play your very best or close to your best," I said.

"Well, of course. Doesn't everybody?" she asked incredulously.

"I'm not so sure about that," I said. "There are lots of different purposes for practice. Sometimes you need to work on your consistency, sometimes you need to work on your shot placement, sometimes you need to work on your technique, sometimes you need to work on your power. Yet if you keep your same standard, you really can't improve in any other area except practice at performing your shots the same way every day."

"You mean I'm not really working on all those other parts of my game?" she asked.

"I don't see how you can if all your attention is focused on how the shot turned out," I said. "You certainly aren't working on technique or speed or power. You only are concerned with the shot outcome and what you 'should' do. What about the days you aren't doing what you should? It seems you get so frustrated by not 'shoulding' that you get nowhere. Perhaps if you were able to accept some flaws in your practice game, you might take the risk to work on these other parts of your game."

"I don't like making mistakes," she said. "I don't want to be average. I want to be great."

"Everybody makes mistakes. It's knowing how to fix them that leads you to improve," I explained. "Beating yourself up for making mistakes is not going to make you great. It sounds like you worry that if you accept any kind of error, you will end up being average. I'm not asking you to ignore the mistakes, rather suggesting you analyze the mistake, turn it into a correction, and let it go. Then you can get to work on perfecting the correction. You might want to think about using a different approach to meet your practice goals."

"How?" she asked.

"Try giving yourself certain periods of time in a practice session to work on different skills, like serve placement or shot consistency. You tend to only acknowledge those aspects of your game when you are playing badly and need to beat yourself up about something," I said. "But this new approach builds in more structure and clearly more realistic expectations into your practice. Try keeping track of these different parts of your game. One way is to make a checklist and rate yourself on a scale of one to ten in each category. You also might want to keep track of how you feel each day using a similar scale. For instance, if you feel pretty lousy, either mentally or physically, you should not expect to play out of your head. On the other hand, you shouldn't expect to be awful. On a day you feel lousy, you need to set specific goals that are achievable and challenging. A challenging goal on a day you feel lousy will be far different from a challenging goal on a day you feel outstanding. You will be choosing different purposes for practice while still pushing yourself through frustration. This is a more effective use of your practice time."

FAST FACTS

➡ Perfectionism has been found to be a significant predictor of precompetitive anxiety. (7)

All athletes need to be reminded that there are different purposes for practice. Instead of just trying to produce great outcomes, the athlete needs to acknowledge and reward the steps to producing the outcomes. Athletes tend to want to show up at practice every day feeling great and producing spectacular physical feats. Even if this were possible, great days don't fully prepare athletes for the rigors of competition, because athletes don't usually spend time analyzing why it went so well. On good days, effective workers identify what they did to produce such great outcomes. On bad days, they change their outcome expectations, finding a purpose for practice that is achievable yet challenging. They work with their situation, using it to help them improve an aspect of their game that may not get much attention. They don't get caught up in what they should be able to do, instead, accept what they are doing and move ahead from that point.

QUICK QUESTIONS

How do I help her balance school and sports?

This is a question I hear from parents all over the country. As a young athlete progresses, the amount of time necessary for practice increases and so do the demands of school. Add in other activities such as drama club or student government, and there is virtually no time left in the day to do much of anything else.

"I feel like I'm constantly nagging her to make sure she gets her homework done before practice, because if she doesn't, then she has to get up early the next morning to do it because practice wipes her out," one mother told me. "I feel like a drill sergeant more than a mother. It's not that she doesn't try, it's just that there's so much to do in so little time. I like that she wants to be involved in other activities besides school and sports, but how do we fit it all in?"

Athletes ask me these questions, too. I find that just about any high school girl wants to know how to find a workable balance. And right there is the key. Balance. Not every activity she does gets equal time. It's just not possible. Balance is about give and take, setting priorities and then following through. At the height of soccer season, she will probably have to spend less time socializing with friends and more time trying to get her body to recover from intense workouts and more time finishing homework on the weekends. When soccer season is over, friendships might then become the priority over soccer.

The mistake most athletes make is that they don't have a plan on how to use their time effectively. They tend to deal with what happens as it happens. They may understand that they have homework and practice on the same night, but without planning in advance, usually one or the other suffers. It is not easy to teach children to think ahead, plan, and recognize that making choices in life is a constant process.

One way to start teaching these skills is to sit down with the athlete on a Sunday or Monday night and sketch out the activities scheduled for the upcoming weeks. If the second week ends with a big game or competition, for example, she might choose to devote extra time and energy to homework during the first week. If during week two there is no game or meet, she might choose to spend more time with friends or on outside projects or just goofing off. Planning for the weeks ahead is a great way to make parental expectations clear and considered. She learns to juggle what is important to her, to her family, and to her coaches and then acts accordingly. It's about creating balance rather than hoping balance happens.

Start by having her keep track of every activity for an entire day, charting how much time she spends on a certain activity and how high a priority it is in relation to her goals. For example:

Morning

Wake up
Finish homework (30 minutes, high priority)
Shower, brush teeth (30 minutes, high priority)
Eat breakfast (5 minutes, high priority)

Watch morning cartoons (15 minutes, low priority)
Feed dog (5 minutes, high priority)
Call friend to see what she's wearing (15 minutes, low priority)

Have her continue through school, afternoon, and evening. Then take a look at her sheet and make sure she has labeled some fun tasks as high priority. Most of her time is going to be spent on activities marked with a high priority. Help her figure out how to better structure the day to make sure she has a balance between what she wants to do and what she needs to do to meet her goals. If, for example, she's on the telephone for forty-five minutes but has marked it as a low priority, she might want to try and cut back to twenty minutes, especially if she needs more time on a high-priority activity. It may seem as if friends are always sacrificed, but there is a way to help with this. If you let her "borrow" time from chores to spend with friends, the next time she needs more time for homework, chores, or practice, for example, she just "borrows" it from friendship time. This way, she is learning that there are choices she must make in order to manage her time effectively and still feel she has control over her own life.

Good Rules She Should Follow

- Establish priorities by setting goals.
- Make sure fun activities are high priority at times.
- Strike a balance between low- and high-priority activities.
- Delegate and plan ahead.
- Be flexible.
- Remember that a sacrifice made today doesn't have to be made repetitively.
- Priorities change.

Coaches can help, too, by emphasizing that academics rank ahead of athletics. The coach can make sure practices and games aren't scheduled during classes and relax training during stressful test weeks. Evening games or meets are ideally scheduled for Friday or Saturday nights so that the athletes have time over the weekend to recover.

QUICK QUESTIONS

Should withholding sports be used as a form of punishment?

Most parents and coaches who stress a balance between sports and academics communicate to athletes that sports participation is a privilege, not a right. When nonsport responsibilities are not met, such as schoolwork, household chores, and family concerns, then sports participation is often taken away, even if it is detrimental to the team. Girls who understand priorities and responsibilities learn quickly that by not taking care of business at school or home, they hurt not only themselves, but their teammates. It's usually a lesson learned quickly that doesn't need repeating.

THESE GIRLS TAKE FOREVER TO GET INTO A SERIOUS PRACTICE MODE

Robert is the high school track coach for both the boys' and girls' teams. He is proud of his ability to treat both teams equally, especially when it comes to working on skills, conditioning, and technique. However, he began to notice a distinct difference between the two teams.

"The boys come to practice and they jump right into what they're supposed to be doing," he said. "But the girls, they come, they talk, they socialize, they mess around until they're behind. What can I do to get them ready to practice?"

Boys and girls may have different needs in terms of getting ready for practice. Boys tend to see activity as a means of social interaction, whereas girls very often prefer to have time to feel connected through group discussion rather than just group activity. This doesn't mean they aren't ready or prepared to practice. They are just getting ready in their own way. For girls, social interaction with their teammates may be an essential reason for their sports participation. It's important to value the social aspect of sport by structuring socialization into practices, thereby maintaining the girls' interest in track. I suggested that the coach start practice ten minutes earlier so the girls could socialize and feel connected before the real drills. Social time can also be structured into the workout by using an activity like stretching to promote social interaction and warm-up simultaneously.

Although young women athletes must train hard in order to succeed, they also want to have fun and feel connected to those around them. When these special needs are met, athletes tend to be happier, and in my experience, happy athletes are more productive. Of course, each need doesn't have to be recognized every single day. When practice is going to be intense, inform athletes of the expectation and give them a reason to get moving quickly, such as letting them go as soon as all the drills are completed correctly, or provide hope that tomorrow will be a lighter workout where they will be able to work together on certain drills.

FAST FACTS

➡ Of girls aged nine to twelve, 84% listed themselves as self-motivators, while 76% received additional motivation from their mothers. Also, 58% were motivated by their fathers or friends.(8)

QUICK QUESTIONS

How can I get her to play aggressively?

There are differences between behavior that is considered aggressive and acceptable and what is considered too aggressive and inappropriate. Playing an acceptably aggressive game doesn't mean using power to overpower another player. It does mean using power to raise her own level of play.

An athlete can become confused by being directed, on one hand, to control her emotions while, on the other, being asked to play with great emotion. She needs to be able to see others play aggressively without breaking the rules or intending to harm someone. When she exhibits intensity in her game, reinforce this style of play. It is helpful to guide athletes to unleash emotion on the field during plays and let off steam after the play is completed.

Have her think of someone she knows who is very confident and plays with a lot of intensity. Then ask her to pretend she's that person and while practicing bring to life the posture, thoughts, and intensity of that imaginary person.

Mental rehearsal in the form of imagery can also be helpful. Teach her to see plays in her head, so when she is confronted with new or unexpected situations, she has thought about how to react and can actually see herself playing aggressively.

Very often, an athlete knows how to be aggressive but forgets to think about playing aggressively. Have her at least five times a practice think about being aggressive. She can use her body language as a way of showing this aggressiveness. When playing aggressively, athletes tend to keep their shoulders down and back and their eyes focused on a specific area. It is extremely helpful for an athlete to be able to identify a behavior that can help her change her intensity level rather than just hoping to play aggressively. Even if her mind is doubtful, her body can project confidence and set her up for aggressive play.

FAST FACTS

➡ A study of 212 girl soccer participants from two different age-group leagues, under 12 and under 14, suggest that young athletes' aggressive behavior is related to their team's "moral atmosphere," including team aggressive norms, players' perceptions of these team norms and coach characteristics, and players' moral motives for behavior.(9)

WHAT ABOUT TRAINING IN ANOTHER STATE?

Chris is a fourteen-year-old figure skater who has been asked to move to another state to live and train with new coaches. Her mother doesn't want to uproot the family and her father can't move because of his job. The coaches say Chris has the chance, if she trains hard and properly, to become a member of the national team, even an Olympian. She's got the physical skills, but her parents wonder if she's mentally ready to handle such a big change in her life?

. . .

There are no right or wrong answers here, only tough questions. In order to make a decision about sending a child away to train, parents need to have an understanding of what factors are driving their decision making. Chris's mother is contemplating sending her daughter away to train for better coaching, but who is driving this decision? Is this something Chris wants or her parents want? Is providing Chris with the best opportunities to excel in her sport something her parents highly value, or is keeping the family together—even at the expense of Chris's pursuing her sport—more important to the family?

Before making any kind of decision regarding sports, Chris's desires, needs, and wishes should be heard. If Chris does not want to train in another state, moving doesn't need to be considered. If she does have aspirations of training away from home, a clear understanding of her reasons is warranted. Is it because she wants to be the best? Does she want to move with her other skating friends? Does she want to remain with a certain coach? A child's rationale for wanting to move away from home is critical to the decision-making process. This doesn't mean that her ambitions will drive the decision. Frankly, most teenagers do not want the responsibility of having to make such a life-altering decision. Regardless, their input needs to heard.

I don't think you can ever know if an athlete is mentally ready for such a huge life change. I don't even know if parents are ever mentally ready for this change. When she does move, there is a tremendous sense of loss, even if everyone believes this is the correct decision. It's essential for parents to prepare their daughter and themselves for this great loss.

If the athlete moves, her life will be centered on training. Yet it's important that both parents and athlete understand that training away from home will not guarantee the creation of an Olympian or even a national contender. It's up to parents to consider whether they can help their daughter feel good about her athletic pursuits even if she does not attain the lofty goals that have been set.

It's best to work into these situations slowly. Try sending her to camp or away with friends for a week. Next, perhaps for the summer. Let her ease into the process of separation with the idea that each move is a trial run. That way, if she becomes homesick and decides to return home, she won't feel as if she failed.

Prior to the move, select living arrangements, see her school, meet her teachers, find her a doctor, and look at the athletic facilities. This helps her ease into the move and lets her know you care about creating a comfortable and safe environment. Once the move is made, it is important that the connection between parent and daughter is maintained. Parenting from long distance, indeed, is a challenge. It is good to set a schedule for phone calls and visits. Discussions naturally will revolve around sports and how her day as an athlete unfolded. But even when she is away from home training to be a superstar, parents must continue to acknowledge all parts of her personality.

FAST FACTS

➡ Mary Lou Retton moved away from home to train and says, "Knowing my parents were just a phone call away gave me such a sense of security. The whole family was involved in the decision, but the ultimate choice was mine."(10)

QUICK QUESTIONS

Should I take my daughter to see college or pro teams play?

It seems natural that your daughter might want to be exposed to athletes playing at a higher level. But don't force her to go to games if she doesn't seem interested. When you do go, make sure that you point out important parts of the game that she might miss. For example, it's okay to say, "Wow, she's got a great jump shot," about the star player. But it is also important to point out how the player who only got into the game for a few minutes played harder than anyone else, or how a player who misses the first free throw shakes off the disappointment and makes the second. These are the aspects of sports that are easily overlooked yet are the lessons your daughter will use throughout her life. If you value those mental aspects of the game, your daughter will be more likely to value them as well.

The training environment contributes to the way in which athletes see themselves and their sports experience. Practice habits set her up to succeed in competitions. If she is able to deal with frustration and setbacks on a daily basis, she will show much more grace in dealing with competitive situations. Training provides the opportunities for her to learn how to process mistakes, develop strategies to communicate information to the body, communicate with teammates and coaches, and develop a healthy work ethic. When she can value these aspects of practice rather than solely being concerned with the outcome, she will mature as a person and an athlete.

6

Mind Games: Improving Performance as She Advances

I always have to move on. I can't dwell on the past. If I were to dwell on that I probably would have lost. I probably would have been thinking: "Why didn't I hit that? I should have hit that." I would have freaked out, which is really ridiculous to do something like that when you can just stay calm, stay quiet, just continue.

—Serena Williams

Brianna Scurry paced back and forth in front of her goal as she prepared for a penalty-kick shootout that would decide the 1999 World Cup Championship. The United States and China had played to a 0–0 tie, and close to 90,000 partisan fans were on their feet in anticipation of one of the most dramatic finishes in women's sports history.

As she paced, Scurry was talking to herself, although her lips weren't moving. In her head, she was reminding herself about when she stopped a spectacular shot by the Swiss and the Brazilians and the Italians, different pressure-filled situations in which she had been victorious.

"This is my goal, my house," she repeated to herself over and over, taking deep, steady breaths. "Nobody is coming in my house today."

As she paced and talked, her five teammates—who would get chances to take penalty kicks against the Chinese goalie—were reminding themselves, too, about times they had been victorious in similar game endings—kicks in the air that hit the back of the net, kicks that slanted sideways past the diving goalie, kicks that caught a corner and caromed across the goal line.

"I thought about how well I had been kicking PKs in practice," said Brandi Chastain. "I had a lot of confidence."

In the end, each U.S. team member made her penalty kick—and Scurry stopped a kick from one of the Chinese players to give the United States the World Cup championship.

The American women won showing tremendous physical prowess. Yet much of their success could also be attributed to the mental strengths they called upon not only in the championship game but throughout the World Cup tournament.

As athletes advance in their sport, it becomes crystal clear how influential the mind can be in altering performance. High-level athletes have very few skills left to learn and therefore spend the majority of their efforts learning how to execute and perfect the skills they "own." As a result, it is increasingly important that they take advantage of sports psychology strategies used to enhance performance, which I refer to as the "mind games."

In Chapter 2, I introduced the Pressure Loop and the important concept of differentiating between those aspects of performance that are controllable versus uncontrollable. An athlete who is aware of the many factors that affect her performance is said to possess internal control. Two internal factors discussed earlier that can actually alter the way an athlete sees, thinks, and feels about herself are her perceptions and thoughts. In order for an athlete to develop internal control, maintain an open mind, and use her thoughts to move ahead, she must master a set of skills or "mind games." These "mind games" consist of such techniques as relaxation, visualization, self-talk, thought stoppage, reframing, goal setting, and focusing. Although parents and coaches are not expected to teach these specific techniques, they can consistently model effective thinking and support the idea of mental training.

Generally, I recommend the application of mind games for athletes who have already mastered the concepts of the Pressure Loop and therefore are ready for the next step, which is to implement the ideas of the internal loop into training and competitive settings.

Parents can have a major impact on their daughter's success by reinforcing and placing value on the mental aspects of sports performance. Changing the way an athlete thinks and feels about her performance and herself is not an easy task, nor does it happen overnight. Yet when an athlete's mind is opened to a new perspective, thereby changing her thoughts and performance, it is a powerful sight to see. In order for parents to assist their daughters in getting started with mental training, parents themselves must have a keen awareness of the factors that affect performance.

INTERNAL CONTROL

Earlier I discussed the importance of identifying factors about performance that are directly controlled by the athlete. This can be a difficult task even for adults. Try to answer this question: What kinds of things about you affect your work performance? Internal and controllable factors such as thoughts, perceptions, reactions, focus, preparation, confidence, conditioning, emotions, images, precompetition routines, and goals are controlled by the athlete and do have an impact on performance.

Once an athlete can identify the factors that she controls about her performance (i.e. perceptions, thoughts, reactions, focus, preparation, etc.), it's time for her to be taught some mental skills so that she can actually make use of these internal factors. For instance, an athlete can change her perceptions by using a method called reframing, or alter thinking through self-talk, or control her emotions by learning relaxation and visualization techniques. Mental skills like these provide athletes with tools that strengthen the way they see, think, feel, and ultimately perform.

MASTERING PERCEPTIONS

The first controllable aspect of performance that an athlete must strengthen is her perception—more simply, the way in which she chooses to see herself and her situation. Changing her perception, or reframing a situation, can significantly affect performance. It is important to teach athletes that they have many choices when it comes to their thinking. In order to reinforce this point, I use the following exercises.

Perception Exercise

Sometimes a young woman becomes so fixated on one view of herself or her situation that it becomes almost impossible for her to acknowledge or see other perspectives. She assumes that the way she see things is the only way they exist. Reality becomes what she sees, not how things really may be.

Take a look at the picture on the following page. I promise this exercise does not say anything about your personality—so no need to worry about what you are supposed to see! You may have seen a picture of a young-looking woman, but there is another picture there too, a picture of an old-looking woman. She almost looks like a witch. The young woman is a more detailed picture, so most people see that one first. If I first showed you a single-image picture of a young woman and then showed you the double-image picture, you would still most likely see the young woman first. And if I showed you a picture of an old woman first, then the double-image picture, in the double-image picture you would see the old woman first. This is because you look for what you expect to see. We are all conditioned to see things in certain ways.

Principles of Perception

- We are all conditioned to see things in certain ways, and those things we are conditioned to see tend to be what we see. That is why if you first look at a picture of a young woman, when you look at the double-image picture, you will seek out what you have been conditioned to see—a young woman. Conditioned responses to events can sometimes be obstacles to achievement. For instance, I don't know very many athletes who after a poor performance go home and say, "Wow, that was a great learning experience." Although this kind of response would be helpful, athletes tend to respond to their bad performances with statements such as, "I can't believe I messed up. How could I do that? I really stink." This is a conditioned response that most likely occurs with frequency but does little to guide the athlete in moving past her sense of disappointment.

- We create our own reality based upon our perceptions and our outlook. Therefore, even if our perception is incorrect, it is important and affects us because it is what we choose to see. For instance, many people think this exercise says something about their personality. When you jump to that conclusion, you become consumed with thoughts about what it means that you saw the old woman versus the young woman. If this is all you open your mind to see,

the point of the exercise is lost, because you are too busy trying to psychoanalyze yourself. Your perception gets you stuck in one way of thinking.

- Sometimes our perceptions can cause us problems, especially when we get stuck in the way we see a situation. As we age, we become more and more conditioned to see things in one way. We close our minds to other ways of looking at ourselves, our friends, our situations. We tend to rely on what we have known and learned in the past.
- Athletes must be reminded that there is always another way to see a situation. We just tend to stick with what is familiar to us. The familiar often feels more comfortable and reliable, even if these thoughts and approaches aren't helping us produce the desired results.

Perception Exercise for a Group

Tell the group they are going to play a game. The object of the game is to get the most points. They are each going to find a partner and turn and face their partner. They are to rest their elbows on a table and grab their partner's right hand. (They are in an arm-wrestling position.) They get a point any time one of either person's arms touches either side of the table or breaks a 45-degree angle. They have ten seconds to get as many points as possible.

Everybody will arm wrestle. Why? Because as soon as you demonstrate the face-to-face position with elbows resting on the table, people are conditioned to think of arm wrestling. Arm wrestling is an activity in which two people compete. But to meet the goal of the exercise they don't have to arm wrestle. If they work together and move their arms back and forth, they can with no effort amass thirty points in ten seconds. So what happened to the goal? People forget about the goal because they are wrapped up in thinking about arm wrestling. As soon as you demonstrate the arm wrestling position, people assume they are to compete. They forget that the goal is to get the most points and the most effective way to get points is to work together. They get locked into thinking in the same old way they always do, even if it isn't the best way to meet the goal. To be a great performer, athletes need to be able to find new and more effective ways to meet their goals, which often requires them to see themselves and their situation in an unfamiliar way.

HOW DO PERCEPTIONS AFFECT PERFORMANCE?

The way in which perceptions affect performance is that athletes' perceptions and actions need to match or athletes will feel uncomfortable. In sports, very often athletes get stuck in seeing themselves only one way. This is especially true for adolescent girls, who often feel a tremendous amount of pressure to conform to external standards and this pressure leaves them feeling depressed, moody, and self-critical. Therefore, their self-evaluations can be quite negative and they are quick to believe if they feel bad it must mean they are bad.

For example, an athlete who believes she can't do a skill but then goes out on the field and successfully completes that skill is left trying to make sense of the inconsistency between her perceptions and her actions. Nine out of ten times, she will attribute her athletic success to luck. You will hear her say, "I can't do it. I just got lucky." This preserves her self-perception, which is that she cannot do the skill.

In order to make her perceptions and actions match, she has two choices. First, she could change the very way she sees herself. She could say, "Wow. I guess I was wrong. I really can do this skill." However, it is extremely difficult for teenagers to change the way they see themselves. They get locked into their beliefs and actually try and find support for their self-perceptions.

Rather than changing the way she sees herself, she may attempt to find support for her negative self-perception. She may go and mess up the skill so that her perceptions and actions are consistent and she can come back with proof or evidence that she really can't do the skill. You may hear her tell you, "See, I told you I couldn't do it." She uses the failure to strengthen her negative self-perception. This leads to more self-doubt.

Perceptions Need to Be in Line with Actions

PERCEPTION	ATTRIBUTION	ACTION
Can't do it	Luck	Does It
Can do it	Perception Change	Does It

Perceptions Affect Thoughts

The way athletes choose to look at a situation determines the types of statements they choose to say to themselves. These thoughts, in turn, affect performance. For example, when athletes look at practice as sheer torture, they arrive at training thinking about how hard it is, how tired they are, how they don't want to be there. This makes it difficult for them to have an enjoyable or successful practice. They are choosing to look at everything they don't like about the situation. Another example is an athlete who decides she cannot complete a drill. This athlete will dwell on all the reasons she can't and the bad consequences associated with being unsuccessful. This type of thinking does not set her up for success.

Athletes convinced that they can't execute a skill need help in changing their self-perception. If they can just find another way to look at the situation, they will be more likely to choose thoughts that will help them be successful. However, instead of finding the best or most effective approach, athletes tend to be consistent. They use the same approach, even if it doesn't work. They keep taking the same action, yet expect a different result. Athletes need to learn to open their minds and look at the same situation in different ways.

PERCEPTION	THOUGHTS
Can't do the drill	Going to mess up and disappoint coach, get cut
Possible that I can do the drill	Done it before, breathe, keep my leg straight, eye on the ball

Perception ⟶ Affect ⟶ Thoughts ⟶ which Affect ⟶ Performance

SHE DOESN'T LEARN FROM HER MISTAKES

Kathryn was a fifteen-year-old nationally ranked figure skater whom I had been working with for a few months. She had high expectations for herself and tended to perform quite well in pressure situations. However, in several competitions throughout the year she had been having trouble with her combination jump in the technical program. A miss of this required element amounted to a four to six-tenths deduction from her score. It was now the national championships, and Kathryn was practicing a few hours before she would compete in the technical program. She missed every combination jump she tried. Her coach walked away frustrated and complained to me, "She keeps making the same mistake. She just doesn't learn."

I met Kathryn in the locker room where she was crying and talking about all of the externals she couldn't control. She knew her coach was mad and she worried about disappointing her parents and all the friends and relatives that were coming to watch the competition.

I decided to help Kathryn by attacking the way she was looking at the situation. It was clear that all she was seeing were the missed jumps. This outlook was causing her to think about all the reasons she might mess up, which was most likely going to lead her to mess up and have a miserable few hours.

I asked Kathryn about the combination jump, "How many triple toe loop double toe loops do you land on a daily basis?"

"I guess about five a session," she said.

"And you skate about three sessions per day, so that means you hit fifteen combinations per day. And how long have you been doing that jump consistently?" I asked.

"My gosh. For at least two years," she said, puzzled.

I began to calculate. She skated six days per week, so she had done a grand total of 8,640 triple toe double toes. When I announced this number, Kathryn looked shocked and momentarily stopped crying. A new way to look at the situation.

"What kinds of things do you do eight thousand times?" I asked.

"I wake up. I brush my teeth," she said.

"Yes, you brush about two times a day. You are doing this jump fifteen times a day. Have you ever brushed your teeth and had the tooth brush slip and jam into your gums?"

She nodded, "Yes."

"Well, do you wake up the next morning worried you don't know how to brush your teeth?"

She laughed, "Of course not."

"Do you analyze your brushing technique or hire a coach to teach you a new technique?"

"No."

"Of course you don't. Why not?" I asked seriously.

"Because," she said, "I know I know how to brush my teeth."

I said, "Well, I think you know it's possible that you could land this jump. You have done it eight thousand times."

What I did was give Kathryn a different perspective. She went from crying to laughing. I opened her mind to see that hitting her combination jump was possible and maybe even probable. I wasn't interested in persuading Kathryn that she could do the jump. I had no idea whether she would land it or miss it. I wanted Kathryn to accept the fact that she couldn't predict the outcome and instead merely acknowledge that it was possible she could do it. Once she opened her mind to possible success she could shift her thinking from all the reasons she might mess up to thoughts and actions that would guide her to success. Kathryn ended up landing the combination jump. I don't know if her change in perspective determined the outcome, but I do know that for the two hours she sat in her room waiting to compete, she was a much happier athlete. Instead of beating herself up for past mistakes and potential future mistakes, she kept herself focused on how to land that combination. She chose a new way to look at the situation.

Typical Misperceptions

1. She thinks she must be loved or approved of by every person she sees as significant in her sport: An athlete won't receive the approval of all authority figures, nor will everyone like her. She must accept that one's worth is not determined by being loved and approved of by everyone. It's critical that she is reminded of her own goals and makes sure that she surrounds herself with people who understand her goals and are willing to guide her toward achievement.

2. To be worthwhile, she must achieve in all possible respects: A young woman needs to recognize all aspects of her personality and

not measure her worth solely on her accomplishments. There are times she will fail, and these challenges must be recognized as opportunities for growth.

3. She is devastated when things in sports don't go her way: It is disappointing but not devastating when expectations are not met.

4. If she pleases others, she is successful: This puts others in charge of her destiny and renders her powerless. She can't control the reactions of others, only her own. It can be incredibly frustrating to try and meet all of the different expectations people may place upon her. Instead, teach her to consider the views of others with her own.

5. If something is or may be threatening, she thinks she should keep dwelling on it: Worrying and worrying about the uncontrollable serves no purpose. Instead, tell her to identify what can be controlled and use the internal factors to respond.

6. She thinks she should be dependent on others: Others are there to help guide and support her in meeting her goals. However, she needs to learn to trust her own thoughts, opinions, and feelings. This is the foundation from which self-esteem is developed.

7. Her past behavior is all-important in predicting her present behavior: A bad performance in the past does not guarantee a bad performance in the future. The way in which she processes the poor performance and responds to it is all-important.

8. She should be upset over the problems of others: She must be reminded to take responsibility for her own actions and reactions. It is one thing to feel empathy for someone; it is totally another to take responsibility for their feelings.

9. She thinks that beliefs held by respected authorities are always correct: She needs to learn to consider how the views of others fit with her own opinions. Instead of just espousing the beliefs of an authority figure, encourage her to reflect upon the situation and add her own valuable ideas.

10. She believes that effort and persistence should always pay off: Effort and persistence are two internal factors that provide an athlete with her best shot at being successful. However, an athlete needs to know how and when to apply her effort and persistence. There are many other internal factors that also affect performance.

TEACHING PERSPECTIVE AT HOME

A wonderful role for parents to play is to provide children with different perspectives. When parents reframe the situation, it gives athletes a new choice regarding how they see themselves and their sports situations. Instead of spending hours debating whether or not your child made a great play, guide her through the process of looking for ways to see herself and her situation in a productive way.

Helping her to reframe and gain perspective starts with reminding yourself and your daughter to look for opportunity in the failure and mistakes. Typically, when an athlete fails, she does not automatically say to herself, "Wow, I really learned a lot from that terrible performance." Adults can model reframing, by choosing to find benefits in challenging situations. How parents deal with their own work struggles show kids a lot about how to respond to failure. Do you come home and complain about how everyone else messed you up and you might as well quit because it isn't worth trying anymore? Or do you set the example by finding a new approach? Sit down with your kids and brainstorm how you might change the situation. Show them it's okay to be flawed. As long as you can reframe the situation, you can usually make a difficult situation manageable.

After failure, telling your daughter she did a great job is false and she knows it. So don't lie. Validate how your child feels, which is probably disappointed. Point out something that was an improvement. Show her how she can benefit from the experience. For example, "I know today was a disappointing game for you. But, you have never had to play injured before. That was a great job you did trying to block out your worry and concern about your knee. I think today was a terrific learning experience because it made you stronger mentally. You showed that you can recover from an injury and get right into the game. The results will show up soon. What's important is that you strengthened your mental game. I'm very proud of you."

You can assist your daughter in reframing a negative situation into a learning experience by asking her better questions, such as, "What do you really think?" "Is there another way to see this situation?" "How can you benefit or grow from this experience?" "How can you make this better?" These questions help her to find better answers. Avoid why questions such as, "Why did you play so badly today?" These questions put kids on the defensive and keep them fixated on the negative result.

FAST FACTS

➡ Former Olympians ranked many mental attributes over the physical as most important to Olympic success(1):

Dedication	82%
Mental attitude	80%
Perseverance	77%
Competitive attitude	71%
Self-confidence	69%
Physical + talent	37%

MASTERING THE SELF-TALK GAME

Lucinda was a twelve-year-old diver. Her coach was quite frustrated with her because when he taught her she easily made corrections. Yet when she practiced on her own, she didn't pay any attention to her technique. She only cared what the dive looked like. He worried that she might one day get hurt. He asked me, "Is it possible she doesn't know how to think?"

Can athletes not think? Ask an athlete to sit perfectly still and for five seconds just shut off her mind. She won't be able to do it. She will think about not thinking. Athletes can learn to quiet their mind or narrow their thoughts, but they can't completely shut off their minds. My question to athletes is, "Do you pay attention to what you are saying to yourself? Do those thoughts help you get things done?"

There are two voices in most athletes' heads: the critic and the acceptor. The critic reminds her that no matter what she does, she can always do it better. The critic reminds her to never settle for less than perfection and constantly harps on the negatives. On the other hand, the acceptor tells her it's okay to make mistakes and helps get her thoughts focused on how to improve performance.

My experience has been that young women are especially adept at dwelling on why they won't be successful or what they don't have or what

they don't like about themselves. Women search for connectedness in relationships, and one way to feel connected is to share common experiences,
thoughts, and feelings. For example, a group of ballerinas were sitting on
the floor stretching prior to the commencement of class. I walked by to
hear one girl say, "I hate my thighs. They are just too big." Another chimed
in, "Yeah, but you are so lucky because you have great turnout. My turnout
is terrible. No matter what I do, I can't change that." And yet a third friend
said, "You both are lucky because you get good parts. I never even get the
chance to be a real dancer. I'll always have to do character."

Each girl tried to make the other feel better but at the same time shared
a related story of dislike for herself and her situation. When I work with
young women athletes, I often ask them what it is they truly hope to accomplish in sport if there were no limits—their dreams. Nine out of ten
girls respond, "I want to go to the Olympics." Then they spend forty-five
minutes explaining in detail all the reasons they will never get there.

An athlete's self-talk needs to be examined daily, and young women
should be encouraged to start calling each other on the self-destructive stories they tell about themselves. It should not be okay for young women to
talk so freely about what they dislike about themselves. At the same time it
should be okay for young women to talk about what they like without the
fear of being considered arrogant or snotty. It's important for athletes to
evaluate their self-talk and make sure it is guiding them toward goal attainment. The right thoughts don't guarantee success, but they sure do give
an athlete her best chance while increasing the probability that she will enjoy the process.

THEY MIGHT THINK BADLY OF ME

Jessica was a twelve-year-old ice skater who was quite talented. She didn't
perform her very best at competitions, but still skated well enough to receive high placements. While I was working with Jessica, she mentioned
that she didn't like to show off.

"In practice, I don't like to show off much. I'm not comfortable calling
attention to myself," she told me.

"If you had to take a guess at why you think you are uncomfortable,
what would it be?" I asked.

"Well, it's when I'm skating with younger kids that aren't at my level. I don't want anyone watching to think I'm being . . . well, I want to say . . . pompous."

"So, you think that when you show off you are acting arrogant or conceited."

"Yeah. I don't want people to think badly of me."

"So, showing off leads people to feel badly about you? What exactly is showing off?"

"Just skating fast and maybe doing my facial expressions and hamming it up as if I were competing."

"It seems to me that practicing skating with speed and simulating competition are important parts of your preparation. Your ability is your ability and you are out on the ice practicing to make yourself even better. Are you going in the warming area telling everyone for hours how wonderful you think you are?"

She laughed. "No."

"I'm curious as to what you think would lead someone to think badly of a skater who executes what she is capable of doing and works to improve her skill level?" I asked.

"I don't want them to feel bad because I can do more than they can."

Jessica was actually trying to protect other people's feelings. She didn't want anyone to feel upset that they weren't at her level yet. She especially worried about the feelings of the parents who would come and watch. Jessica believed that by changing her actions and diminishing her capabilities, she could make those other people feel good. Even at twelve years old, she felt responsible for the feelings of others. It was crucial for Jessica to understand that it was not her responsibility to make the whole world feel good. How could she possibly skate while trying to please everyone who walked through the door?

"You have three coaches and two parents. That's five people who have certain expectations for you. Isn't that enough? Do you really want to add in trying to please the whole world? The whole world certainly isn't privy to your goals or your action plan. For instance, if a mother of another skater walked in the building and saw you smiling during your program and said, 'That Jessica is such a show-off,' the feedback has little meaning, because that mother doesn't have any idea about the goals you have set or the action plan you have developed to ensure that you reach the goals. As it turns out, practicing your smile is an area of your training that you and your coach have identified as needing improvement. Your coaches and parents know this, so they would not misjudge your actions. Before pointing the finger at yourself and changing your behavior to make everyone else feel good, evaluate the people you are trying to please. Make sure the advice or feedback they are giving fits with what you know to be true. Some people may value certain aspects of skating that are much less important to you. Stay focused on the goals you and your support group have set and try and meet those expectations."

Feelings can be powerful motivators, as are thoughts. In order for self-talk to have a meaningful impact upon performance, young women need to separate what they feel from what they think. Very often a young girl who feels bad will think badly, assuming her thoughts are controlled by her emotions.

In order for an athlete to control her thoughts, she must first recognize her own patterns of thinking. Typically, athletes use three paradigms of thought. Most athletes are familiar with negative self-talk. Everybody, at times, thinks negatively. It's normal and natural. But when overused and not balanced with positive and effective thinking, negative thinking can be devastating to performance as well as to the enjoyment athletes experience.

Most athletes are aware that at times they think negatively. If you ask an athlete, "How do you overcome your negativity?" she will most likely respond, "I try and think positively." Yet, when you tell a frustrated athlete, "Just believe in yourself," it's not uncommon to receive an eye roll as a response. Athletes don't particularly want to think in a negative way but at the same time they are feeling upset and disappointed with their performance, which makes thinking in a positive manner much more difficult. Athletes can learn to talk to themselves in a variety of ways that help separate thoughts and emotions. For example, instead of an athlete saying, "I can't do it. I'll never get it," she might more accurately report, "I'm having trouble with this skill right now. I'm going to keep working on my technique until I get it." In the former statement, the athlete not only is negative but she assigns a permanence to her negativity by saying she will never get it. In the latter, she acknowledges her challenge but remains hopeful for change to occur. By altering her self-talk, an athlete can work through frustration and ultimately perform better.

PURELY POSITIVE—Ask her to think of self-affirming statements that remind her that she can do something. Positive self-talk needs to include kind, accepting, and caring statements that encourage her to "go for it" and feel good about her efforts. One of the most powerful uses of positive thinking is for an athlete to take credit for her successes and identify how she contributed to the great performances. Positive self-talk is most effective when stated in the present and kept very simple. Sometimes athletes will use rhymes or themes. For instance, "Pride produces productivity" was a saying an Olympic athlete used to remind herself to take pride in her accomplishments. If she could be proud of herself and show that self-respect, others would feel proud of her.

*State it in present	"I am happy."
*Keep it simple	"I am going to do this."
*Rhyme it	"Stay tight to keep it light."
*Theme it	"Pride produces productivity."

IDENTIFY THE NEGATIVE—Most athletes are quite familiar with negative thinking. Ask an athlete to tell you all the negative statements she says to herself and within five minutes she will easily have created a long list. She will even laugh at herself for saying such incredibly negative and unhelpful statements. Yet, she will use this type of thinking repeatedly. What follows are some of the patterns seen in athlete's negativity:

*Overgeneralizations	"I don't skate well on Mondays."

When athletes overgeneralize, they take one situation and make it happen over and over again. So, in order to predict how they will perform they use one negative experience and generalize it to many situations. The rationale is, "If I screwed up against the Tornadoes, I guess every time I play the Tornadoes, I'll screw up."

*All-or-nothing thinking	"If I don't hit this, I'm a rotten gymnast."

This is a very black-and-white way of thinking. Perfectionists use this type of thinking to help them justify their negativism. It is either good or bad. There is little room for small improvements. Results are the basis for most judgments. Progress is not considered. There is one standard and it is either met or not met. It's as if they want everything to fit into a little box. I worked with an athlete who at home was incredibly neat. Her sock drawer was color coded. When she skated, she tried to categorize her jump outcomes just like her sock drawer. A jump either fit into the good drawer or the bad drawer, and she didn't even consider a drawer for average. I explained that she was fully capable of doing any one of her jumps if the technique was good. That was an easy task. However, on a few of her harder jumps, her technique had to be just right for her to land the jump. When she landed a jump that had a small technical error or wasn't the best one she had ever done, she would get very upset with herself. Yet I felt it was important for her to acknowledge her success at landing a technically incorrect jump. After all, it was much harder for her to land the slightly tilted jump than the technically correct one. She didn't need to work on landing technically correct jumps, rather, she needed to push herself to learn to land the jump all of the time even if it was technically deficient. However, anytime she did a jump that was less than good, she overlooked it and categorized it as bad. She could never increase her confidence because all-or-none thinking didn't allow her to take credit for anything less than perfect.

*Personalization   "Cindy was laughing at me when I missed that shot."

This type of thinking is very common with a teenager and emerges in early adolescence (eleven to fourteen years) when girls become preoccupied with their appearance and group identity. She thinks others are talking about her or focusing on her insecurities. She takes others' actions and personalizes them to herself. Early adolescence marks the time when kids begin to judge themselves based upon comparisons to their peer group. As she matures, she will become more concerned with her own progress and much more self-referenced.

*Catastrophizing   "What if I don't do well?"

This type of thinking is common at game time. It's the classic what-if syndrome. "What if I mess up?" "What if I don't get to play?" "What if I can't recover from my injury?" These what-if questions are used by athletes to try and predict the future. Athletes are better served by accepting the unknown of performing and trying instead to focus on what they can do to give themselves the best chance of reaching their goal.

*Emotional reasoning	"I feel fat, therefore, I am." "I feel helpless, therefore my problems are impossible to solve."

Emotional reasoning occurs when athletes judge their feelings. An athlete assumes that because she feels something to be true, it is true. For instance, she can feel helpless, but her problem can be very solvable. She can feel fat and in fact be the same weight as yesterday. Kids tend to confuse how they feel with reality. Their rationale is, "If I feel bad, it must be bad." Athletes need to open their minds to see the situation differently rather than using their thoughts to justify and support what they feel. Parents can help by accepting their daughter's feelings and guiding her to use separate, more effective thoughts to move beyond the problem.

HOW TO COMBINE POSITIVE AND NEGATIVE INTO EFFECTIVE

The most often used positive thinking statement is, "I can do it," while the most often used negative thinking statement is, "I can't do it." Although these two types of thinking appear to be complete opposites, they actually have one very important element in common. That is, they are both related to the outcome or result. When thinking positively, athletes are trying, through their thoughts, to predict that the outcome will be very positive. They say, "I can do this and here are all the reasons why I can and will succeed."

Negative thinkers, through their thoughts, try and predict that the outcome will be a failure. They say, "I can't do it and here are all the reasons I can't and won't." The bottom line is that none of us can predict the future. When using positive or negative thinking, athletes keep themselves focused on the outcome. An athlete will expend all sorts of energy predicting that her outcome will either be desirable or undesirable. Meanwhile, her coach enters the picture and says, "Please straighten your arms." Although the athlete hears the correction, she can't possibly make the correction, because at the moment of execution she is either thinking, "I can" or "I can't." She spends the entire practice vacillating between the positive and negative, which serves to do nothing except keep her focused on the outcome. In fact, to get the outcome she desperately desires, her thoughts really need to be on the process. She must think about *how to do it*. This is a third type of thinking, which I have labeled effective thinking.

Examples of Effective Thinking

WHEN SHE IS HAVING TROUBLE MASTERING A SKILL—Effective thinking is used when an athlete gives herself information about how to do the skill. It focuses attention on technical information, positive mental images, and key feeling words. It takes an athlete beyond just thinking "I can do it" to actually taking control of how she does it. When your daughter asks if she can go to a friend's house and you say, "No, not tonight," how does your daughter respond? Does she say, "Okay" and walk out of the room? My guess is that she says, "Why, why, why? Sally gets to go. I promise I'll clean my room and the garage and grandma's house, too, if you just let me go." Basically, your daughter is applying effective thinking. She is trying to figure out a way to get what she wants.

It doesn't matter to me whether an athlete thinks she can or thinks she can't. What is important is that an athlete wants to do it, because athletes who want to meet a specific goal figure out how to get there. How many times have you seen an athlete who thinks she can do it and then doesn't or an athlete who thinks she can't do it but then does? Thinking you can or thinking you can't is not an absolute predictor of performance outcome.

Successful individuals know what they want and figure out a way to get it. They don't dwell on whether they will or won't get it. They direct all of their energies to developing strategies related to how to get it. This same type of thinking needs to be applied during athletic practices. When she can make a shift from the outcome to the how to do it, your daughter will start to make progress and reduce her frustration significantly. Some examples of the components of effective thinking are:

*Technical Information	"Straight arms"
*Metaphors	"Reach for a tree branch"
*Feelings	"Snap," "Lift," "Spring," "Easy," "Smooth"
*Effort	"Push," "Cool it," "Pick it up"
*Images	"As if I were floating on clouds"

Effective thinking keeps athletes focused on how to do a skill rather than on whether they did it or not. During practices, the key is to pick a technical correction for the skill and stick with that correction until skill improvement is attained. In order to think effectively, an athlete must first identify her mistake. Figuring out what is going wrong in a skill is critical to effective practice and overall athletic success. She should identify one error in the skill. An easy way to do this is to pick a body part and analyze its movement as it completes the skill.

Second, she needs to turn the mistake into a correction. Most athletes are fairly skilled at identifying a mistake but not as experienced at turning the mistake into a correction. An athlete needs to direct her body to do what she wants it to do rather than what she doesn't want it to do. If I tell an athlete, "Don't think about pink elephants, don't think about pink elephants," she will most likely think about pink elephants. An athlete who tells herself, "Don't bend over," only reminds herself of the mistake she is trying to avoid. First, she must see herself make the mistake so she can then tell her body not to do it that way. Instead, she needs to turn the mistake, bending over, into a correction, "Stand up straight."

The correction needs to be specific and stated clearly. For example, there are many ways in which an athlete can think about standing up straight. She might think of having her head up or back up. She could also think about standing straight as a pencil or feeling a string pulling her up to the sky. Corrections need to be stated in a manner that is easy for the body to understand. Once a correction is identified, the athlete needs to think about it on the skill attempt.

Finally, to think effectively, she should give herself appropriate feedback. Athletes will commonly give themselves outcome feedback based upon the success or failure of the skill attempt. An athlete who is trying to stand up straight might go out and do the skill and fail. She will then give herself feedback about the outcome by saying, "That stunk. That correction didn't help." However, she is missing the point. By giving herself obvious information, she doesn't teach her body anything about the skill movement. The feedback must be related back to the correction she was trying to make. This shifts her focus to "how to do it" rather than "I didn't do it." After the skill is completed, she needs to ask, "Did I or didn't I stand up straight?" By staying focused on the process, she can start making corrections and eliminating mistakes, thereby improving the skill. Her frustration will be managed, and eventually, the skill outcome will happen.

In order to think effectively, an athlete can take herself through the following process:

Mistake ──────▶ Correction ──────▶ Skill attempt ──────▶ Feedback about the correction

The kinds of messages she sends herself on a daily basis will vary depending upon the task at hand. If she is working on improving technique or trying to manage her frustration, effective thinking will be her best choice. For some, effective thinking doesn't necessarily mean choosing a technical correction. Some athletes find that when they encounter a mental "block," distracting themselves altogether has a positive effect. For instance, a gymnast having trouble "going for" a vault, not committing fully to the skill, might be paralyzing her body with too much technical information. Instead, she might try and replace technical thoughts with non-skill-related thoughts, such as images of her favorite color or shape.

Distraction is only helpful when the body knows how to execute the skill and has actually executed it consistently in the past. Under those circumstances, distraction helps the athlete to get her mind out of her body's way. Once she stops paralyzing her body with technical thought, muscle memory takes over and the skill is completed.

Some athletes use a skill called "thought stoppage" to help them control their self-talk. The idea is simple. A negative or unwanted thought enters her mind and she says, "Stop," or "Chill out," or any other statement she chooses. Then she replaces the unwanted thought with one that is more helpful. The key to thought stoppage is an athlete's ability to catch herself when she starts the cycle of negative thinking. Then she must understand what effective thinking is all about so she can replace the unwanted thought with something more useful. Many athletes just try and block out the negative thoughts but this is extremely difficult to do. It is much easier to get rid of unwanted thoughts when she chooses new, more helpful ones.

➡ A study of 115 professional tennis players who competed in the 1992 Lipton Tennis Tournament revealed that the most common mental training strategies they used were self-talk, goal setting, relaxation, imagery, and a pre–service return routine. The players felt their motivation to compete, ability to maintain concentration throughout a match, and self-confidence affect their performances considerably.(2)

QUICK QUESTIONS

Is goal setting an important mental skill?

Most successful athletes use some type of goal setting. The United States Olympic Committee believes goal setting is as necessary as having a coach. When you get in your car to drive somewhere, if you have a specific destination, you will take a certain route. However, if you don't have a destination, pretty much any route will get you to nowhere! Goals provide direction, help formulate training plans, provide feedback and motivation. When athletes hit obstacles, goals can be especially helpful in reminding them of their reasons for sports involvement.

Most athletes set outcome goals that are the long-term desired result: I want to make a national team, get a college scholarship, be an All-American, win. Fewer people set goals about their performances. Performance goals are related to the skills or parts of the game that need improvement in order for the athlete to eventually achieve the outcome. For instance, an ice skater might need to improve her speed, hold her spins longer, and skate clean programs in practice once a week. At a competition, her performance goals might be to miss only one jump in the program, skate with speed, and immerse herself in the choreography of the program.

Finally there are task goals, which even fewer athletes know about or use. Task goals are the actions an athlete can take in training to maximize her chances of achieving the performance goals. Task goals can also be set for the actual competition. For the ice skater mentioned above to meet her performance goals, she might try in training to remind herself to skate as fast as she can into ten jumps every session, count the revolutions on her spins every time she does a run-through of the program, and use specific self-talk during the more difficult elements of her program. These task goals are the small steps she can take on a daily basis to help meet her longer-term performance goals.

Competitive task goals are the behaviors that an athlete can actually carry out at an event to increase her chances of performing to expectation. Task goals tend to focus on the mental aspects of the sport. For instance, an ice skater who has decided that her performance goal is to skate a clean program might set as task goals to keep her thinking simple by using the self-talk practiced during training, to pace slowly and talk slowly to herself before taking the ice, and to project confidence through her body language.

Lastly, it can be helpful to make athletes accountable for their goals. Allow them to reward themselves if they carry through on the performance or task goals. For example, an ice skater decided that to improve her outcomes she needed to change her training in some way. In the past, she had difficulty motivating herself to do her program with an attempt at every element. Days and sometimes weeks would fly by and she would not skate her program. As a reward, she decided that if she did a full run-through everyday, attempting each and every skill in the program for four consecutive days, she didn't have to do the program on the fifth day. This reward was powerful enough to get her in the routine of running through the program daily and made her accountable for carrying through on the performance goal.

EXAMPLE OF GOAL SETTING WORKSHEET

(adapted from the United States Olympic Committee)

I. Outcome

Think about this competitive season, and pick a challenging but not impossible outcome goal (win, place, reach final round, qualify, etc.).

_____

_____

II. Performance

How do you maximize your chances of achieving that goal? Write down three to five elements you need to complete or improve upon to increase the odds of achieving the outcome you wrote down in step one: (e.g., hit routine, add new skill, programs, improve power or speed).

1. _____

2. _____

3. _____

4. _____

5. _____

III. Tasks

What can you do in training between now and your competition, to maximize your chances of achieving your three to five competition tasks? Write down two things to focus on in training that will set you up to have the performance you desire: (e.g., if your performance goal is to hit your routine, you might do competition simulation or consistency drills where you have only one chance to complete three skills in a row).

1. In training, I will: _____

2. In training, I will: _____

IV. Competition

How do you maximize your chances of achieving your outcome goal at the competition? Write down three BEHAVIORS you can do at the actual competition to increase the odds of your achieving the outcome you wrote down in step one: (e.g., use key words, create a feeling, breathe, listen to my music, keep my thoughts simple, etc.).

1. I will _____

2. I will _____

3. I will _____

V. Enforce Your Goals

You just figured out how to maximize your outcome for this season, so make sure you start today to change your behavior. Pick a reward for completing your practice tasks and a punishment for not doing it (e.g., new CDs, running before school, etc.)

1. If I do my task goal, I will get _____

2. If I fail to do my task goals, I have to _____

Making Sure Your Long-Term Goals Lead to Short-Term Goals

1. What is your dream goal for this season? _____

_____

2. What are the abilities of other athletes who have achieved that goal?

_____

_____

_____

3. Do you have all of those abilities fully developed? Yes _____ No _____

4. If no, which abilities do you most need to work on? _____

_____

_____

5. What will you do between now and the end of the season to develop those abilities? _____

_____

_____

_____

6. What will you do this week to develop those abilities? _____

_____

_____

_____

7. What can you do next practice to develop those abilities? _____

_____

FAST FACTS

➡ A study of 678 Division I male and female collegiate athletes from different regions of the United States investigated the frequency, effectiveness, and importance of different types of goals to enhance performance. Virtually, all athletes practiced some type of goal setting and found the process to be moderately to highly effective. Females generally set more performance goals than males while males set more outcome goals than females.(3)

SHE ISN'T FOCUSED

Focus is a word athletes hear all the time. However, very few athletes truly know what focusing means or how to get focused. Focus is something that is under the athlete's control and related to effective thinking. When an athlete is focused, she has chosen specific thoughts, images, or feelings that she believes will help her to improve the situation or performance. Knowing when to choose certain thoughts and learning how to attend to those thoughts are critical to success.

Jody was a fifteen-year-old gymnast who was on the junior national team. She worked extremely hard but never seemed to get very much accomplished. When she made mistakes in practice, she became angry and expressed her feelings to everyone by pouting, making faces, slapping her legs, and cursing. She would keep pounding away at a skill, continuing to fall or balk, and would become more and more frustrated and agitated. During these times, coaches found her impossible to train.

She would keep practicing the skill over and over again rather than take instruction. She would continue to use an approach that wasn't working, yet she would expect a different outcome. Many of these workouts resulted in a coach kicking Jody out of the gym and sending her home for the day. At competitions, the minute Jody made a mistake, she gave up. Her competition reactions were a direct result of her practice habits. In order to improve her focus in competition, Jody had to learn to focus on a daily basis.

During Jody's episodes of unproductive work, she had no awareness of her thoughts. We worked together to identify her thought patterns. As soon as she missed a skill, she would begin to dwell on the mistakes. She would ask herself questions like, "Why can't I do it?" and "What's wrong with me?" She would tell herself, "You should never miss that," and "You're stupid." One missed skill would become about not being able to do the skill at all, missing it all the time, not being able to do it in competition, and finally not being able to do skills in the other events. Jody became unfocused as soon as her thoughts drifted to the past or the future rather than focusing on the present.

Being focused is about being in the present. Jody's tendency was to dwell on skills that she had already completed. Unfortunately, she dwelled only on the mistakes. Even a completed skill was picked apart for errors. Jody would prepare to improve the skill by keeping her thoughts on the previous missed or flawed attempts or jump to the future trying to predict how her next attempt would turn out. Jody was not giving a 100 percent effort to actually correcting the skill. She was giving a 100 percent effort to repeating her past mistakes.

When I asked Jody how she had coped with frustration, she responded, "I just keep doing it until I hit. Then I feel better." Yet because she never actually worked on improving the skill, it could take her weeks to hit one. Jody practiced lots and lots of skills, but her efforts were ineffective. Jody needed to focus her attention on specific technical thoughts related to each skill attempt. She may not hit the skill immediately, but she would benefit in two ways: by taking the small steps necessary to move herself closer to hitting the skill, and by focusing, she would be taking charge of her emotions.

But first, Jody needed to learn to recognize when her thoughts became unfocused. She had to learn to replace unproductive thoughts with new, more productive ones, and she also had to physically act out her desire to make her situation better by making her body look confident.

A focused athlete differs mentally and physically from an unfocused athlete.

Jody Unfocused	Jody Focused
1. Is unaware that her thoughts are on the past or future	1. Acknowledges that she needs to think about what is happening to her RIGHT NOW.
2. Asks herself questions that have useless answers. "Why am I so bad?" "Why can't I do it!"	2. Asks herself questions that help make the skill better. "What can I think about to make this better?" "What's important now?" "How am I going to get it done?"
3. Body language expresses feelings of defeat, says, "I can't do it." Head down, eyes, down, shoulders lifted up and pushed forward.	3. Body language says, "I'm giving it my best shot." Says, "I would like to feel confident." Head up, shoulders pushed down and back, chest out.

Focusing Exercises

(a) Have her think about how this book feels under her hands.
(b) Ask her to think abut how her feet feel in her shoes or socks.
(c) Tell her to listen to one sound in the room.
(d) Then turn on the television or radio and ask her to repeat a, b, and c above.
(e) Find a window or door that has a screen on it. Have her look directly at the screen and think about what she sees—the color, the design, the bugs.
(f) Have her look through the screen and think about what she sees outside—the grass, the houses, the ground.
(g) Ask her to switch her focus back and forth looking at the screen and looking through the screen.

I'm sure that the girl doing this exercise was easily able to focus on the book, feet, and sound in the room. I am also confident that even when the television or radio was competing for her attention, she was still able to think about the book, feet, and sounds. She might have noticed that when her attention was focused on one particular thought, such as her feet, all other thoughts or sounds did not completely disappear from awareness. She will find that she can look outside and totally focus on what she sees through the screen. However, the screen does not disappear from her awareness. She knows it is there, even if she is not focused on it at the moment. At any time, she can switch her focus and look at the screen.

Focusing does not mean eliminating all other thoughts. It does mean being aware of other thoughts, yet directing attention on something specific related to what is being done at the moment. How many times has she been told to get focused for competition by getting rid of all the distractions? To think only about her sport? The problem with this strategy is that life is full of distractions. The better alternative is to learn how to respond to the distractions and to maintain a clear focus. Focused people concentrate on action rather than activity. In other words, they are aware of their thoughts and make themselves respond effectively to the situation.

FOCUSING TECHNIQUE

Jody had to learn to use her thoughts to take action and change the situation. In three easy steps, Jody learned to **ACT**.

A—Acknowledge that she is in a situation that led her to think ineffectively.

C—Choose to think about something that enables her to take action. It should be one simple thought related to the skill she's working on at that moment. Thoughts must be related to the present rather than to past errors or future errors that keep her focused on activity. Instead, she needs to take action.

T—Toughen her body to set herself up for success. Typically, when she is unfocused, she allows her body to turn inward as if she wants to curl up in bed under her comforter. This is a self-protective stance, but does little to assist her in making a positive change. When she puts her head up, chest out, shoulders down, she brings to life feelings of confidence. This is a learned skill called body language presentation.

. . .

Focused athletes are able to respond to difficult situations by recognizing that their thoughts are either on the past or future and refocusing their thoughts on the present. Focused athletes tend to be choosy regarding their thoughts. In other words, they don't just let in any and every thought. They select their thoughts carefully to best meet the demands of the situation. When they are presented with a particularly challenging situation, they don't keep responding in a way that produces a negative result. Instead, they apply the skill of thought stoppage by checking their thoughts, saying "Stop" or some other key word to begin to filter out the unhelpful thoughts, and replacing old thoughts with new and effective ones. They narrow their thinking and bring it to the present tense. The more easily athletes can apply this skill in practice, the more likely they will be to transfer the same skill to a competitive setting.

Thoughts are not the only way in which athletes can get focused and improve their competitive performances. The pictures athletes see in their mind also can be used to change performance, deal with frustration, and improve skill level. I am often asked about the effectiveness of imagery and visualization.

DO IMAGERY AND VISUALIZATION WORK?

This is a question I get a lot from parents who are trying to find a way to help their daughters perform better. Much has been written about imagery, which has also been called visualization and mental rehearsal. Judging from the athletes I've worked with and the research, it does work and work well when done properly.

Imagery allows an athlete to create a performance in her mind using all of her senses. The best way to get her to understand its effectiveness is to have her take a piece of thread and attach it to a paper clip. The paper clip should be dangling like a pendant on a necklace. Have her hold the thread between her thumb and forefinger, with the paper clip hanging at the bottom of the thread. Have her picture the paper clip moving back and forth. With no motion of her hand, the paper clip will start to move back and forth. Next, have her move it side to side and then in a circle using visual-ization alone. Finally, ask her to close her eyes and picture the paper clip moving in the direction of her choice. When she opens her eyes, the paper clip may be moving in that direction.

This exercise clearly demonstrates to an athlete the power of her mind. The brain sends messages to the body via impulses. The impulse gets to the end of the finger and fires, thereby moving the hand and the paper clip. When visualizing performances, a similar type of muscular activity can be initiated. The mind actually fools the body into thinking it is performing motor skills. Of course, you can't visualize your way to the Olympics, but it can be a great addition to regular training.

HOW IMAGERY WORKS

Athletes who can vividly image their performances seem to be able to use similar neural pathways when they actually perform. Those athletes who have more difficulty creating a picture in their mind will experience less muscular activity while using imagery. Imagery can help athletes better understand the movements required of them. By practicing the skill in their mind's eye, they become familiar with the steps needed to create a successful skill or play. In this way, athletes are able to prepare themselves for the demands of the situation. For instance, an offensive soccer player can picture herself responding to various defensive strategies. Imagery can reduce stress or prepare athletes for stressful situations. By picturing differ-ent types of situations, athletes can see themselves dealing with stress in a safe and nonthreatening environment.

Creating a picture in the mind's eye can stimulate learning, increase con-fidence, and aid in physical and emotional recovery. There are two types of imagery, which are differentiated by the type of perspective used. External imagery is used when athletes imagine seeing their performance from out-side their body, as if they were watching from the stands. There is less em-phasis on how the movement feels and more on how it looks.

Internal imagery is used when athletes imagine their performance from behind their own eyes. Athletes see only what they would ordinarily see while playing the game or performing. The emphasis tends to be on how the skill feels. This type of imagery has been found to be used a great deal by elite athletes and has been theorized to produce more neuromuscular activity than external imagery. Many athletes switch back and forth between internal and external. However, the type of imagery perspective used is less important than the vividness of the picture.

IMAGERY GUIDELINES

The more vivid the image, the more effective the imagery. Athletes can create a more vivid image by using all of their senses in addition to picturing themselves doing a skill. For instance, she needs to visually see the defense and focus on the ball, and kinesthetically feel the sensation of her body as it moves. She can try to hear the crack of the bat or sound of the perfect golf drive. She can feel the grip of the racket and smell the chlorine in the pool. She might try to taste the salty sweat in her mouth and bring to life the emotions of elation, pride, and satisfaction.

A visual image—like a videotape—can be stopped, repeated, or slowed down. Imagery can be done at different rates of speed. If an athlete is trying to visualize the ideal performance, it should be done at the speed at which she hopes to perform the skill. When trying to make corrections to a skill, athletes can slow the pace down to try to see the technical components of the skill. Many athletes don't use imagery because they only see themselves making mistakes. In order to change the pictures playing in their mind, these athletes will have to practice imagery on a regular basis. However, they can begin by using imagery to help picture the corrections of the missed skills. In this case, the athlete would actually stop the picture in her mind in order to focus her attention on the correct movement of one part of her body.

Visualization may break down at the point at which the skill is not clearly understood. It can be harmful to skill development to visualize something an athlete doesn't clearly understand how to do. The material for imagining must already be stored in the brain from previous experience or practice efforts. Although athletes may be unable to see themselves perform the skill, they may have the capability to picture someone else doing the skill. This can be a good starting point for athletes to work into being able to picture themselves performing ideally.

Imagery can be used to plan ahead and react to various situations. These can include physical adjustments in intensity levels or strategies as well as mental adjustments such as changes in focus or reactions to unexpected events. Athletes can re-create experiences or places with which they are already familiar or create a picture of how they think it might be. Also, athletes can use their self-talk while visualizing. The specific self-talk phrases can be thought about silently during the visualization just as they would be during the actual performance.

Imagery Uses

- Experience self performing better (stronger, faster, more accurately) than ever before.
- Describe new competitive environments in detail so athletes feel as if they have been there before (more experienced teammates can do this for less experienced ones).
- Imagine self responding in a certain way to specific situations or plays.
- Imagine self making technical corrections or practicing a certain skill.
- Imagine situations that have caused problems in the past and replace old responses with new and more effective ones.

When to Use Imagery

- Use in conjunction with physical practice or as a supplement to physical practice.
- Use as an effective and helpful substitute for physical practice when fatigued or injured.
- Use to practice other mental fitness skills such as positive mental attitude, energy management, and active awareness.
- Use to prepare for practice.
- Use before or after a game/competition.
- Use during breaks in the game or practice.
- Use during practice to correct a certain skill.
- Use during personal time to relax and decompress.

FAST FACTS

➡ A study was conducted examining different types of imagery interventions in relation to sport confidence. Findings show athletes who visualize task performance while trying to feel the emotions and physiological responses connected to competing tend to be more successful than athletes who imagine completion of the task as an isolated event.(4)

RELAXATION AND IMAGERY

Relaxation is often an excellent precursor to imagery. Relaxation helps quiet the mind and prepare athletes to create the desired images in a vivid and clear manner. Imagery is a re-creation of an athlete's "reality." It's about athletes knowing how they want things to be and re-creating these scenarios in their mind. Pairing imagery with relaxation can be helpful for athletes unable to quiet their doubts enough to see themselves completing the skills to the best of their ability.

ABOUT RELAXATION

There are two types of relaxation exercises. One, known as progressive muscle relaxation, was developed by Dr. Edmund Jacobson. It involves the tensing and releasing of various muscle groups. Another involves visualization combined with slow breathing. In each, an athlete can be coached by another person, or she can tape-record the instructions. It is important to know that relaxation, like imagery, is a learned skill and requires regular practice.

Here's how to get started:

- Assume a comfortable position, preferably lying down with joints flexed.
- Breathe slowly and easily.
- Pay attention to how each part of the body feels as muscles are systematically tensed and released.

Progressive Muscle Relaxation

Clench your jaws (as you breathe in), notice the tension, hold for
three seconds, release and breathe out. Repeat.

Shrug your shoulders tightly (as you breathe in), notice the tension,
hold for three seconds, release and breathe out. Repeat.

Tighten your stomach muscles (as you breathe in), notice the tension, hold for three seconds, release and breathe out. Repeat.

Clench your right hand into a fist (as you breathe in), notice the
tension, hold for three seconds, release and breath out. Do the
same with left hand. Repeat.

Flex your right arm to tighten the biceps (as you breathe in), notice
the tension, hold for three seconds, release and breathe out. Then
do the same with your left arm. Repeat.

Then, tense your right quadriceps muscles (as you breathe in), notice the tension, hold for three seconds, release and breathe out.
Then do the same with your left quadriceps. Repeat.

Tense your right calf muscle (as you breathe in), notice the tension,
hold for three seconds, release and breathe out. Then do the same
with your left calf muscle. Repeat.

Point your right foot downward to tense (as you breathe in), notice
the tension, hold for three seconds, release and breathe out. Then
do the same with your left foot. Repeat.

To Finish:

Take a deep breath, filling your abdomen first, then your chest.

Hold your breath for a moment and then slowly exhale, emptying
your abdomen first, then your chest.

Repeat this three times and center your attention on your breath.

Imagery-Based Relaxation

Let your eyes begin to close . . . and as they close, take a deep breath. A
deep breath all the way down into your abdomen. Now you can begin to
relax every muscle in your body. Your face begins to relax . . . you are let-

ting go of any tension. Your forehead becomes smooth . . . smooth and relaxed. Letting go of any concerns and any worries . . . very, very smooth
and relaxed. Your cheeks are beginning to relax. . . . letting go, letting go,
letting go of any tension. And now your jaw begins to relax . . . becoming
looser and more and more relaxed. As you let go of the last bit of tension
in your jaw, you may begin to feel your lips part.

Your neck begins to relax . . . as if a warm wave of relaxation is flowing
through your neck, taking all the tension away . . . letting go of any tension . . . nice and relaxed . . . a wave of relaxation flowing down the right
side of your neck . . . and the back of your neck . . . and the left side of
your neck . . . and down the front of your neck . . . your neck is feeling
smooth and relaxed.

And now your shoulders . . . letting go of any tension . . . allow every
muscle in the shoulders to deeply relax . . . letting go of any tension . . .
your neck and shoulders feeling totally relaxed. And your arms, too, are becoming more and more relaxed. Just allow a warm wave of relaxation to
come into your arms . . . warm wave of relaxation moving down your biceps . . . deeply relaxing all the muscles in your arms . . . the wave of relaxation is taking away all of the tension . . . carrying away all the tension out
through your fingertips.

You're letting go, letting go, letting go of the last bit of tension.

Now your legs begin to relax. Just allow a warm wave of relaxation
to move through your quadriceps . . . taking away all the tension . . . a
warm wave of relaxation into your knees . . . and down through your
shins . . . deeply relaxing . . . a warm wave of relaxation around your
ankles . . . deeply relaxing all of the muscles in your legs . . . all the
tension carried out through your feet and toes. Your entire body relaxing and letting go. You begin feeling almost drowsy . . . feeling peaceful and calm . . . You are drifting and floating . . . drifting and floating,
feeling drowsy, peaceful, and calm. Your body feeling loose, limp, and
relaxed.

As you drift, so relaxed and calm . . . you see a staircase. I am going to
count backward from ten to one and as I count, you will walk down the
staircase, becoming more and more deeply relaxed with each step you take.
Ten . . . drifting deeper and deeper into total relaxation . . . nine . . .
eight . . . more and more deeply relaxed . . . seven . . . six . . . feeling

peaceful and calm . . . five . . . drifting deeper and deeper . . . four . . . three . . . more and more deeply relaxed . . . two . . . and one.

Your whole body is now pleasantly and comfortably relaxed. . . . I'll give you a few moments to go back to any muscle group that needs extra attention.

RELAXATION, IMAGERY, AND HEALING

Judging from ancient healing and spiritual traditions, imagery may also play a role in promoting healing and managing pain. When athletes are in pain, whether emotional or physical, the pain tends to dominate their attention. It becomes hard to remember a time they didn't feel pain, and they wonder if it will ever go away. It seems as if the discomfort will be permanent and everlasting. Although some people do experience chronic pain, in most cases the pain will go away eventually.

It can be helpful for an athlete to see her body as healthy and strong. Sometimes the only way an injured athlete can even begin to imagine herself recovered is through the use of imagery. Instead of directing all her energies and focus to the injured areas, attention can be directed to seeing the area healed and functioning well in a sport setting. The athlete begins to replace old negative pictures of herself and her injured body with inspiring pictures of her healed and well-functioning physique.

Although injury has been identified as a physical shock, the bodily symptoms can be exacerbated by the psychological trauma. Just as physical injuries differ from one athlete to another, so do the emotional responses to injury. Injured athletes often lose regular contact with teammates, partners, and coaches, which can lead to feelings of isolation. The once highly praised athlete goes from hero to zero. Sometimes the only way she can remain active in her sport is through the pictures she creates in her mind's eye.

In order to assist an injured athlete through recovery, it's important to have her set goals and picture herself attaining the different stepping stones to rejuvenation. She may need assistance in reframing the situation and finding a way to reinterpret the injury. Listen to the way she talks about the injury and attack any irrational thinking that is detrimental to healing. Help her to think logically about the injury by interjecting reason into the emotion and get her focused on recuperation through the use of guided imagery and relaxation training.

For most athletes, suffering an injury is difficult both emotionally and physically. However, the mind can help guide her through the healing process. The mind needs to be well prepared to respond once the body is healthy and ready to go. Athletes who actively take control of their rehabilitation programs and use their minds to facilitate these goals become a driving force and inspiration in their pursuit of recovery. All great endings have humble beginnings. As the ancient Chinese proverb states, "A journey of a thousand miles begins with a single step." The key to a successful injury recovery may very well rely within the athlete herself.

FAST FACTS

➡ A study of thirty-two former sports medicine clinic patients with either knee or ankle injuries found that 19 percent of the athletes had exceptionally fast recoveries. These subjects evidenced high scores on positive attitude, outlook, stress and stress control, social support, goal setting, positive self-talk, and mental imagery.(5)

Behavior to Watch for from Injured Athletes

- Obsession with the question, "When will I be able to play again?"
- Denial in the form of, "Things are great"; "It's no big deal"
- A history of coming back too fast or too slowly from injuries
- Dwelling on minor somatic complaints
- Remarks about letting the team down or guilt about not being able to contribute
- Dependence on the therapy process
- Withdrawal from teammates, coaches, friends, or family
- Statements that indicate a helplessness in impacting recovery

Assisting the Injured Athlete

- Understand and listen to the athlete's perspective on her injury.
- Avoid premature confrontation about self-defeating behavior related to injury.

- Help the athlete gain accurate information about her injury and recovery process.
- Discuss the changes she may go through as part of rehabilitation and transition back into sports.
- Help the athlete set appropriate goals and develop coping strategies, such as relaxation and imagery.
- Provide the athlete with positive feedback regarding implementation of these coping skills.
- Discuss possible setbacks and plan strategies to cope with them.
- Prepare for a recovery target date.
- Keep the athlete involved with the team or sport in some way.

FAST FACTS

➡ A 1998 study on imagery reported no significant difference between genders in use or frequency of the technique.(6)

CAN YOU USE VIDEO AS A REPLACEMENT FOR IMAGERY?

Video has many uses and can actually be used in conjunction with imagery. Some athletes can have difficulty creating a mental picture of themselves. Videotaping an athlete in action and having her review the tape can assist her in creating a clear image of how she looks while practicing and performing.

I have also found video to be helpful for athletes who just cannot see themselves performing the correct skill or movement. For example, a gymnast who at one time performed a release move on bars with ease suddenly lost the correct feel of the skill and could no longer do it correctly. We turned to old videotapes of her performing the skill beautifully. As she watched the video of herself, she repeated a key word, such as "tight" or "quick." After watching the video repeatedly, she returned to the gym. As she prepared to do the skill and while she actually did the skill she would repeat the key word to herself. Instead of picturing the incorrect movement, she could now picture the correct technique as performed on the tape. Eventually, she was able to reproduce the skill successfully.

· · ·

The key to training the mind is practice. Some "mind games" are easily defined and applied, like relaxation and imagery. An athlete can learn the
skill and practice it daily or weekly. Others, such as reframing, are harder
to work into practice sessions, and athletes will need some guidance in using this as a tool to enhance performance. Providing an athlete with another outlook or just asking a simple question like, "I wonder how you
could use this experience to make you better?" are ways to help her reframe. Using effective self-talk can be done daily to help alleviate her frustration and prepare her to compete. When she has practiced responding to
her frustration in a positive manner, it certainly makes it more likely that
she will be able to respond in a similar way at game time. Relaxation, imagery, self-talk, thought stoppage, focusing, and goal setting are the mental tools athletes can apply to assist them in meeting their many sports
challenges. These mind games are lifelong lessons transferrable to almost
any endeavor she pursues.

7

Crunch Time: How to Help Her to Do Her Best When It Counts

It didn't feel like I was ready even though I was physically ready and well trained and all that, my mind, it was smoking. It was on fire and I couldn't really put it out at that point. Fear is not something you can hide away from.

—Michelle Kwan, speaking about
the 1997 National Championships

Athletic competition can be a frightening endeavor for athletes of all levels and ages. On game day, athletes hope they can execute their skills to the best of their ability at that given time. They can only hope, because it is impossible for them to predict the actual outcome. Often, I explain that competition is like trying to walk through a door when all that is known about the other side is that it is a dark, open space. If we know what lies on the other side of the door, we can walk through it with little fear. However, when on the other side of the door is an unknown dark space, we will experience fear and tentativeness while trying to pass through it.

Competing is much like walking through a door without being privy to what is on the other side, because before an event, athletes don't know how they will perform. Athletes, parents, and coaches each can take guesses about the outcome, but they cannot actually predict it (unless, of course, they are psychic). The unknown makes competing a nerve-racking endeavor.

Athletes tell me, "I'm so scared and nervous to compete. I know I shouldn't be nervous, but I am." Why shouldn't they be nervous? Where did they learn that nervousness was bad? Practice is where athletes work on skills and don't experience much nervousness. On the other hand, competition is all about athletes executing skills while feeling nervous. It is not only understandable that athletes feel nervous before performing, it is the very presence of nervousness that defines competition. The key to performing and competing well or walking through that door is how successfully athletes are able to respond to the feelings of nervousness.

SHE IS SO SCARED BEFORE A COMPETITION

Ellen is a sixteen-year-old ice skater who is extremely talented. She is, almost without exception, the best skater in her division. However, she has trouble skating up to her ability during the competition and is constantly beaten by far inferior skaters. Ellen's parents called me.

"She can do everything in her program during practice, but before competition she gets this look of panic," her mother said. "We can't seem to help her. She just bites our head off if we suggest anything. She's got a big competition in a week. Is there anything we can do?"

This is not an uncommon problem nor an uncommon time frame in which I have to work with an athlete. As a matter of fact, many athletes seek my assistance immediately before a big event with the hopes that they can improve their competitive outcomes.

When I met with Ellen, I asked her to tell me about a competition in which she had skated exceptionally well.

"Well," she said. "I would say it's been a really long time. I used to skate great until I was about twelve years old. Then I just started falling apart at every competition."

This was not surprising. Many athletes are proficient competitors at young ages. They tend to trust in their abilities because they have developed only a few high-risk skills, and therefore have the tendency to practice consistently well. As athletes get older and improve, expectations rise and so do their worries about potential mistakes. Instead of missing one jump, a more advanced skater has the potential to miss three or four.

I wanted to find out from Ellen what kinds of thoughts she had when she skated very well, and compare that mind set to her present competitive thinking. My guess was that during competitions Ellen overanalyzed rather than letting her skills happen as if she were on automatic pilot. When athletes become consumed solely with the outcome of performance, they tend to overanalyze or think about everything and anything in the hopes that something will help them control the result. I asked Ellen to reflect back to a time she had skated very well. If she could relive positive competitive experiences and identify the thoughts, feelings, and images that helped create them, then improving performance would just be a matter of reapplying an old approach to a new situation.

She told me, "When I was younger, I didn't think about anything. I just went out there and did it like practice. It was easier then. I didn't have all these triple jumps to worry about and nobody expected me to do much."

"You weren't really thinking a whole lot, it was just happening?" I reflected.

"Yeah. Pretty much," she said. "It's not like that now. Even if I try not to think, I can't stop it. My dad says that I get too nervous when the pressure is on. I skate great at exhibitions and shows because I don't get nervous. But at competition, I get so nervous my stomach gets tied up and I choke."

Ellen and her parents were making a critical mistake in their evaluations. Ellen and her parents had attributed the competitive outcome to the presence or absence of nervousness. Ellen's perception was that when she didn't feel pressure, she skated well, and when she did feel pressure, she choked. In reality, this was a totally incorrect assumption. It wasn't the nervousness that changed Ellen's performance, rather, the shifts in Ellen led to changes in performance. In other words, when Ellen felt nervous, Ellen changed in some way. Most likely, her self-perceptions and thoughts changed, which in turn produced changes in performance.

"In exhibitions, when you're not nervous, what do you think about?" I asked.

"Not much," she said. "It's like practice. I just do it. I know I'll skate well."

"How about at competition?" I asked.

"I think a lot," she said. "I try and get really focused and remember all the things my coaches have told me. I worry a lot too about how I'll do and what will happen if I mess up."

· · ·

Ellen was not a bad competitor, she just didn't know how to compete. She believed that to skate well in competition, she needed to think and try really hard. The more important the competition was to her, the more she would think and try to control the outcome. Ellen assumed incorrectly that in practice she didn't need to think much because she had lots of opportunities to get it right, but in competition when she only had one chance to do it right, she'd better think a whole lot to ensure that it would go well.

The formula for good performances is actually the exact opposite. The more important and pressure-filled an event, the more minimal the thinking. It is best for athletes to try and rely on the simple thoughts that lead them to trust what they have trained their bodies to do. Competition is really about giving up control and instead trusting that the hard work and preparation will pay off. Unfortunately, Ellen hadn't been taught this formula, nor did she know how to implement it, because she had never practiced "competition thinking." All Ellen needed to learn to do was apply the thinking that worked for her in exhibitions to competitions. She knew how to perform—she just didn't know she knew.

In order to identify the most effective competitive thinking for Ellen, we began by clearly defining the goals for the upcoming event.

"Ellen, do you have an outcome goal for this competition?" I asked.

"I want to win," she said. "But I know I'm not supposed to think about winning," she added quickly.

"Actually, it's good that you have a clear vision of what outcome you would like to create. It's always easier to hit a target you can see. However, in order to win, you also need to define performance and task goals."

"You mean like how I hope to skate?"

"Right. What type of performance do you think you need to have to win?"

"I need to skate two clean programs with good speed and choreography," she said, making it clear she had already thought this through.

"Sounds like you've spent some time thinking about your goals. Can you tell me about the average programs you skate in practice. Is it a clean program—one miss, two misses?" I asked.

"In practice I usually only make one mistake in the long and do a clean short. Once in a while I'll miss two things in the long, but that doesn't happen much anymore."

"So, on average, you have one miss in the long and a clean short?"

"Yeah, I'd say that's right."

"Well, then, realistic performance goals would be to skate clean in the short and skate clean or hit seven out of eight elements in the long. Now we need to create your mental game plan or task goals. These are actions you can take to give yourself the best chance of skating a clean short and long, which in turn will give you the best chance of winning," I explained.

It was difficult for Ellen to decide which thoughts would help the most, because she had never before created and practiced a mental game plan. Instead, she just worried about remembering everything in the hopes that something would be helpful. The mental game plan would be three simple tasks that she would execute and trust to give herself the best chance of performing well and ultimately the best chance of winning.

Since it was vital that Ellen keep her thoughts to a minimum, we came up with one technical key word for her most difficult jumps. In between the jumps, she had specific spots where she would focus on her breathing. During the remainder of the program, she chose to pretend she was a character from the story her music told.

These were the only three tasks Ellen was to think about during the program. Her thoughts were to remain simple, and every time she ran through the program in practice, she was to use these simple thoughts. Ellen was no longer going to paralyze her body with overanalysis of technique. Instead, she was going to trust that she had done all of the work and that her body would come through for her. Whenever she felt any doubt, she would just remind herself of the three task goals. That was the simple mental game plan she was to follow.

By setting task goals, athletes eliminate the need to overanalyze. They know exactly what they will focus on because they have been practicing those thoughts or mental game plans on a daily basis. Whether they are competing at the Olympic Games or a regional event, their thoughts should remain the same. Once they have determined the thoughts that give them the best chance of performing well, they practice the mental game plan daily. This makes it a natural part of their routine and increases the chances that they will rely on those same thoughts to carry them through pressure-filled moments.

FAST FACTS

➡ A study consisting of 251 male and female high school, intercollegiate, and college-age recreational sports participants revealed that sport participants higher in ego orientation (focus on comparing oneself to and defeating others) were more likely to experience concentration disruption prior to or during performance. In general, women were more task oriented (focus on improving relative to own past performances) than men, and were more likely to report worrying and being physically anxious prior to or during competition.(1)

WHAT IS NERVOUSNESS?

Nervousness, which is technically known as arousal, is a physiological response by the body. Nervousness is the degree of excitement an athlete experiences; it runs on a continuum from deep sleep to intense excitement. Nervous athletes describe themselves as having butterflies, dry mouth, sweaty palms, stiffness, jelly legs, increased heart rate, and quickened breathing. Many times you will see aroused athletes yawning, which is incorrectly interpreted as fatigue. Actually, as athletes' heart rates increase and breathing quickens, they yawn to take in more oxygen and slow their breathing.

Nervousness is the way in which the body gets ready to perform certain activities. Although nervousness can make athletes feel uncomfortable and different, it does not necessarily affect performance negatively. As a matter of fact, people can experience nervousness or arousal before events they are looking forward to as much as about events they fear. Prior to competition or games, athletes get nervous because they are unsure of how they will perform. Their bodies sense they need some help in dealing with this unknown situation and begin to get aroused to prepare the athlete to fight. Through a series of signals, the adrenal gland is stimulated and hormones released. The hormone most commonly known to athletes is adrenaline.

Adrenaline can be helpful to performance, because it can act as a quick burst of energy, allowing athletes to perform beyond their usual capabilities. However, adrenaline also produces many of the physiological changes that lead athletes to feel uncomfortable, fatigued, and uncoordinated. These physiological changes often worry athletes and lead them to react to their emotions rather than the situation. Their feelings and their thoughts become one and the same.

Nervousness is a process in which athletes begin to feel the physiological signs of arousal. The time frame in which they feel the nervousness varies from athlete to athlete. Some experience it days before a game or competition, while others experience it the minute before or during actual play. The nervousness makes athletes' bodies feel different than they do during practice. Athletes don't particularly like the way they feel when nervous. This dislike, coupled with people around them asking, "Are you nervous?" and telling them, "Don't be nervous," leads athletes to believe that they must get rid of the nervousness. When athletes try to stop the nervousness, they quickly find their efforts to be futile. The athlete who cannot stop the nervousness becomes even more anxious and ends up being nervous about being nervous.

Athletes begin to assume that because they feel nervous, which is bad, they will most likely perform badly. Since they don't know how they will perform, they use their nervousness to predict that they will have a poor outcome. When they feel bad, they think ineffectively and equate how they feel with how they will perform.

This starts a cycle of negative thinking, which produces fear or anxiety. So, the athlete has become anxious over what she feels in her body and what she thinks in her mind. By the time she is ready to perform, she has convinced herself that because she is nervous she is doomed to failure.

The perception that nervousness means an athlete is in for a poor performance is thoroughly inaccurate. In fact, it is the presence of nervousness that differentiates practice from competition. In practice, athletes work to improve technique and skills and experience minimal to no nervousness. In competition, athletes no longer work on skills, rather, they execute skills while feeling moderate to high levels of nervousness. Athletes who are executing skills with little nervousness are most likely home practicing. I tell athletes that if they want to compete without nervousness, they should stay home and practice. Competition is all about performing skills while feeling nervous.

The relationship between nervousness and performance is most often explained by what is called the inverted U hypothesis. According to this theory, as nervousness increases, performance also improves—up to a certain point. After that, further increases in arousal cause performance to decline. In other words, there seems to be an optimal arousal level for athletes that varies individually. Moderate levels of nervousness seem to be the best. Very low or very high levels of nervousness will not produce the best performances. Where the moderate level is for each athlete depends upon the athlete. If you think of low arousal as one and high arousal as ten, then one athlete might perform best within a one-to-three range, while another might perform best right in the middle, around a four-to-six range. It just depends on the athlete.

Low Nervousness   High Nervousness

If an athlete is very worried and her nervousness continues to increase, there will be a dramatic decline in performance. Therefore, in order to have an optimum level of nervousness, an athlete needs to control her thoughts. Think about riding a roller coaster. You may experience feelings of nervousness before the ride. However, if you like roller coasters, you will interpret these feelings as excitement. Physiologically, there is no difference between excitement and nervousness. The difference is a result of the way in which the athlete perceives these feelings.

Typically, athletes start feeling nervous, and begin to think, "Oh, no. I'm so nervous. I'm going to mess up." The nervousness, which is present to help performance, now hurts performance. Athletes who respond well to their nervousness have learned to accept it and make statements such as, "The nervousness is my body's way of getting ready to perform," or "I'm really excited to play."

Some young athletes naturally respond to the pressure of competition with more anxiety than others. This is known as trait anxiety. People with high levels of trait anxiety usually experience more fear in specific situations than those with low levels of trait anxiety. If an athlete is told to kick a penalty shot to win the game and she possess a high level of trait anxiety, she will experience a great deal of worry and concern, whereas if she has lower levels of trait anxiety, she will perceive the situation to be a great opportunity and will be excited by the possibility of winning for the team.

The type of event and how athletes perceive the event will also influence their nervousness. A swimmer might experience a great deal of fear and worry at a qualifying meet and very little worry at a nonqualifier. Ask athletes what they feel at different types of competitive events, so they can learn to manage their varying levels of nervousness. Many athletes make the mistake of thinking they will feel the same way every time they perform. If athletes have had a very good performance, they incorrectly assume that in order to perform at that same level, they must replicate the exact amount of nervousness. The truth is, they need to accept whatever degree of nervousness they feel, and use their thoughts and mental game plan to execute their skills regardless of how they feel.

FAST FACTS

➡ Researchers have noted that more experienced and successful athletes interpret precompetition anxiety symptoms as facilitative of strong performance. Mental skills such as self-talk, goal setting, and imagery are successful strategies for restructuring negative interpretation of anxiety.(2)

TECHNIQUES TO MANAGE NERVOUSNESS

Although nervousness is necessary for optimum performance, there are certain outlooks and techniques that can be used to assist athletes in coping with the physiological and psychological effects.

- Minimize Outcome—Athletes who have excessive anxiety may need help in reducing their muscle tension and turning around self-destructive messages. It can be beneficial to deemphasize the outcome and minimize the importance of the event. For example, at the Olympic Games, as an athlete was getting ready to take to the ice, her coach said, "Do it for your country." Although this statement was intended to be motivating, many athletes might feel burdened by being reminded of the tremendous importance the whole world placed on this event. Instead, an athlete can minimize in her mind the significance of the event. Yes, even when it's the Olympic Games.

- Minimize Thinking—Some athletes overthink, virtually paralyzing their bodies with too much information. These athletes need to get focused on a few simple tasks. Remind them to keep their thoughts concise, using a few key words or phrases. Reliance on practiced self-talk, combined with seeing competitive situations in a less threatening way, can help athletes to manage their nervousness more effectively. Instead of interpreting the nervousness to be a predictor of failure, they see it as their body's way of getting ready to respond to the situation. Once they accept the nervousness, they can focus on a few key thoughts that enable their bodies to get in the flow and perform automatically with little help from the mind.

- Perform on Demand—It is critical to provide athletes with opportunities to practice performing. Give them chances to simulate stressful situations. In practice, coaches often ask athletes to perform on demand. They require athletes to complete a certain number of skills in a certain time frame or to avoid some type of extra practice. Other kinds of perform-on-demand exercises include mock competitions, scrimmages, and inviting peers or friends to watch. Some athletes even like to imagine a competitor and determine what type of performance they need in order to beat the imagined opponent. They try to perform to the expected level and keep track of how often they are able to beat the imagined competition. These stressful situations can produce some feelings of nervousness for athletes, and it is therefore in the athletes' best interest not to require such drills on a daily basis. More importantly, perform-on-demand coaching is most effective when coaches and athletes together devise a mental game plan to help handle the created pressure. Athletes can check to make sure they have a specific key word or phrase, image, or breathing technique that will guide them through the exercise. If the athlete is trying to work on managing her physical tension and fatigue, she might want to learn such techniques as relaxation, centering, and breathing along with learning how to project confidence through her body language. Eventually, she can incorporate these techniques into her actual training and put them to the test during her perform-on-demand coaching sessions. These types of activities encourage athletes to control their arousal and minimize immediate performance results.

- Mental Game Plans—It is critical that athletes identify the type of self-talk that produces the best performances for them. Athletes use self-talk in a variety of ways. Some use general key phrases, such as "I can do it" and "I've done it lots of times before." Others prefer more technical reminders such as, "Keep up your speed," "Follow through," "Keep your eye on the ball," "Watch the defender," "Scan the field," while others are more comfortable using feeling words— "Be aggressive," "Float," "Nice and easy," "Charge," "Power." Some will like to try to create a certain feeling or see an image in their mind. Still others prefer to distract themselves and think about anything but sports. Some athletes may make use of all of these different types of self-talk. Have athletes test out a variety of self-talk statements and decide which they like the best. Usually, whatever works in practice is what they should use in competition. These self-talk statements become their mental game plan. The biggest thought that gets in the way during competition is the outcome. Athletes think, "Oh, my. This is my chance to win. I don't want to mess up," instead of thinking about how to win and perform well. The key is to develop and practice a mental game plan. Far too many athletes think about nothing in practice and then get in the game and begin sending messages to their bodies that are new and unfamiliar. The mental game plan needs to be prepared and practiced, not decided at game time. When an athlete knows exactly what to focus on, she can devote her energies to trusting both her mental and physical training.

- Breath Control—When the body becomes aroused, physiological changes take place and can make the athlete feel uncomfortable. For example, nervousness may cause breathing to become shallow or, in cases of panic, very rapid, as seen in hyperventilation. When breathing quickens, the amount of oxygen to the brain is reduced, which can result in dizziness, headaches, and tingly sensations. Athletes can learn to control their breathing and thereby control how they feel. Abdominal breathing is a skill that must be learned. Have her lie flat on her back and place her hands over her abdomen. Ask her to distend her abdomen as it protrudes out as far as possible. Then, have her suck in her abdomen as far as possible. Most children will breathe in as they suck in their abdomens and breathe out as they distend it. Actually, the correct way to do abdominal breathing is to breathe in through the nose as the abdomen distends and breathe out through the nose as the abdomen falls back in. The exhalation should be heard. Remind her to imagine air being forced into her body when she breathes in and to imagine the tension leaving her body when she breathes out. Have her repeat the exercise for twenty breaths. Abdominal breathing, like any precompetition exercise, needs to be practiced and perfected before being implemented in the competitive setting.

- Body Language Presentation—Some athletes put their feelings on display through the way they hold their bodies. When athletes become tense and scared, it is common for their shoulders to rise and fall forward and for their jaws or fists to clench. A quick and easy technique for athletes to reduce such tension is to alter their postural stance. Athletes who clench their jaws can be taught to part their lips slightly and rest their tongue gently on the roof of their mouth behind the front teeth. For those who clench their fists, have them clench their fists tightly for five seconds and release. Then have them place the fingers of one hand on top of the other with the palms facing upwards. The thumbs of each hand should be gently touching. Athletes who tend to act out negative emotions by hunching their shoulders can be reminded to stand tall with their shoulders pushed down and back. Sometimes it can be helpful to remind athletes to remove facial tension by lifting their eyebrows and opening their eyelids. All of these postural changes can be performed in conjunction with abdominal breathing.

- Pacing—Some athletes like to prepare themselves to compete by pacing. Very often athletes who pace can walk themselves into a frenzy. When pacing, it is most effective for the stride to be firm and commanding yet controlled. An athlete walking frantically in circles is not sending the message to her body that she is in control. If you encounter an athlete pacing swiftly or talking quickly, slow her down by modulating the tone and speed of your own voice. Talk more slowly and with less voice inflection. Also, athletes can be taught to find a neutral stance, which they use as an indicator that they are in control of both mind and body. When the tension hits, they let it flow for a few moments and then assume their neutral stance, reminding themselves that they are in control.

- Precompetition/Pregame Routines—A precompetition routine is a plan of action that helps athletes control their nervousness. A routine makes the unpredictable aspects of competition more predictable. The athlete doesn't know how she will perform but does know how she will prepare to perform. By planning out her precompetition actions, she puts herself in control of getting ready. Routines also help the athlete remain focused on factors about her performance that she controls, such as her thoughts and body language. She doesn't need to worry about thinking or doing all of the right things at the last minute. Instead, she follows her predetermined plan. A routine may include a series of physical and mental exercises that serve to warm up mind and body, such as stretching, jumping rope, visualizing, deep breathing, talking to teammates or friends, pacing, sitting, coloring, playing cards, listening to music, walking through routines or plays, humor, team chants, and watching or not watching opponents. Routines should be developed based on the athlete's needs and are used to help keep the athlete comfortable both physically and mentally. Stretching and warming up the body is critical just as is keeping self-talk simple and focused on key words that facilitate trust in physical preparation and abilities. Make sure athletes don't start their routine too early. Many athletes arrive at a game one hour prior to the scheduled start and go through their routine. In about ten minutes, they feel ready and focused. The problem is that the game doesn't start for another fifty minutes. Prior to using the pregame routine, have an athlete test it out in practice and evaluate its effectiveness.

- Mastery Scripts—Routines may include something called a mastery script, which helps athletes begin to think about and believe in the possibility of creating a great performance. An athlete can write out a script detailing exactly how she hopes the game/competition will happen. Stressful situations are not acknowledged; rather, the script describes the ideal situation. While developing the script, the athlete imagines how she would like to think, feel, see, and act during the upcoming event. Athletes can include in the script their precompetition preparation or can just create the ideal performance itself. Mastery scripts help balance worry with positive thoughts and outlook.

FAST FACTS

➡ Two studies of tennis coaches found that they used a variety of skills to increase athletes' beliefs that they could successfully complete a task. Coaches used liberally rewarding statements, verbal persuasion, conditioning drills, and modeling of other successful players. They encouraged positive self-talk and emphasized that feelings of anxiety are not fear but are a sign of readiness and that failure results from lack of effort or experience and not from a lack of innate ability.(3,4)

Example of Mastery Script for a Figure Skater

It's a few minutes before I perform. I look around and see that lots of people have come to watch me. This is my opportunity to show off all of my hard work. I feel comfortable in this rink. I am waiting to skate the long program and I begin to feel my nerves kick in. I like this feeling as I know the adrenaline my body is producing will help me out. I remind myself that doubt in and of itself will not make me perform badly. I am a well-trained athlete and have practiced to be mentally tough. I have confidence in my ability to keep my thinking simple and focused on the present. I feel ready to go, physically pumped up and mentally collected.

As I prepare to perform, I take a nice deep breath. I scan my body and make sure I am projecting confidence by pushing my chest out, putting my head up and shoulders down. I take another deep breath from my ab-domen and say to myself, "Nice and easy." I can feel the confidence. Just as I finish saying, "Nice and easy," my concentration narrows to my mental game plan. I am thinking really well. As I begin performing, I notice I'm focused (in the present), doing what I have trained myself to do. Not judg-ing what is happening, just executing. I feel solid and strong and trust my-self. It feels great to let the performance happen!

FAST FACTS

➡ The experience athletes have when they are fully immersed in their sport, performing effortlessly as if their bodies are on auto-matic pilot, has been referred to as "flow."(5)

ALL I DO IS THINK ABOUT EVERYTHING THAT WILL GO WRONG

Donna was an eighteen-year-old swimmer who had experienced a great deal of competitive success, but as her abilities improved, so too did the ex-pectations. Donna had always been confident in her athletic abilities, but this year was different. Expectations for her performance had dramatically increased, and Donna was having to learn how to compete with some doubt. She had struggled through her last few meets. Her mother called with the hope that I could give her a confidence boost.

Donna spoke to me about feeling unlike herself when she swam. I asked, "Can you describe the last meet where you did feel like yourself?"

"Well, it just felt easy. There weren't many expectations for me. I knew what time I wanted to swim and was really working on trusting myself. Practices went well and I felt calm and relaxed at the meet."

"It sounds like when you didn't feel the weight of expectations, you were able to set a clear goal and focus your attention on how to achieve that goal, which in this case was to try and trust your training."

"Yeah, I think that's right."

"How about when you felt the weight of expectations. Was your ap-proach similar?"

"No, I thought about winning and impressing everyone or not impressing everyone. I can remember at the last meet sitting in the hotel room seeing myself swimming really slowly. I could see myself messing up the turns, and I don't even remember trying to stop thinking about it. I just replayed it over and over again in my head. I never thought about that until now."

Just by analyzing a good swim, Donna had recognized some of the critical mental factors that impacted her performance. Unfortunately, the expectations could not be eliminated, so Donna would need to develop some coping skills. As it turned out, she already possessed some effective ways to deal with the pressure. When the perceived expectations were minimal, Donna naturally responded by setting clear goals and creating a mental game plan. However, when the expectations were perceived to be high, she buckled under their weight partly because she didn't set goals or develop a game plan. She took a new approach which was to sit in the hotel, rest, and think about everything that could go wrong at the meet. Certainly, not the way I would recommend for an athlete to prepare to compete. Yet many athletes ready themselves in this very way under the guise that they are resting and getting focused.

Donna and I discussed a more effective pre-meet routine. If she was going to sit in the hotel and think about everything that could go wrong, it seemed that getting out of the hotel room was the better option. Often, athletes need to stay busy to keep their minds off of the upcoming event. Athletes who think and rethink the competition may have a hard time remaining positive and eventually drift to the negative. When athletes have a mental game plan for the meet, they can easily deal with the doubt by reminding themselves to trust their game plan, which most likely will involve some specific self-talk words or phrases. However, athletes that just hope they are able to get focused usually are thrown by the doubt and negativity that slowly creeps up on them. They don't know what it is they are going to do to give themselves the best chance for success, and with no clear game plan to stop the doubt, it can spiral out of control. It always seems funny to me that athletes wait until five minutes before an event to get focused. They would never wait until five minutes before an event to physically train. Yet you see athletes who have never even given a minute of time to mental preparation trying to come up with quick fixes right before a big event. Mental preparation is best done weeks and months in advance.

Then, five minutes before the event, the athlete executes the mental plan rather than trying to create it.

The great part of competition is that athletes are not required to think. Instead, they are directed to let it all go and play with reckless abandon. No matter what, the spectators clap, and there are no laps to be run or weights to be lifted, just a bed waiting at home. These realities make competition in many ways a simpler endeavor than practice. Yet athletes try to make competition into something quite complicated. Uncomplicate it by reminding athletes that competition is a time of simplicity.

FAST FACTS

➡ Professional golfer Nancy Lopez sticks with this philosophy. "The simpler I keep things, the better I play."

HER OPPONENTS CONSTANTLY TRY TO THROW HER OFF

Audrey is a fourteen-year-old golfer who is just learning the hard knocks of elite competition. During the first round of a recent tournament, she was setting up for a three-foot putt, which she normally would make easily, when her opponent casually walked by and said, "Boy, your butt looks big when you putt."

Shaken, Audrey not only missed the putt, but fell apart and recorded the worst round of her career. She talked with her golf coach about the sting of her opponent's words, and he responded by saying, "Get used to it, because it gets worse."

Her mother called me the next day wanting to know how to help Audrey deal with the negative comments of other players and friends. It was an interesting question and one that I'm getting more and more as women and young girls become more and more competitive. The stakes are higher, the competition greater, and unfortunately the tactics used to gain an edge may have become lower.

Men and boys have often used trash-talking in the war of athletic intimidation and may even be praised for rattling their opponent. I've often noticed that boys compete, argue, make fun of one another, and even fight, and rarely let those events interfere with their friendships. On the other hand, one innocent comment by a girl misinterpreted by her girlfriend can sever a friendship forever. Many girls worry that their friendships will be threatened by their athletic talents and successes. Part of being a girlfriend is connecting with your friends, and one way to do this is to share similar experiences, feelings, thoughts, and opinions. It may take time for girls to learn that true friendships are about valuing differences as much as similarities.

The competitive environment can clearly reveal such differences and therefore has the potential to tear apart friendships. A girl's personality on the field may differ considerably from her personality off the field. Carol Gilligan's landmark study, "In a Different Voice," explored the contrasting manners in which girls and boys reacted to competitive situations. She asserted that since girls place high value and importance on social relationships they may experience competition to be a threat to those relationships.(6) At some point in her career, she may grapple with separating herself as a player from herself as a friend. Psyching out opponents may be viewed differently from one player to the next. One athlete may see it as a challenge of the game, while another may see it as a personal attack on a friendship. Psyching out opponents is a well-known tactic in athletic competition, and as unfortunate as it may be, it is necessary for athletes to learn to deflect their intent.

First, Audrey needed to understand what she could and could not control about her athletic performance. Whether it was a comment from a competitor or bad weather conditions or a lousy draw, Audrey would have to be able to identify such distractions as uncontrollable and learn to shift her attention to those factors under her control.

"Focusing on the controllable aspects of performance has a critical impact upon shaping your performance," I explained to Audrey. "What kinds of things do you tend to worry about related to your performance?"

"I really worry a lot about my competitors. What they think of me and what they say. I don't want anyone to be mad at me or think badly of me. I really don't like anyone to be upset with me."

Audrey's biggest worry was about other people, especially her competitors (external). Audrey had little power to change what her competitors said or did, and by consuming herself with worry about them, she prevented herself from developing a plan to alleviate the worry. Audrey's external focus kept her centered on what she saw as the problem—her mean-spirited competitors. This external focus and ongoing worry led her to feel out of control.

I asked, "Audrey, how do you feel when you spend so much time worrying about people you can't change or control?"

"I start to feel really nervous, scared and almost helpless."

"Have you ever described yourself as stressed-out?"

"Of course," she laughed

"Next time you think you are stressed-out, check in with your thoughts. I will guarantee you that you are dwelling on things you can't do anything about. You are stuck on the externals."

Audrey was not only worried about what her competitors thought of her, she actually took responsibility for their reactions. If Audrey did well, she worried that her friends would get mad. She viewed their anger as her responsibility. In order to remain their friends, she felt she had to make them feel better.

I explained, "Audrey, part of athletic competition is about learning to respond to a variety of situations and emotions. Have you ever done really badly and been upset?"

"Sure," she responded wondering where I was going with this.

"And how did you respond to that disappointment?"

Audrey thought for a moment and said, "I was upset for a few days and kept thinking about what I did wrong. Then I talked with my coach and we figured out what I needed to work on about my game. We focused on the short game and I changed my swing a bit. I remember getting better after that experience."

"I don't hear you saying anything about being mad at your friends or blaming them for your poor play. You processed your defeat like a champion. You accepted it and got focused on what you needed to do to improve. It wasn't your friends' responsibility to make you feel better. You had to choose how to respond and learn what the best way was to process the defeat. Your friends need to do the same. Part of athletic competition is learning how to use disappointment and anger to move ahead. Just as you took responsibility for dealing with your emotions, you need to let your friends do the same."

Once Audrey agreed to let her friends be responsible for their own actions, we talked about how the "big butt" comment affected her game. Audrey expressed great doubt about her capabilities, and it became clear that she spent much of the tournament trying to predict how it would turn out. When her competitor told her that her butt looked big, she became consumed by thoughts about her looks. She finally determined that she had a "big butt," didn't like the way she looked, and had better change her stance to make herself look better and therefore stop the taunting. The more consumed Audrey became with thoughts about her appearance and how others saw her, the less she was focused on how to execute. She didn't rely on her mental game plan, but instead chose to let her thoughts remain centered on her opponent and at the last moment actually made technical adjustments to her swing. Audrey's thoughts lingered on the comments of her opponent, making her feel worse and worse. The worse she felt, the more negative she became, and finally she used these feelings and thoughts as indicators that a poor performance was inevitable. Audrey's game was affected by the way in which Audrey reacted to her opponent's comments. When the distraction occurred, Audrey changed her game plan and technique rather than hunkering down and forcing herself to execute her mental and physical game plan with precision. At the moment she needed to rely on her training the most, she instead decided to come up with a new strategy.

Audrey asked, "So, you mean I should just ignore what those girls say to me? That's so hard to do."

"It is hard to do, but you don't just ignore their comments. What you do is identify that you cannot control what they say, but you certainly can control how you react to what they say. Ask yourself if you really want to allow name-callers to take you out of playing your game. My guess is that instead of focusing on how you could react effectively to the comments, you just chose to play back their remarks in your head over and over again. Did this in anyway help you play better?"

"I never really knew I had any other choice," she said. "It was as if they took over my thinking and there was nothing I could do."

"Right, but who controls your thoughts?"

"I do. Right?"

"Right."

When the taunts began, Audrey not only needed to try and tune them out but to shift her focus from their words to a replacement thought—such as reviewing specific information she'd received during practices, improving her body language to show she was trying, visualizing the correction, using deep breathing to reduce tension, or anything else under her control that might help her be successful.

One strategy I suggested that Audrey use to help her stay focused on the controllable was what I call a "coping script." A coping script doesn't describe the ideal situation like a mastery script does, but instead prepares an athlete for the unexpected, anything that might throw her off or distract her from the task at hand.

I told Audrey to write down a way she thought she could deal with not only the trash-talking opponent, but anything that might disrupt her thought process, such as a loud noise or a bad putt.

"For example," I said, "Think of something like, 'I will take a deep breath. I will make sure my shoulders are down and back. I will project confidence through my body language. I will then remind myself that I need to focus on myself. I'm prepared and ready to perform.'"

Coping scripts help athletes prepare to deal with just about anything, making the unexpected a little bit more familiar. A coping script details stressful conditions and an athlete's responses. With the mastery script, an athlete describes the flawless ideal performance. Coping scripts are designed to help athletes rehearse mental strategies to deal with the unexpected or challenging situation. The technique of thought stoppage can be included in the script and employed as a strategy to alleviate potential anxiety. It might be helpful for Audrey to read the script prior to her next match as a reminder that she is in charge. This helps shift her attention from the uncontrollable to the controllable, providing her with a strategy to deal with distraction—be it an opponent or herself.

Example of a Coping Script

I am trying to qualify for the finals at a golf tournament. I need a birdie on this hole to get to the finals. I hate this hole because of the water. Last time I hit right into the water. I stop for a second and look at where I want to put the ball. Suddenly, I remember the comments of some former opponent who likes to tell me my butt looks big. Now I really begin to wonder if I can make the shot. I stop myself for a second before starting my preshot routine. I tell myself, "Stop." I remind myself that I am well prepared and that I don't want to let someone else take me out of my game. I picture myself making a great shot and remember how nice and easy that feels. I repeat the words "Nice and easy" to myself. I decide to focus my attention on where I want to put the ball. I know where I want it to go. I scan my body language and take a moment to just stand still feeling my nervousness. I then begin my preshot routine. I take a few practice strokes repeating my key words. I begin to have all sorts of doubts. I see myself hitting it into the water. I stop, take a step back, shrug my shoulders. I tell myself to trust my swing. I take a deep breath and see myself as if I were in a bubble. My own world. I start my routine again and will do so as many times as I need to. I execute my routine and the last thought is on creating a nice and easy swing. Getting refocused on myself is what competition is all about.

FAST FACTS

➡ A study of 115 professional tennis players who competed in the 1992 Lipton Tennis Tournament found that self-confidence and fan behavior affected the performance of female players more than male tennis players. Higher ranked professionals attributed significantly more of their performance to psychological variables than lower ranked players.(7)

HOW CAN WE HELP HER BECOME EVEN BETTER IN COMPETITION?

Jennifer is a thirteen-year-old soccer player whose parents don't know much about sports. She's immensely gifted physically, and they called me asking what they could do to help her use her mind to enhance her physical prowess.

"She's good," they said. "We know that. But we heard that there are techniques to help make her even better by helping her concentrate on different things."

They wanted my suggestions.

Dealing with athletes who aren't experiencing problems can be an even bigger challenge than dealing with athletes who have them. When she's already achieving, it is difficult to find the "right buttons to push" to help make her even better. Parents, coaches, and athletes can get stuck in the old adage, "If it ain't broke, don't fix it." These young women, however, are usually very coachable and receptive to new ideas and activities, especially when they trust that trying them can't hurt and might, in fact, help.

When I met with Jennifer, my first goal was to get her to talk about her success as an athlete to be sure she could identify how she was creating her positive outcomes. I asked, "Jennifer, can you describe to me some of your best games?"

"I pretty much feel like I play better in games than I do in practice. I get really excited and the adrenaline carries me through the games. I'm a confident player."

"What kinds of thoughts help you to raise your level of play?"

"My coach tells me really good stuff in practice and that builds my confidence for games. I try to talk to myself like he would talk to me. When I do something wrong, he calls me on it, but also lets me know he saw my good effort and gives me some technical advice or strategy to try and let me know I'll eventually get it. I have friends on other teams that are always complaining about what they don't do right, but I feel pretty good about the way I play and practice. I don't always do it right, but that's what practice is all about."

Jennifer had a great perspective about practice, and the descriptive feedback from her coach had a positive impact on her attitude. Since Jennifer could already identify some internal factors helping to create the successful performance, I spent time pointing out the aspects of her perspective that seemed to positively affect her play. As we talked about the different applications of perceptions, Jennifer admitted that she did, at times, become anxious during certain parts of the game. I asked her to be more specific.

"When the opponent has the ball on a breakaway, or when I have the ball in open field and must make a quick and precise decision. Sometimes it's hard to handle when I feel as if I have to do something quickly to get my team to win."

Since we had already talked about perceptions and Jennifer seemed to remain open to new strategies and problem solving, I decided to focus our attention on her thoughts. As Jennifer described in detail the challenging situations, it became apparent that she had no idea what to think about, so she just thought about everything and anything. For these specific situations, I recommended that Jennifer have a simple and precise mental game plan. Instead of allowing these situations to throw her, she would have a preprogrammed way to respond. Of course, this didn't guarantee success, rather, it gave her the best shot at it. Jennifer and I created a "self-talk script" for the specific game situations that proved difficult. To create a self-talk script, the athlete chooses specific key words or images to remember and recite in her mind during certain plays or points in the game or to use when she feels doubtful. These are words or phrases that can also serve to refocus thoughts when her mind starts to wander and act as a reminder to trust the training rather than overanalyze technique and strategy.

Because soccer is a sport that changes constantly, I suggested to Jennifer that she create phrases that she could rely on during the situations in which she felt most anxious. For example, on the breakaway, as she's chasing the player she might say to herself, "Go with her, go with her, go with her." Before getting the ball, she might say, "Take a quick look, take a quick look," and when she feels the pressure to "do something," she might best be served by saying to herself, "Look for deeper balls," or "Smooth and easy . . . smooth and easy," as a reminder to take her time and make smart decisions.

Once Jennifer created phrases that worked for her, she was to use these phrases in practice situations so they would become automatic in games. Self-talk scripts are the result of combining coping and mastery scripts and therefore are especially useful immediately prior to competition. I suggested Jennifer sprinkle the self-talk phrases throughout a coping/mastery script and read it as a part of her pregame routine. These type of scripts can be read aloud or recorded on a cassette tape and listened to through headphones. When using tapes, it can be fun to record favorite music in the background. The physical energy she gets from the music is combined with the verbal messages that help get her mind focused—a nice way to warm up both mind and body.

Example of Jennifer's Coping Script with Self-Talk

Ineffective Self-Talk:

"I never do well against this team. It seems like I always blow it when I'm in open field. Everyone is counting on me to make the big plays. If I don't get my team to win, I'm going to be really upset. No one will respect me. I know the other team is talking about me. I really want to do well today. What if I don't? I don't want to make bad decisions.

Effective Self-Talk:

"Last time I played this team has nothing to do with this time. I am a year older and very much different. The only way last time will impact me is if I let it. I'm well prepared, and once I get out there the fact that it is a certain team doesn't matter. I'm not going to allow them to take me out of my game. All I am doing is exactly what I do in practice. Just keep it the same. I'm going to focus on how to do well. I don't have lots to think about, just 'Nice and easy,' 'Take a quick look,' and 'Keep it the same.' The less thought the better. I'm going to present myself with lots of confidence by keeping my shoulders down, and remember to take it nice and easy. I'm going to take a deep breath to release some of the tension I feel. When I encounter difficult situations, my thoughts will come back to my key words. 'Nice and easy, take a quick look, keep it the same.' My goal is to rely on my key words and not change my approach. I'll trust myself. I can picture myself making the right decision. I've seen myself deal with that situation a million times. Just keep it the same. Those girls keep looking over here. That is great. If they are thinking about me, they aren't thinking about themselves. That means I'm thinking about me and the other team is also thinking about me. That certainly is good for me. I am prepared and ready to go. I am a great competitor and when I am challenged all I need to do is keep playing with the same intensity. 'Just keep it the same. Nice and easy.' I'm going to trust that my training will carry me through. Right now, I need to be patient, because once I get going I'll get absorbed in the game and forget about my worries. I am ready and prepared so there is no use overthinking it. I just need to do it like practice. I'm prepared so I don't need to do anything new or different. Just keep it the same."

Every athlete has to decide what works best for her. When encountering a difficult situation, overthinking athletes tend to change their approach entirely. Planning out their self-talk for these specific situations serves as a reminder to rely on the practiced approach. Some athletes like to talk to themselves about specific techniques, while others like to see the play in their head, while others prefer to create a feeling or distract themselves from thinking at all. I have worked with athletes who don't feel prepared until they write out a coping script, and I have worked with athletes who know exactly what they will think about and don't want any kind of reminders. There is no one right way to prepare, and athletes need to remain flexible to altering their mental game plans as needed.

FAST FACTS

➡ Twenty-eight elite-level athletes from seven sports were interviewed about the factors they perceived influenced their experience of flow state (performing as if one's body was on automatic pilot). The factors identified included preparation, both physical and mental; confidence; focus; how the performance felt and progressed; and optimal motivation and arousal level. The majority of athletes interviewed perceived the flow state to be controllable, or potentially within their control. A large percentage of the factors seen to facilitate or prevent flow were perceived as controllable; however, factors seen as disrupting flow were largely seen as uncontrollable.(8)

8

Her Changing Body, Her Changing Self: The Spectrum of Eating-Related Problems

I come from a generation of women who didn't do sports. Being a cheer-leader or a drum majorette was as far as our imaginations or role models could take us. We grew up believing—as many girls still do—that the most important thing about the female body is not what it does, but how it looks.

—Gloria Steinem

A young ballet dancer is so thin and weak she can't practice. A soccer player has gained so much weight she's ineffective on the field. The mother of a tennis player sees her daughter eat all the time and yet her daughter continues to lose weight.

These examples are illustrations of eating disorders, which are a common and serious problem among young women. Many people believe eating disorders are physical problems, and they are partially correct. Mainly, however, they stem from psychological issues from which young female athletes are not immune simply because they are participating in sports. In fact, in many sports, weight control is crucial. Even when good nutritional habits are taught and stressed, there are many young female athletes who have not learned how to satisfy their emotional needs in healthy ways and turn to binge eating and starving as coping mechanisms. Once the cycle begins, it is extremely difficult to break.

Athletes, like most girls who develop eating disorders, initially suffer from low self-esteem and have difficulty believing that their feelings and thoughts are important and valuable. And as they reach adolescence, they become increasingly vulnerable. One study by the American Association of University Women indicated a marked decline (as much as 30 percent) in self-esteem in preadolescent and adolescent girls compared to the self-esteem of girls in elementary school.(1) This is especially true in sports when an athlete derives her identity exclusively from her sport involvement and doesn't value other aspects of her personality. So when she doesn't do well in sports, which is inevitable, very often she turns to what she can control in order to cope. Because those internal controllable aspects of performance are so difficult to identify and apply, she grasps onto the one factor in her life that she sees as under her control—her weight. She begins to think that if she just lost weight she would feel better about herself and eventually start winning. And when she does well, she discounts the accomplishment and instead worries about future performances.

Girls going through puberty are changing in height, weight, and body shape. This can lead to increased self-consciousness about their bodies and the desire to try and stay small and undeveloped. Also, sports that are subjectively judged may leave athletes questioning whether their body size affects their score. Although sports judges do not consider body size in their deductions or start values, many athletes perceive that to win they must look the same as their role models or those who are winning. These athletes equate thinness with fitness and feel that the only way to win is to be thin.

Very often coaches ask athletes to lose weight. A study of forty-two collegiate female gymnasts found that 75 percent of the twenty-eight gymnasts who were told they were too heavy by their coaches used potentially dangerous weight loss techniques. Another study of elite female athletes found that 67 percent of those who dieted to improve performance did so to comply with coaching recommendations.(2) This can be potentially dangerous in athletes who are perfectionists and are vulnerable to eating disorders in part because they show little balance in their approach to sports and life. They do everything in the extreme. If you tell a perfectionist to lose weight, she will want to be the thinnest player on the field.

Young women susceptible to developing an eating disorder may feel the need to seek approval from others such as coaches, parents, and teammates. They may also feel unusual stress about competition, even during practices. Participation in a sport where coaching decisions are based upon weight leaves some women at risk, as does a circle of friends and family who continually talk about weight as related to body image and as a necessary way to improve performance. Other personal characteristics that can predispose a young woman to eating disorders are when she considers weight loss as a competition, is too mindful of others' comments, and has ineffective coping skills.

SHE IS PAINFULLY THIN

Eating disorders are often mistakenly thought of as strictly physical problems. They're not. When a young girl won't eat or binges then purges, she usually is facing something bigger. Sometimes it is intense pressure. Sometimes it is fear. Often it is about control. Consider the case of Terri, a sixteen-year-old dancer living away from home and training at a prominent dance school.

The school's nursing staff had informed me of their concerns regarding Terri's weight. She was painfully thin, and they suspected she had an eating disorder. I watched Terri in class that day and saw they were right—she was thinner than the other dancers and appeared to look extremely frail, yet she danced effortlessly.

I began to worry, however, when I was told that Terri's instructor was extremely pleased with Terri's body and found her to be an outstanding talent. And when I spoke by telephone to Terri's mother, she said she really wasn't worried about Terri's weight, but did express concern that the other dancers might be jealous of her daughter's thin physique.

"They all wish they were as thin and talented as Terri," she said.

I met with Terri several times without discussing her health, weight, or food. Often girls with eating disorders shy away from people who want to help. They have great fear that others will instruct them to eat more and that they won't be able to stop and will gain weight. I sensed this fear in Terri and knew I needed to establish a relationship built on trust before broaching the topic of her health.

One day I noticed Terri was sniffling quite a bit and appeared to have a cold. I used this opportunity to ask about her health.

"The nursing staff keeps telling me I'm too thin," she said.

I was surprised she so willingly turned the subject to weight.

"What do you think?" I asked gently.

"I think I'm thin, but not as thin as some of the other girls here," she said. "My teacher says I'm the perfect weight."

I asked what she ate on an average day.

"I don't eat," she answered. "If I do, it's half of an apple or a couple of pretzels."

Terri continued to tell me that she was extremely fearful of gaining weight, which would bring criticism from the other dancers and her instructors. But Terri also admitted that she knew she had a problem. She was sick and often lacked energy. She cried a lot at night. But she was surprised that nobody else seemed to think she had a problem.

"They have to know. Why hasn't anyone until you tried to help me?" she cried.

Terri's obsession with weight, I learned, had begun when she was a child. When Terri turned twelve, her mother began comparing her daughter's body with the bodies of other children. Her mother bought a fat counter book and became obsessed with the types of food Terri ate. Terri became obsessed, too, but simply chose not to eat rather than worry about what it was she was eating. She had two menstrual periods at age twelve, and then they stopped as her weight dropped.

Ironically, at the same time, her performance improved, and she attributed these improvements to the fact that she had become very thin. At age thirteen, she vowed to get even thinner.

One summer she went away and gained weight. She told me she felt healthy and had much more energy. But when she returned to training, her instructors were upset and ordered her to lose weight. She went back to her old eating habits. Now, she weighed a mere eighty-five pounds, well under an acceptable weight range for her height.

Terri was desperately trying to please everyone in her life and receiving mixed messages from her mother and instructors. Terri associated not eating and pleasing others with success. It became apparent as we talked that Terri was miserable.

"I can't take it here. I need to go home," she sobbed.

I asked her when she began feeling that way.

"My parents visited last weekend and I realized how much I miss them.

It's hard being here having to do everything on my own," she said. "My parents are so happy that I'm here. I'm the pride of the family, so I just lied and told them everything was great."

I asked how she felt about staying at the school just to please everyone else.

"I keep thinking if I please everyone else, then I will be happy, too," she said.

By depriving herself of food, Terri felt in control, disciplined. She didn't come from a family where conflict was resolved. Instead, "bad" feelings like wanting to go home were just ignored so tranquility and equilibrium within the family was maintained. Terri was overconcerned with external appearances, a lesson reinforced by her environment. Terri expressed feeling out of control, and saw not eating and the perseverance through the hunger as signs of controlling something in her life. She was terrified of failing and disappointing her parents, who had pinned their own hopes and dreams on their daughter. Instead of facing these concerns, expressing them, and finding ways to cope with the stress, Terri turned to food to cope. She became consumed with not eating and the quest for thinness. All of her problems and worries were balled up into one issue: food. She kept thinking that if she remained focused on losing weight and "controlling" her eating, this discipline would alleviate the feelings of helplessness and sadness.

I told Terri that I wanted her to go through a complete physical examination and advised her to do so at an eating disorder clinic in the area. She said she wasn't sure.

It was necessary for Terri to learn how to listen to her own needs and wants. The problem was that she had denied them for so long that she really didn't trust her own thoughts, feelings, or desires. I asked her many questions about her life and what she—not her parents, not her friends, not her instructors—wanted. At first the concept was hard for her to grasp, even with minor decisions.

For example, at the end of one discussion, I asked her, "What are you going to do now?"

"I should go back to class," she replied.

I asked, "What would you like to do?"

She laughed and said, "I want to go home and relax."

I replied, "Would you feel okay doing what you want to do even though it is not what you think you should do?"

Terri's concept of what she should do had been shaped by her need to please others. To put herself in control, it was critical that she first and foremost consider her needs and then see how those desires fit with the wishes of others. I was trying to teach her to place importance on her own feelings and thoughts. The more she could value these, the more likely she could take her life back into her own hands.

Terri admitted that she was tired of not eating and obsessing about what she did eat. It was critical that Terri get a definitive diagnosis and begin proper treatment immediately. We discussed her options such as staying at the dance school and attending an eating disorders clinic nearby or returning home and being evaluated by a team of doctors there. Terri wasn't sure she could look in the mirror every day and be in an environment that compared girls' bodies while also maintaining a commitment to nourishing herself.

Terri quickly decided to leave. She asked me to help her talk with her parents and I agreed. I sat with her as she called her parents and informed them that she wasn't sure if she wanted to dance or ever return to the school, but that she wanted to take control of her life and regain her health.

They were shocked but agreed to let her come home and also agreed to take whatever actions necessary to support her recovery.

After Terri left, one of the dance instructors called me and was quite angry. She proceeded to tell me that eating disorders do not exist and that she could have dealt with Terri herself.

"If you tell someone they have a broken arm, they will think they have a broken arm," she said. She continued to say that Terri's parents should not have been notified, because parents overreact to these things. This meeting made it clear to me that some of the important people in Terri's life were misinformed and uneducated when it came to eating disorders.

I did find an eating disorder specialist in Terri's hometown and she was, in fact, diagnosed with anorexia nervosa. She chose to enter an outpatient treatment program. She called me periodically and sounded happy. She said eating was still a struggle, but that she was making progress. She had decided to teach some dance classes. I congratulated Terri on being able to listen to her own needs and desires, and thought teaching would be a great way to express her love for dance while still allowing herself to heal. Terri had tried for so long to please others that she let these people define what she wanted and who she was. How do you meet your own needs if you never acknowledge you have any? Terri finally found her own voice and was listening to it. She was able to get help and start on the path to recovery because, unlike most anorexics, Terri recognized that she had a problem and made a decision to fight her illness. I often wonder how she is doing.

FAST FACTS

➡ Approximately 1% of all females have anorexia nervosa and 1–3% have bulimia nervosa (binging and purging). The prevalence of these two diseases is even higher when only adolescent and young adult females are considered.(3)

ANOREXIA NERVOSA

Anorexia begins with dieting that gets out of control and leads to drastic weight loss. The essential features of anorexia nervosa are the following:

1. A refusal to maintain body weight over a minimal normal weight for age, height, and special activities.
2. Intense fear of gaining weight or becoming fat, even though underweight.
3. Disturbance in the way in which one's body weight, size, or shape is experienced, e.g., the person claims to "feel fat" even when emaciated, believes that one area of the body is "too fat" even when obviously underweight.
4. Amenorrhea (the loss of three or more consecutive menstrual periods).

People diagnosed with anorexia say they feel fat or that parts of their body are fat, when they are obviously underweight or even emaciated. They are overly preoccupied with their body size and usually dissatisfied with some feature of their physical appearance. Anorexics lose weight by a reduction in total food intake, often paired with excessive exercise. Frequently, there is self-induced vomiting and laxative or diuretic use. About one-half of anorexia patients also suffer from bulimia. Anorexics may feel inadequate, anxious, worthless, depressed, and desperate. Other common feelings associated with anorexia include anger, irritability, sullenness, defiance, loneliness, low self-esteem, panic over weight gain, and suicidal thoughts.

Some of the predisposing factors for anorexia nervosa are a stressful life situation, perfectionism, and the need to please. The disorder tends to occur during puberty, and although the incidence of males with anorexia is on the rise, 90% of anorexics are females who are typically bright students from middle-class homes.(4)

Anorexics usually come to professional attention when weight loss (or failure to gain expected weight) is marked—for example, when a doctor notices that a girl weighs less than 70% of the expected weight for her height. When she is underweight, other warning signs surface, such as hypothermia (low body temperature), bradycardia (slow heart beat), hypotension (low blood pressure), edema (swelling), lanugo (neonatal-like hair), and a variety of metabolic changes. In most cases, amenorrhea follows weight loss, but it is not unusual for amenorrhea to appear before noticeable weight loss has occurred. This is especially true for athletes training intensely or with low body fat ratios. Physical signs and consequences include dry or yellow-gray skin; dull, brittle hair; loss of muscle; icy hands and feet; cold intolerance; liver and kidney damage; loss of bone minerals; constipation, digestive discomfort, abdominal bloating, dehydration, muscle cramps, tremors; dental problems; and death.

FAST FACTS

➡ The risk of developing disordered eating is thought to be higher in athletes in endurance sports where a small body type is advantageous and sports with weight categories.(5,6)

QUICK QUESTIONS

How can coaches approach the topic of weight?

One of the toughest issues for coaches is how to approach the topics of weight and fitness. Coaches do need to be conscious about what they say about weight and how they say it. Weight should not be the primary topic of discussion. Instead, address the real issue, which is the health and fitness level of the athlete. Coaches must remind themselves that weight is not a reliable measure of body composition. It's important for coaches to avoid linking performance with weight and refrain from ridiculing or making light of an athlete's weight concerns.

Coaches can have a positive impact on an athlete by validating the pressure she may be feeling. Coaches might not agree with an athlete's feelings but should never discount or judge them. Often, athletes with eating disorders assume their own feelings are wrong and therefore never express them. By helping an athlete to express herself honestly, a coach can teach her that her thoughts and feelings are important and worthy of discussion.

Coaches can be a source of information by providing educational materials in their office or gym or by sending them home with the athlete. Athletes can be required to have preparticipation physicals, and it's imperative that coaches establish relationships with health care professionals who have experience working with athletes.

Many times the most difficult part is getting a child the necessary help and support. For those athletes at risk, parents and coaches need to work together to get professional assistance. This may sometimes mean having to use playing time or even practice as leverage. The main goal is to get the athlete into a system that is specifically designed and qualified to treat eating disorders.

What is most often recommended now is to find a team of health professionals that includes a medical doctor, nutritionist, and psychologist. Since eating disorders are rooted in psychological dynamics, it is critical to include a mental health professional as part of the team.

I SEE HER EAT, BUT SHE'S SO SKINNY

Diana is a sixteen-year-old tennis player whose mother is concerned because she is extremely thin. "I know she eats, because I cook for her," her mother said. "But she's so skinny. Is there something wrong?"

Diana's mom was perceptive to pick up on the inconsistency between Diana's eating and her weight. However, this inconsistency in and of itself is not a reason to be alarmed. I asked Diana's mother if she noticed anything else unusual.

"Have you noticed Diana leave the table after meals and go to the bathroom?" I asked.

"No, she usually goes into the den to watch television or do her homework," she said. "Now, I don't see her at school so I don't know what she is eating there. The only meal I cook for her is dinner, and like I said, she seems to eat it. I do cook low-fat meals, because she won't eat anything else. She eats tons of vegetables, like cucumbers and peas. If I cook anything fatty, she refuses to eat it. So I try and have her involved in choosing foods she wants me to cook. In the morning, she usually grabs a bagel or piece of fruit, but I don't actually see her eat it. I'd say this whole low-fat thing started about six months ago. Yet now that I think about it, on weekends she has her friends over and they order pizza and eat junk food."

"Have you noticed any fluctuation in her moods lately?" I wondered.

"Well, she does seem kind of up and down," she said. "Sometimes she is really happy and the next minute it's like something just hit her and she is, well, she can be downright nasty."

"How about sports?" I asked. "Has she mentioned anything to you about tennis?"

"She doesn't really like to talk about tennis with me, so I just avoid it. But her teammate was over the other day, and they were talking about this speech the coach gave all about how important it is to stay lean. The coach thinks that the leaner you are, the quicker you move. The girls were trying to tear apart the coach's argument by coming up with all the great tennis players that in their mind aren't skinny, but everyone they mentioned seems pretty thin to me."

Diana's mom gave me some pretty good information, and my guess was that something was going on. Diana was only eating one low-fat meal a day, eating much higher fat foods on weekends, having mood swings, and playing sports in an environment that equated thinness with fitness and success. Those observations, paired with the fact that bulimia usually begins between the ages of 16 and 20, led me to believe Diana was probably in the beginning stages of an eating disorder. Many times bulimia is initiated by an event, situation, or person that gets the young woman to start thinking about body shape. When she links body shape with certain positive outcomes, such as popularity, achievement, and control, very often an eating disorder ensues.

Based on Diana's mother's description, my guess was that Diana was restricting her food intake in the attempt to lose weight. The restriction led to some binge eating, which in turn led to some form of purging. Diana's eating was up and down, from starving to binging, and her moods followed these ups and downs. Often what happens is that the binge eating intensifies the need for the bulimic to starve herself, which in turn increases the likelihood for another binge.

During the first year of bingeing and purging, bulimics tend to lose weight. This often leads the bulimic to continue her practices, which leads her to binge and purge more often. However, about one-third of calories taken in during a binge are retained after purging. So, as bingeing increases, so do the calories that are absorbed. Weight may begin to rise, and the bulimic's fears of gaining weight are intensified.

Bulimics tend to have an intense fear that they will suddenly "blow it" and gain a lot of weight. Many life events can trigger this anxiety about getting fat. Bulimics who have difficulty controlling their feelings or dealing with their frustrations often begin to obsess over a potential weight gain. Instead of being able to identify and deal with their feelings, they put all of their emotions into their fear of gaining weight. This fear leads them to extreme dieting, which starts the binge-purge cycle. The dieting temporarily compensates for the binge, but since intense dieting is a form of self-starvation, the bulimic becomes obsessed with food and eventually binges.

I recommended to Diana's mother that she make an appointment for her at a nearby eating disorder clinic. That way she could receive a proper diagnosis if needed and have available to her a team of people to initiate treatment. However, Diana's mom felt Diana would be resistant to any kind of help. In these cases, it can be a good idea to go through a physician who works in conjunction with an eating disorder team. The physician can be the one to make the referral to the psychologist or counselor. It was my guess that Diana was in the early stages of the eating disorder and with proper and immediate treatment would have a full recovery.

BULIMIA NERVOSA

Bulimia is recurrent episodes of binge eating, rapid consumption of a large amount of food in a short period of time; a feeling of lack of control over eating behavior during the eating binges; self-induced vomiting, use of laxatives, or diuretics; strict dieting, fasting, or vigorous exercise in order to prevent weight gain; and persistent overconcern with body shape and weight. In order to qualify for the diagnosis, the person must have had, on average, a minimum of two binge eating episodes a week for at least three weeks.

Eating binges are typically planned, and food with high caloric content is consumed. Usually, the food is eaten inconspicuously or secretly, and food is gobbled rapidly with little chewing. A binge is most often terminated by abdominal discomfort, sleep, social interruption, or induced vomiting. When not bingeing, the person usually restricts food intake, making them hungry and vulnerable to the next binge. Vomiting alleviates the physical pain associated with abdominal distention and reduces post-binge anxiety and guilt over the food intake. During a binge, people can eat from four thousand to eight thousand calories in less than two hours. Some binge and vomit two times per week, while others do it several times a day. It seems athletes in particular use both food restriction and self-induced vomiting to control their weight. This combines behaviors of both anorexia and bulimia.

Although binge eating may be pleasurable at the moment, self-criticism, guilt, and depressed mood follow. The bulimic may feel out of control, embarrassed, ashamed, guilty, depressed, and even desperate.

FAST FACTS

➡ A recent study has found evidence that bulimic women have altered brain chemistry, possibly from birth, which puts them at higher risk for eating disorders. Dr. Walter Kaye found that recovered bulimics had too much serotonin in their bodies. Bingeing and purging actually reduce serotonin activity, so Kaye speculates that those activities may be bulimics' unconscious way of trying to regulate serotonin levels and relive the anxiety and obsessiveness.(7)

TIPS FOR PARENTS

Parents can serve as a good example by modeling healthy eating behaviors and speaking about their own bodies in an accepting manner. It's best to avoid comments about body size and shape. Instead, try communicating acceptance of your daughter as a person first and an athlete second. When she feels pressure, help her to identify the stressors and problem solve rather than relying on weight loss as the answer. If you suspect she needs help, take yourself out of it by finding a professional to make the proper evaluations and treatments.

Once she is diagnosed with an eating disorder, there are some actions parents can take to assist in recovery. Be careful to let your child make her own food choices and avoid discussions that focus on food intake or weight. Try to be a positive role model of healthy nutritional habits and encourage the entire family to be involved in meal preparation.

Allow your child to take responsibility for her recovery. In the process, avoid comparisons with other children or friends. Be sure to validate your daughter's feelings and encourage her to adapt her own values, standards, and beliefs. Let her know it's important that she consider how the viewpoints of others fit with her own. Don't force her to adapt your way of thinking.

Invite her to share her thoughts and feelings about a variety of issues and ask for her advice and opinions. When it comes to decision making, assist her in exploring all of the ramifications of a decision and the consequences, but leave the final decision to her.

Love your child unconditionally by valuing her as a person, not just an athlete. At every turn, point out the life lessons of sports. Try and remind yourself that you are part of her support network, and don't try to live out your own dreams through your child. It's critical to keep sports in perspective and view it as one aspect of your daughter's life. Pay attention to her diverse interests. If she doesn't seem curious, take her to museums, read books with her, visit other cities and monuments, value education, art, and spirituality.

Be sure to defer to the health professionals and their diagnosis or advice concerning the best course of action, and be prepared for the illness to have a long duration.

QUICK QUESTIONS

Are there environmental warning signs?

Be tuned into what is happening in the training environment. Public weigh-ins, posted weights, punishments for weight gain are all unnecessary and unhealthy practices. If a coach is concerned about your daughter's weight, that needs to be discussed with you and a plan of action defined. Otherwise, your daughter may resort to unhealthy practices in an attempt to meet the coach's demands. Very often athletes may need to get in better shape, but it's irresponsible to ask a young woman to do so without any guidelines. You need to be there to find the appropriate assistance.

Coaches today are more and more sensitive to the issue of eating disorders and the role they play in it. However, you do have a right to question a coach who weighs your athlete. What is the purpose for the weigh-in? Typically, athletes are well aware of their weight, so weigh-ins tend to be the coach's way of keeping track or making the athlete accountable. It's best to take yourself and the coach out of this process. Hire someone, like a nutritionist or exercise physiologist, who can deal with this issue. By involving a third party, a vast array of problems can be avoided, including having the coach connect performance and weight, having athletes think the coach's approval is based upon weight, having teammates and training buddies compare weights, and having a coach demand weight loss without providing any guidelines.

GETTING HELP

It's very common for athletes and parents to be in denial about an eating disorder. A girl may deny or minimize the severity of her illness and be uninterested in getting help. However, when health is threatened, athletes need to get immediate attention. At times, I have asked coaches or parents to step in and leverage something in order to force the athlete to get the assistance she needs. For example, coaches have told athletes they can't practice until they are seen by an appropriate specialist.

On the flip side, it can be dangerous to take sports away. Parents with children in treatment have told me they want their child to quit sports. They see sports as the cause of the problem and want to get rid of what they perceive to be causing their child pain. Yet sports can be the one motivator in that child's life. Taking it away can be an incredible loss and too difficult for the child to handle. It may be appropriate to allow the child to continue in her sport while getting treatment. On the other hand, many athletes trying to recover from an eating disorder find it difficult to accept their bodies while in a training environment that is anything but accepting.

WHEN SHOULD SHE GET PROFESSIONAL HELP?

When the physical warning signs of an eating disorder are apparent, a referral to a trained professional needs to be made immediately. However, it is also essential to make sure athletes are educated and assisted in dealing with the stress they face. When athletes are having difficulty putting themselves in control of their lives and coping with stress, professional attention is warranted.

Athletes may experience pressure about their performance, appearance, training or their own expectations. Performance pressures that you want to make sure she is equipped to handle include striving to be the best; seeking approval from coaches, parents, and teammates; vying for playing time; and participating in competition, with all its stresses.

The environment may also present some challenges for athletes. Red flags to watch for include coaches who make decisions or give approval based upon weight, who hold weigh-ins, or who demand weight loss without guidelines or assistance, as well as significant others who speak about size and shape.

At times, athletes can have difficulty dealing with their changing body and appearance. Take note when she begins to diet and talks about weighing a specific number of pounds, links performance to weight loss, or views weight loss as a competition.

The way an athlete thinks about herself and her situation can leave her vulnerable to developing disordered eating behavior. If she is a perfectionist, make sure she has some strategies to maintain balance and learns to keep things in perspective, especially the comments of others. Keep an eye out for external thinking, especially excessive worry about outcomes. Make sure she places importance on what she thinks and feels and expresses these personal opinions. If you perceive that she is having trouble dealing with any of these issues, you may want to ask for professional assistance or recommendations.

When it's time to seek help, there are many resources available. You can ask your family physician for referrals, call a hospital that has an eating disorders program, call your local women's center, or look in the yellow pages under mental health services. There is usually a local mental health association listed in the white pages or a psychologist information and referral service. The school counselor can be a good resource and usually has well established relationships with a variety of mental health professionals in the community. Eating Disorders Awareness and Prevention, Inc. provides educational materials and referrals.

THE WEIGHT CAME ON SO FAST

Jordan was a competitive gymnast and club field hockey player until an injury ended her gymnastics career. In gymnastics, Jordan, thirteen, had to be very weight-conscious. Once her gymnastics career was over, she believed she could now eat all the foods she had been denied. Without the daily four-hour workouts in the gym, her weight shot up quickly and when field hockey season came around, she was easily twenty pounds over-weight. Her mother called me one day wondering how to talk to Jordan about losing the extra weight without alienating her daughter or triggering a potentially harmful reaction like anorexia or bulimia.

I wanted to approach this issue two ways. First came the physical weight gain. Jordan's parents could broach the topic with her, but the conversation absolutely needed to focus on health and fitness. I told her mother, "You can talk with Jordan, but you want to avoid any reference to her weight. If you mention her weight gain, she may get defensive, and it won't be a pro-ductive conversation. You might want to try and throw the topic out for discussion. For instance, you might ask Jordan, 'Hey, I know you are get-ting ready to start field hockey. How do you feel about your fitness level?' See if she opens up to you and talks about her weight gain or how she feels about her body."

Parents can express their concern for their children's health and fitness level without making it a simple weight issue. When it is addressed in this manner, a whole host of options for help are available. In other words, you don't want this issue to become a power struggle between mother and daughter where Mother is saying, "You're too heavy" and Daughter is re-sponding, "No, I'm not." So removing yourself from the process as quickly as possible is helpful.

If the discussion were to revolve around helping Jordan get in shape for field hockey, her mother could suggest investigating the kinds of strength and conditioning services available in the community. I suggested starting with an exercise physiologist who could give Jordan a clear idea of her fit-ness level. This type of professional will do a body composition test, which is a much better measure of fitness level than weight. Once the evaluation is complete, the exercise physiologist can design a program to work on Jor-dan's fitness level through strength and conditioning training. They could work together to set goals, one of which might be to lose some weight or reduce body fat. Many exercise physiologists have access to sports nutri-tionists, and the physiologist could make this recommendation if necessary to help Jordan reach her fitness goals.

This strategy gives Jordan input and control over her fitness regime and takes Mom out of the process. The last thing that a thirteen-year-old wants to do is report her weight gains and losses to her mother. Instead, Mom can show support of Jordan's commitment to get in shape and be a good role model of healthy eating and exercise habits.

The second part of this issue is emotional. Jordan experienced a traumatic life event. She had a major injury that forced her out of a sport she loved. When athletes leave sports, especially due to an unexpected injury, a profound sense of loss may be experienced. I wondered how Jordan had dealt with her feelings about no longer participating in gymnastics.

"Has Jordan talked with you about being forced out of gymnastics?"

"No, not really," she said. "She never liked to talk to me about gymnastics. She just accepted what the doctors told her. There were a few tears, and that was it. She threw herself into her social life and other activities she hadn't had time for before."

I explained to Jordan's mom that my guess was that Jordan had been repressing a lot of her feelings, and unexpressed emotions don't simply go away. I expressed concern that Jordan might be eating to comfort herself and to help deal with conflicting feelings. Jordan might not have had any idea why she was eating more and more. I hoped that I would be able to meet with Jordan, but Jordan's mom wasn't sure that she would go for the idea, even if it was to help improve her sports performance. I asked if Jordan had any relationship with the school counselor. Her mom remembered that the counselor used to be a field hockey player in college. I recommended that Jordan's mom call the school counselor and encourage the counselor to build a relationship with Jordan. They would have an easy time connecting over sports, and once a relationship was built, perhaps the counselor could assist Jordan in gaining an awareness of some of her feelings and teach her more effective coping skills.

QUICK QUESTIONS

My daughter has always been overweight. Should I sign her up for a sport where there is a lot of running to help her lose the weight?

When trying to get your child involved in fitness programs, the goal should be to encourage health habits that will last a lifetime. Most experts agree that children who develop positive exercise habits will be more likely to continue these habits as adults. If you want your children to derive the physical benefits from sports, they will be more likely to do so with activities they enjoy. For instance, if you choose to put your child into soccer because she will run a lot, but she dislikes soccer, she will probably not continue playing for long. Because of her dislike for the game, she may not be open to seeing the potential fitness benefits. Perhaps she really likes to play softball. Although there is not much opportunity for aerobic exercise, she might be willing to do extra drills in order to improve her skills for a game she really enjoys.

It's important for you as parents to value activity and movement rather than inactivity. You can throw out choices, letting your daughter know why it is beneficial to play sports or take a fitness class. Let her know that it's important to be physically active to live a healthy life. Give her choices of activities with which she can be involved to stay physically active and fit.

I would make sure to approach the topic in a delicate way. Stick with the issue, which is health and fitness, rather than telling your daughter outright that she needs to lose weight. You want to prepare her for a lifetime of healthy living and physical activity. Evaluate your own lifestyle choices. Your healthy influence has to stand up to competition from television, the Internet, video games, and fast food. Remember, unhealthy habits have to be learned. So create an environment that values movement and healthy eating and encourage children to participate in developing their own exercise and fitness programs.

FAST FACTS

➡ According to Kenneth Cooper, MD, 11 million children from ages six to seventeen are considered obese.(8)

SHE'S STARTING TO CUT BACK ON FOOD

Anne Marie is a healthy, fit fourteen-year-old who is active in several different sports. Her mother has always stressed healthy eating habits, and Anne Marie rarely indulges in junk food or overeats. Her mother believed she had a normal, healthy appetite until Anne Marie started ninth grade at a new, much larger school and began to eat less and less. Several days a week she came home with most of her lunch uneaten and refused a snack before heading to basketball practice. Her mother worried that this pattern might lead to an eating disorder.

I was happy to find that Anne Marie's mom was picking up on some of the warning signs of eating disorders. After all, the best cure for eating disorders is prevention. I did feel there was reason for concern, especially given the prevalence of eating disorders in young women. Research suggests that at least 40 percent of all white, middle-class normal-weight girls attending suburban high schools are actively engaged in losing weight in order to become very thin.(9) The age of onset for eating disorders is variable, but the peak ages for anorexia nervosa seem to be fourteen to eighteen, while those for bulimia are sixteen to eighteen. Prevention is critical, and we had a very good shot at it in Anne Marie's case.

There are two types of prevention. Primary prevention is the attempt to keep eating disorders from ever happening by eliminating or at least reducing risk factors. Secondary prevention is the early identification of a problem, appropriate referral, and immediate treatment for those who are in the initial phase of an eating disorder. Anne Marie had just over the last few weeks started to restrict her food intake. She was beginning to engage in disordered eating patterns, but certainly had not yet developed a full-blown eating disorder. I thought we had a pretty good shot at primary prevention.

Since there is no one cause for eating disorders, it is important to identify the factors that place a young woman at risk. The more risk factors that are present, the more likely the young woman is to develop an eating disorder. Risk factors can be placed into two categories. Those factors that predispose someone or leave her vulnerable to developing an eating disorder are called predispositions. Precipitants are those personal behaviors and external stressors that account for the emergence of the eating disorder at a specific time. In other words, Anne Marie could have certain predispositions for an eating disorder, but without a precipitant would most likely not actually engage in disordered eating behaviors. Anne Marie's mother had attributed her sudden restriction of calories to the stress of moving to a larger school. However, when I talked to Anne Marie, a few predispositions also emerged.

"Anne Marie, your mother tells me that she has always stressed healthy eating. How do you see your own attitude toward food?"

"Yeah," she said, "she always has told us to eat healthy, but at the same time she is kind of psycho about it. She doesn't cook anything that has fat in it, and we never have any sweets around the house. Whenever I'd go to a friend's house, she would always remind me not to eat anything sweet. I'm always worried about what I shouldn't be eating."

"What kinds of discussions do you and your family have about physical appearance?" I asked, concerned.

"We don't say very nice things about fat people," she said. "I remember my mom told me that someone really fat just doesn't have any self-control. I figured not eating certain things just showed my mom that I could have control over what I ate. It's like she was real proud of me for eating what she calls healthy. Also, my friends and I are always commenting on the girls that are really skinny. It seems like the boys like them more."

It became clear that although Anne Marie's mom thought she was stressing a healthy diet, she was actually teaching Anne Marie how to restrict her food intake and equating restriction of food with a personality trait—control. Anne Marie was beginning to equate thinness with certain consequences. If she was thin, it made her mother happy. If she was thin, other girls would envy her. If she was thin, the boys would like her better. Suddenly thinness had a whole lot of positive consequences attached to it, and all of the consequences were related to external approval. Unfortunately, the environment had set the stage for Anne Marie to define herself in terms of thinness, self-control, and approval from others. These all happen to be predisposing factors for eating disorders.

Although it may seem illogical to others, Anne Marie's sudden quest for thinness seemed perfectly logical to her. She believed that losing weight was good and gaining weight was bad. Weight gain showed a lack of control, and therefore was in her mind "disgusting." Anne Marie's perception of herself was starting to be determined by her weight and body shape. Weight loss was connected to control, and being in control was something Anne Marie valued, as was gaining approval from family, friends, and peers. The problem with these assumptions was that they were rigid and simplistic. In other words, all of Anne Marie's worries and desires were simplified into one thing—thinness.

There are many precipitating events leading to eating disorders. In Anne Marie's case, two struck me. First, there was puberty. Anne Marie's body was beginning to change, and people were starting to take notice. Her uncle said, "Wow, you're really getting big." Although her uncle was commenting on her growth spurt and development, Anne Marie took his words at face value and used it to reinforce in her own mind that she must be getting fat. It was difficult for Anne Marie to get used to her changing body. A lot of her athletic friends had not started to develop yet, and she felt helpless to stop her ever-changing body.

Second, Anne Marie had moved into a larger middle school. Although for many this is just a transition, for Anne Marie the move produced feelings of anxiety. She felt a profound sense of loss, not only of friends but of the comfort she had felt with her former teachers, administrators, school building, and peer group. She had moved away from what was comfortable to something that was far from comfortable. In her new school, Anne Marie worried about what the other kids, teachers, administrators, and coaches would think of her. She had no idea what their expectations of her would be. Could she live up to them? What if no one liked her? Did she have to prove her intelligence and athletic ability all over again? Would they judge her on her past performance in school and athletics? What if she didn't measure up here? There were so many questions, which led to emotions such as fear, anxiety, loneliness, and helplessness, and as Anne Marie started to look for answers to those questions, she locked on to the one thing she could come up with that put her in control. She thought if she could lose weight, she would feel better. All of her worries and anxiety would disappear, because she would be in control. In her mind, she knew that if she lost weight, there would definitely be some positive consequences.

I decided to refer Anne Marie to an eating disorder specialist. Her issues were not specifically sports-related, and I also felt the family might benefit from family counseling. As Anne Marie began to separate from her family, she needed to learn to trust her own thoughts and feelings and to value self-approval along with external approval. Her parents would benefit from learning how to promote this self-reliance and put Anne Marie in control of dealing with her emotions. As a result of the early recognition, my guess is that Anne Marie did quite well.

QUICK QUESTIONS

What are "eating disorders not otherwise specified"?

Anorexia nervosa and bulimia nervosa have very strict diagnostic criteria. Many people do not neatly fit into the specified definitions of these disorders yet still engage in many of the disordered thoughts and behaviors that are part of these serious diseases. Those who cannot be diagnosed with anorexia or bulimia but engage in disordered eating behaviors are placed into the category of eating disorders not otherwise specified, because although they are not on the far end of the continuum, their eating behavior does pose health risks.

Athletes who become engaged in disordered eating behavior often justify their actions. The disordered behavior may help them forget about their stress for a moment and put a stop to excessive worrying. When they become consumed with weight, it may seem as if all other problems are placed neatly into one package—appearance. Many athletes become consumed with weight loss as a way to feel in control of their performance, while others see it as providing a rationale for why certain things don't go the way they had hoped. For others, being consumed with their weight and appearance makes them feel better than other people. Disordered eating has been described by some as the one thing they do for themselves where no one can tell them how to do it or what they are doing wrong. By restricting food intake, athletes narrow their choices and establish a sense of control. Sometimes the weight loss keeps a young woman looking like a child so she doesn't have to grow up and live up to more expectations. When weight loss occurs, many receive attention and positive reinforcement. For others, food fills a void when they feel lonely, bored, or isolated. Some see food as safe and comforting, while others view it as numbing them from the emotions they don't know how to confront. Sometimes a young woman will say that everything in her life seems better when she doesn't eat. She buys into a false sense of security, believing that she will find happiness when she loses enough weight.

FAST FACTS

➡ The proportion of female athletes with disordered eating has been reported to range from 15% to 62%.(10)

SHE DOESN'T THINK SHE DESERVES WATER

I got a call one day from a mother who was alarmed and startled by a statement her daughter had made one night after soccer practice.

"She told me she didn't drink any water the entire two-hour practice because she kept getting beaten during the one-on-one drills and didn't think she deserved water," the mother said. "I couldn't believe that she would think of water as a reward."

The critical issue here was not whether the water was a reward or punishment but what the feelings were that initiated the two-hour lack of rehydration. Some athletes will not drink fluids during practice for a physical reason, such as feeling it weighs them down or makes them heavier. What these athletes have lost sight of is that in drinking, they aren't taking in extra fluids, they are replacing lost fluids. Athletes need to be well educated regarding the impact hydration has on performance.

Muscles in a well-hydrated state should be between 70 and 75 percent water. Lack of hydration can cause sore muscles, reduce endurance, increase weakness, and reduce training benefits. Water is used to take nutrients into working muscles as well as remove toxic metabolic by-products of energy metabolism. Most sports nutritionists recommend drinking ten to fourteen ounces of water one to two hours before the start of practice. During exercise, three to four ounces should be drunk every fifteen minutes. After exercise, 16 ounces of water should be taken in for every pound lost during exercise. In hot and humid weather, athletes can sweat off up to six pounds per hour. They can go weeks and even months without certain vitamins or minerals before noticing any effect, but without adequate water, performance may be affected in less than an hour. If an athlete has waited until she is thirsty to drink, she has waited too long.(11)

I have found that once athletes are educated about the necessity and uses of water, they tend to increase their fluid intake. It's a simple thing to do to improve performance. However, in this case, the restriction of fluid intake was not just for physical reasons.

This athlete was restricting the amount of water she drank as a way of dealing with her feelings of inadequacy. She was pushing herself physically to become a better soccer player, but on this day was not getting the desired results. She was getting beaten, and in her mind that was failure. In order to overcome these feelings of failure, she had to do something that would make her feel good and prove that she was a dedicated and committed athlete. Her actions were examples of certain qualities that have been mentioned as contributing to athletic success. By restricting water intake, she was pushing herself even though it hurt, sacrificing something, and staying committed to something, and she could recognize herself for the control she showed. Her actions were a way of proving to herself and maybe to others that she had the drive and self-control necessary to be a successful athlete. It was her way of feeling better about having not shown her success through her athletic skills.

This glorification of self-control is a driving force for many with eating disorders. By seeing the body as the enemy, they try and resist the body's natural urges to eat and drink. This seems to be in the pursuit of thinness, but very often it is really in the pursuit of self-control. Perfectionism, achievement, ambition, and sacrifice are all highly valued in our society. This often sends the message to young women that in order to be successful they must sacrifice, strive for perfection, achieve, and be in control at all times. Instead, what young women need to know is that these qualities are important for success, but not in the extreme.

In order to be a great soccer player, a girl may at times have to sacrifice going to a late night party or an afternoon by the pool, but she doesn't have to sacrifice everything. Athletes need to strive to better their skills, but they don't need to beat themselves up if they don't attain perfection. And, more than achievement, athletes need to know how to fail and accept failure as a part of the achievement process. It's about finding a balance.

This young soccer player, in an attempt to feel successful, took all the qualities of success to the extreme. Anything in the extreme has the potential to be damaging. Once she became aware of the origins of her behavior, she could find more effective ways to deal with her feelings of failure. By not drinking, she was actually contributing to her performance decline rather than changing it. She viewed getting beaten during practice to be a failure, and this perception led her to overlook certain aspects of her game that had actually improved. By punishing herself, she eliminated any chance of enhancing her performance. Instead, she needed to accept the loss. Loss is the one constant in sport, and punishment is unnecessary. What is necessary is for her to look at her level and quality of play and make physical and emotional adjustments as needed.

QUICK QUESTIONS

How do I help a friend?

Encourage her to tell a trusted adult about her concerns, such as a coach, trainer, nutritionist, psychologist, counselor, physician, parent, or school nurse. Let her know she has the right to confidentiality. Be supportive, encourage others to help, and provide your friend with educational information. If it seems appropriate, set up a meeting with someone the athlete trusts and with whom she has good rapport. Talk to your friend about specific observations that cause concern and assure her you will be there to help. Avoid talking about weight gain or loss. Instead, show interest in your friend as a person by stating your observation, such as, "I'm concerned about you. You seem really preoccupied and sad lately." Realize you can't make her better. The recovery is up to her.

SHE HASN'T HAD A PERIOD IN THREE MONTHS. IS THIS NORMAL?

No. Check with your doctor immediately. Amenorrhea is the absence of three or more consecutive periods in previously menstruating females. This is of concern, because it is often associated with low estrogen levels. The low estrogen may cause bones to lose calcium, which can lead to stress fractures and premature osteoporosis. If there are no signs of pubertal development and no period by age fourteen, medical evaluations are recommended. If there are signs of puberty and no menses by age sixteen, a medical exam is suggested. Amenorrhea occurs in 2–5% of the general population of women of reproductive age, but various studies have found the prevalence in athletes to be as high as 40% or more.(12)

WHAT IS THE FEMALE ATHLETE TRIAD?

Recently, the Female Athlete Triad has received a great deal of attention. The triad consists of three medical disorders clinically identified by the American College of Sports Medicine in 1992. The potential consequences of the triad effect not only athletic performance but the long-term health of the athlete as well. The three components of the triad are

- Eating disorders
- Amenorrhea (no period for three or more consecutive months)
- Osteoporosis (bone loss)

These three components are interrelated. Eating disorders may lead to a negative energy balance, which means that the amount of calories consumed is less than the amount of energy expended. The body interprets this negative energy balance to mean it's starving. Since the body is starving, it thinks this wouldn't be a good time to reproduce. So it shuts down reproduction capability by stopping the menstrual cycle. The menstrual cycle is shut down by a series of events beginning in the area of the brain known as the hypothalamus. This process is not fully understood, but when menstruation stops, estrogen levels are decreased. This decrease in estrogen combined with decreased dietary calcium intake signals the bones to release calcium to replace low levels in the bloodstream. This may result in bone loss or formation of unhealthy bone.(13)

It is generally accepted that the development of amenorrhea and as a result later osteoporosis are secondary to the disordered eating. The prevalence of the triad is unknown at this time. The triad is not easily cured. Very often the key signs are seen through the symptoms and warning flags from eating disorders. Pay attention.

FAST FACTS

➡ While inadequate nutrition is a common cause of amenorrhea in females with disordered eating, it is not the only cause. Some of the many other causes of amenorrhea include pregnancy, anatomic abnormalities of reproductive organs, thyroid and other endocrine diseases, and psychological and physical stress.(14,15)

➡ The prevalence of premature osteoporosis in female athletes is unknown. In female athletes with disordered eating and amenorrhea, the prevalence of osteoporosis appears to be higher, especially in athletes with low body weight and low body fat.(16)

STRESSING NUTRITION

There are over fifty nutrients that your body needs on a daily basis. Over time, inadequate intake or omission of any of these important nutrients can have a negative effect on health and performance. There is no one perfect diet for athletes. A good diet maintains hydration, provides adequate calories, and supplies the fifty nutrients in the necessary amounts. An adequate diet is essential to maintaining energy levels, developing muscles, and increasing endurance and strength. It is always best to go to the doctor or a licensed nutritionist with concerns about your daughter's eating habits and needs. They can set up a program specifically for her that can help prevent problems down the road. Here are just a few things to consider:

There are six basic nutrients to consider when choosing a balanced diet for anyone, but especially important for a young female athlete. Water makes up close to 75 percent of the body's weight and is immensely important in regulating a body's temperature and cell functions. It carries nutrients to the cells and waste away from them.

Most vitamins are chemical substances that the body does not manufacture and must be obtained through diet. The major vitamins, which regulate chemical reactions within the body, are vitamins A, B complex, C, D, E, and K.

Iron, magnesium, phosphorous, sodium, potassium, chromium, and zinc are examples of minerals that regulate body processes. They, too, are not manufactured within the body and must be obtained through diet.

Carbohydrates are the primary source from which the body draws energy during exercise. About 60 percent of an athlete's daily calories should come from the carbohydrates found in fruits, vegetables, breads, and grains.

Vegetable fats and animal fats are sources of energy used primarily during low-level activity or long-term activity, such as long training runs. Nutritionists often recommend that these make up about 25 percent of an athlete's daily calories. Animal fats are usually saturated, which can contribute to heart disease and some cancers. Vegetable fats are more easily digested.

Protein is perhaps the most important nutrient for building muscle and synthesizing hormones. Protein can be found in fish, poultry, meats, dairy, nuts, and various beans. Nutritionists recommend that 15 percent of the daily diet consist of protein calories, which are broken down into amino acids and distributed to muscles and other tissues.

Most nutritionists advise eating a balanced diet, including a variety of foods low in fat. Skipping meals does not promote weight control, but proper food choices does. Athletes should go no longer than four hours without eating. Athletes learning how to make healthy choices can try selecting foods by color. When they choose a combination of orange, yellow, green, and red foods, they are likely to get more fuel. When recommended by a physician, athletes can use a vitamin and mineral supplement. It's important for athletes to schedule a refueling snack after two and a half to three hours of practice and to stay hydrated by drinking water. If an event lasts longer than two hours, an athlete may benefit from a sports drink. The United States Olympic Committee recommends that fluid replacement drinks be 4–8% carbohydrate (fifteen to eighteen grams per eight ounces of fluid). Have athletes experiment with sports drinks during practice before using them at a competitive event.

WHAT'S BEST FOR A PRECOMPETITION MEAL?

There is no one right meal for every athlete. Most often, nutritionists recommend that athletes eat a meal rich in carbohydrates and drink plenty of water. The morning of the event, she should eat breakfast about three hours before competition time to allow the food to digest. Usually something light works best. If she is extremely nervous before competition, nutritionists suggest making sure she eats well the day before, perhaps having an extra-large snack in the evening instead of breakfast. Also, foods such as bananas, apples, and yogurt can be eaten up to an hour before competition because these foods are easily digested and will give her energy during the game. Stay away from greasy or fried foods, especially in between games or competitions. It's tough to avoid the nachos and hot dogs at the concessions, but ultimately she'll feel better and maybe even perform better as a result.

SHOULD SHE TAKE CALCIUM SUPPLEMENTS?

Doctors and nutritionists recommend that adolescents get about 1,200 milligrams of calcium a day—the equivalent of four glasses of milk. If she's not drinking that much milk, they recommend that she takes 400 milligrams of calcium in supplement form once a day. Again, always check with your own doctor first.

9

Serious Issues: The Dark Side
of Sports Participation

These kids get to the point where they are willing to trade sex for attention, affection, kindness, gifts or money. . . . They don't tell because,
correctly, they recognize that society doesn't understand what happened
to them, doesn't understand the seduction process.

—Kenneth Lanning, FBI supervisory agent

Open the newspaper on just about any day and the headlines scream
out the stories of sexual abuse, harassment, homophobia, drug use,
and other serious problem issues in women's sports. The examples are
seemingly endless:

- Two former University of North Carolina soccer players, Debbie
  Keller and Melissa Jennings, accused University of North Carolina
  coach Anson Dorrance of inappropriate behavior that included un-
  invited sexual comments and creating a hostile environment. Dorrance has led North Carolina to fifteen NCAA titles and the
  United States to a Women's World Cup championship. He has denied the allegations.(1)
- In 1997, two former Syracuse University tennis players filed a sexual harassment suit against the school and sought $762 million in
  damages. A settlement was reached in March of 1999, three days
  before the trial was to begin. At issue were repeated massages given
  by the coach in his office and on road trips.(2)
- In 1991, cyclist Katie Schaudt, then fifteen, filed charges with po-

lice alleging that her trainer, Robert Nash, sexually assaulted her for two hours on a farm road, where they were working out.(3)

- Gergana Branzova of Bulgaria was shocked when some of her teammates at Florida International University asked her out.(4)
- LSU softball coach Cathy Compton lost her job because of an "unhealthy" relationship with one of her players, according to the school's athletic director.(5)
- Olympic swimmer Michelle Smith of Ireland was recently banned from her sport at the age of twenty-eight, after testing positive for steroids.(6)
- Three former University of Massachusetts women's basketball players filed a lawsuit against the school, saying their coach's yelling, insults, and obscenities made their personal lives unbearable. They are seeking $45 million in damages.(7)

Female athletes today face a myriad of serious and potentially dangerous problems and issues that threaten not only their experience in sports, but their lives. A young woman who is sexually abused by a coach or harassed by a teammate or opponent can carry emotional scars with her for the rest of her life. The damage can escalate for the young woman who chooses to use drugs or illegal anabolic steroids to enhance her athletic performance. These are issues that young girls are dealing with on an increasing basis. They are frightening and real. And they cannot be ignored.

HE MADE ME THINK I HAD NO CHOICE BUT TO HAVE SEX WITH HIM

Barbara was fifteen when she was fondled and kissed by her volleyball coach. She was seventeen when he raped her. It all began when he started paying extra attention to her, lavishing praise on her, promising that with his coaching, she'd be an Olympian. All she had to do, he said, was trust him. And do what he said.

On an out-of-town trip, the coach called Barbara and asked her to come to his room to discuss strategy. When she arrived, he was wearing only a bathrobe. After she closed the door to his room, he grabbed her and kissed her and thrust his hands up her shirt. Frozen with fear, Barbara told no one of the incident.

"I didn't know what to do," she testified to a state agency investigating child abuse. "You have to understand: I trusted him completely. More than anyone in the world."

Two weeks later he convinced her to meet him at a hotel so they could talk privately.

"As an adult I know how stupid it sounds now, but he promised me we were just going to talk volleyball," she said. "He pulled off my pants. He held my arms and hands down. I pleaded with him to no avail. He had sexual intercourse with me. I bled. It hurt worse than anything I had ever felt."

Later it was learned that the coach had sexually molested several additional underage players. One testified that she reluctantly submitted to having sex with him because she believed he controlled her future. He had disciplined her harshly and then "apologized and said he had to do that to make me a better player and that I needed to obey his coaching to be the best." He abused her sexually over a period of two years.

Another woman said she had sex with him because she felt helpless, that she had no choice. "I was scared to death—scared to tell him no," she testified. "I didn't think anybody would believe me."

Tragically, these stories are too common in today's society. It is generally thought that one in four women in North America were molested in childhood and that one in five are survivors of adult sexual assault.(8) Abuse in sports can happen, too. In fact, sports can provide opportunity for abusers because of the nature of relationships between adults and athletes. Especially when the adult is a coach or teacher.

Athletes by nature want to please their coaches, to gain their approval. And actually, pleasing the coach is an important tool in training—if an athlete can please the coach in practice, she then is more likely to replicate that behavior in a competitive setting. But there are times when the lines are crossed by coaches who use their power and influence to convince a young girl that "pleasing" means sexually as well.

Many girls are blinded by wanting to gain their coach's favor so badly that they are incapable of recognizing when the coach has overstepped the boundaries. The most severe examples are like those of Barbara, who fell victim to repeated sexual abuse without being aware, until much later, that she was a victim. The Women's Sports Foundation regards romantic and/or sexual relationships between coaches and athletes as an abuse of professional status and power.

Their policy states, "Romantic and or sexual relationships between coaches and athletes undermine the professionalism of coaches, taint the atmosphere of mutual trust and respect between coach and athlete, and hinder the fulfillment of the overall educational mission of athletics. The Foundation views it as unethical if coaches engage in romantic and/or sexual relations with athletes under their supervision, even when both parties have apparently consented to the relationship."(9)

The pattern of behavior of abusive coaches can be confusing. In the beginning, as coach, athlete, and parent establish trust, the coach's behaviors may be quite positive. For the majority of coaches, these behaviors are genuine and a building block for a long-term productive working relationship. However, the abuser will eventually break the bond of trust and act in an unethical or in the most tragic circumstances an illegal manner. The abuser may appear to do some of the following:

- The coach seeks out the trust of the athlete. The reason behind this is that the more trust he has, the less likely the athlete is to complain or even tell someone else. Often the athlete fears being ridiculed by other athletes if she tells, so she figures it is better to stay quiet.
- The coach also seeks out the trust of an athlete's parents. The more the parents believe in the coach, the more likely they are to allow him to spend time with the athlete.
- Once the coach gains the athlete's trust, the coach is likely to suggest spending private time with the athlete on the pretense that it will help her sports performance.
- Once the trust is established, the abusive coach crosses the line of healthy coach-athlete interaction and coerces the athlete into having sex or performing sexual acts to stay in favor with the coach. Often, the coach will use threats and intimidation in addition to

vows of love to assure that the abuse continues. Without intervention, the abuse can be long-term and extremely damaging.

It is vital to teach female athletes at an early age about behavior and actions that are unacceptable. Although parents may find these topics uncomfortable, it is necessary to educate children about the differences in appropriate and inappropriate touching, flirting and harassment, and teasing and bullying. When it comes to discussions about touching, make it clear that some touches are okay while others are hurtful. Children involved in sports may often be touched as part of the learning process, to ensure safety, and to celebrate victory, as is the case with hugs or handshakes. When talking to children about touching that is *not* okay, explain that adults should never ask to touch children's private parts and that the child is not to blame if an adult crosses this boundary. Let children know they should report such an incident immediately and that parents will believe them.

Children can be encouraged to trust their instincts and tell an adult "no" when the adult suggests something she knows is wrong or unacceptable. It is helpful to convey to children that their bodies are their own and they have the right to decide who will touch them and when they want to be touched. It's critical to children's safety that they learn to trust their own feelings and when they feel unsafe, to remove themselves from the situation immediately. In order to increase the likelihood of this behavior, identify for children support people to whom they can turn and talk when feeling unsafe or threatened.

Warning signs that a coach might be sexually interested

- The coach invites the athlete to his house without anyone else present or suggests training sessions on an ongoing basis where no one else is present.
- The coach makes inappropriate remarks about her body or discusses inappropriate topics with her, such as sex. Often the coach will divulge things about his own personal life with his wife or girlfriends. Very often your child will report these, as they may make her uncomfortable.

- The coach tries to "recruit" you as a parent, lavishing praise and compliments about your daughter that seem extreme, especially when couched with the phrase, "As long as she does what I say . . ."

QUICK QUESTIONS

How do I keep her safe?

One of the most effective steps to take is to find out if the league or sports club has a harassment/abuse policy and procedures in place. If not, think about implementing some. Also, check out the coaches. Extensive background checks can be made on potential coaches. In Texas, for example, the Volunteer Center of Dallas County conducts criminal checks for youth leagues and more than seven hundred organizations, providing complete national arrest and adjudication records for $4 per name if the coaching candidate signs a release form. Some leagues make signing the release form mandatory and you could speak with your league about implementing such a policy. To protect the candidates, designate one person to handle the checks, such as the league commissioner, and be sure to set guidelines as to what past crimes are automatic exclusions, such as crimes of a violent or sexual nature.

The league may have developed a job description for coaches, which should place some limits on their authority. Ask if the coach is a member of a coaching association that has a code of ethics. Very few sports organizations have developed a coaches' code of conduct. However, the United States Olympic Committee does have an established coaching code of ethics.

Pedophiles are known to stalk sidelines of sporting events and practices to find victims. Therefore, take precautions such as using symbols rather than names on bags or sweats, and avoid printing names on the backs of uniforms. Remember that sexual abuse and assault is a crime of opportunity, so don't freely distribute rosters that include phone numbers and addresses. A 1996 Justice Department study of more than 43,000 sex offenders convicted in cases involving children found that only one in seven molested a child who was a stranger.(10)

Be wary of closed practices that occur on a regular basis. Never let a girl train with a coach in total privacy or at his home alone. Let coaches know they're being watched, and make sure you watch closely. A 1997 *Sports Illustrated* article detailed the parental outrage over the arrest of a local gymnastics teacher. At an emergency town meeting, they told police there was no way the coach could have been acting inappropriately, because they had watched workouts in his gym. And yet the coach later pleaded guilty to two child abuse charges and two sex-related charges.

Furthermore, stay informed about scheduling and procedures. Abusive coaches will try to gain the power base with the athlete and confuse onlookers by not allowing them to know what's happening with the team. Although you don't have to be the person to supervise practices, other people should be present during practices and travel.

Be aware of being courted. Abusive coaches try to win trust from an athlete's parents by overstating a child's potential and excessively flattering the parent. Abusive coaches also tend to pay more attention to athletes who seem the most vulnerable, such as children whose parents have abdicated parenting responsibilities to the coach. Instead of overreacting to one-time events, keep an eye out for patterns of behavior and remain your child's advocate.

Have frank and open discussions with the coach, and be careful not to put the coach on a pedestal. This shows your child that it is important to have strong personal boundaries and that conflict can be resolved without hostility or "bad-mouthing." Show up at practices and be interested in what is happening. Instead of getting caught up in the technical details of your child's practice, be there simply to ensure her safety.

Make sure boundaries are established and clearly expressed to parents and athletes. Athletes are often asked to sign a code of conduct or rules and standards they must follow in order to be a part of the team. The same policy can be established for a coach.

When it comes to your child, teach her what constitutes sexual abuse and convey to her that it's okay to say no to an adult. Role play with her by giving examples of certain situations and then ask, "What could you do?" Communicate with your daughter and listen to how she talks about her coach. Instead of questioning her about how fast she swam or how many jumps she hit, try asking about her feelings regarding the day. This safe and open communication will help your daughter feel comfortable enough to talk about concerns or worries she may have, especially regarding the coach, and lets her know you will accept her feelings and thoughts and be there to help her deal with them.

Inform your child that you will be the "bad guy" in uncomfortable situations. If a coach asks her to drive to the mall with him and she feels uncomfortable saying no, have her use you as the deciding factor: "No, my mother wouldn't let me do that" or "You need to call and ask my father." Be sure your daughter knows where you can be reached at all times.

WHAT IF I SUSPECT MY DAUGHTER IS SEXUALLY INVOLVED WITH THE COACH?

If parents suspect their daughter is having a sexual relationship with the coach, it's important to make attempts to communicate about the situation with her. If any criminal behavior has occurred (e.g., sexual assault, rape, molestation), report it to the police immediately. It's common for a girl to keep this type of relationship a secret, especially when the abuse is by a coach, someone she knows and trusts. She may appear to be depressed, angry, or fearful; she may deny the relationship or express anger or self-blame. If she feels responsible in any way, she will be less likely to want to report the incident. Parents can expect that she may act out in an attempt to express her feelings rather than directly identify and discuss them. When her behavior is inconsistent and parents suspect abuse, they should get help immediately from an expert, preferably someone with experience in post-traumatic stress and sexual assault.

Parents can encourage her to express feelings by letting her know that they understand how scary and difficult it must be for her and that expressing feelings is a natural part of healing. When parents share their own good and bad emotions, they model acceptance of a full range of feelings, not just the good ones. She may feel it's safer to keep her emotions bottled up, but parents should gently let her know that bottled-up feelings don't disappear. She will need help in dealing with her anger and, if charges are pressed, weathering the process and trauma of a court battle. Share with her stories about other girls who have been sexually abused and how they dealt with it and recovered. Prepare the family through counseling and support of relatives and friends, because she will forever be a different child.

HOW DO I TALK TO HER ABOUT ABUSE?

If you want your daughter to feel comfortable coming forward and telling someone about the abuse, you need to instill this comfort level at home. Make it okay to talk about sexuality. Give her words to use to describe all of her body parts, and encourage questions whenever they arise.

Educate her on how to respond to harassment and abuse by making sure you teach her about touch. Let her know her body is her own and she has the right to decide when to be touched and by whom. Today, coaches are encouraged to ask children's permission to be touched prior to manipulating their bodies. During this discussion, include the topic of secrets and explain that when secrets hurt or frighten her they are not to be kept. Teach her to remove herself from an uncomfortable situation and give her the permission to say "No." Be sure she knows of some trusted adults she can turn to if she is confused by a coach's behavior. Finally, be sure to discuss the importance of trusting her own feelings.

When She Has Been Sexually Abused by a Coach

1. Get involved immediately to provide your daughter with support and guidance.
2. Believe your child and respond calmly.
3. Let her know over and over again that it's not her fault.
4. Validate her for the courage she showed in coming forward and telling you.
5. Report it to the police at once or use the Child Abuse Report Line (Department of Family and Community Services), CrimeStoppers, or Child Protection Services.
6. Take her and yourself to counseling. For immediate attention, call Kids Help Phone or the local rape crisis center.
7. Inform the sports organization or governing body.
8. Read her stories of other young women who have recovered.
9. Be willing to keep talking about it with your daughter even after therapy has ended.
10. Be prepared for it to wound the entire family.

11. Be prepared for differences in your daughter's behaviors, habits, and physical presence.
12. Contact your local programs for victims of sexual assault to receive information, education, and support.

FAST FACTS

➡ 50% of college men surveyed in 1992 said they would force a woman into having sex if they were certain they could get away with it.(11)

➡ 61% of victims are raped before the age of eighteen. Of these, 32% are raped between the ages of eleven and seventeen, and 29% of these victims are under the age of 11.(12)

HE KEEPS TALKING ABOUT MY BODY

Kim is a sixteen-year-old swimmer whose mother was extremely worried because Kim was coming home in tears every night after practice, running into her bedroom, and refusing to talk. Her mother told me she called the coach to ask if something had happened at practice, but he said he didn't have any idea why Kim would be so upset.

Eventually, with a lot of prodding, Kim told her mother what was wrong. Her coach had been making suggestive comments about her body.

"He started by saying how developed I'd become and that I was growing into a real woman," she said. "And then he'd stare at my chest and make his eyes go real big."

Kim was distraught over this behavior from her coach, someone she looked up to and sought approval from. She didn't know what he meant.

"I thought he was flirting with me," she said.

One day, however, he called her a "prick-teaser" and began to make fun of her body. This was repeated day after day. Kim became so humiliated and upset that she wanted to quit the team, but she was afraid to tell anyone why because she didn't want to get into trouble.

"Did I do something wrong?" she asked her mother.

Kim believed she was responsible for her coach's behavior and failed to see that in reality, she was a victim of sexual harassment. Her mother didn't know what to do.

Sexual harassment is sometimes hard for a young girl to recognize, because it is verbal rather than physical. And like sexual abuse, when it involves an authority figure such as a coach, whose approval is so crucial to a young athlete trying to find success in sports, it is hard for her to understand that what he is saying is wrong.

One comment by someone this important to the athlete can shape much of how she feels about herself. When the comments produce feelings of fear, anger, humiliation, invasion, or degradation, then it is sexual harassment. Kim was justifiably confused by her coach's comments and behavior. Did he mean she was sexy or did he mean she was promiscuous? What Kim failed to realize was that whatever he meant, his comments were inappropriate, irresponsible, and ultimately psychologically damaging.

The biggest step young girls must take in stopping sexual harassment is first knowing how to recognize it. They must be taught what are acceptable comments from a coach, teacher, or peer and what are not.

The EEOC Guidelines on Sexual Harassment

"Unwelcome sexual advances, requests for sexual favors, and other verbal or physical conduct of a sexual nature constitute sexual harassment when 1) submission to such conduct is made either explicitly or implicitly a term or condition of an individual's employment, 2) submission to or rejection of such conduct by an individual is used as the basis for employment decisions affecting such individual or 3) such conduct has the purpose or effect of unreasonably interfering with an individual's work performance or creating an intimidating, hostile, or offensive working environment."(13)

Some examples of sexual harassment that occur in sports or school settings include unwanted touching, verbal comments such as name-calling, rating a girl on a scale of one to ten, spreading sexual rumors, and telling dirty jokes. Other actions considered to be sexually harassing include making gestures with one's hands and body, sexual stares, pressuring someone to look at pornography, pressuring someone for sex, touching oneself sexually in front of others, writing or drawing sexual graffiti, and making kissing sounds.

There are some confusing terms when it comes to sexual harassment. There are sexual advances defined as "coming on to someone" or "trying to lure someone into a sex act." Sexual advances are different from sexual favors, which are sex acts performed in return for some kind of reward, such as more playing time or a starting position. Unwanted verbal conduct consists of inappropriate comments about a person's body, clothing, gender, or size, as was the case with Kim. Some coaches still use sexist language, such as plays called "date rape," "fag right," "fag left," or "Saturday night ride," and these could be considered to produce a hostile environment for athletes.

The law is concerned with the impact of the behavior rather than the intent of the behavior. So, by law, sexual harassment is really about how the person is affected by the harassment, not what the harasser meant by the act.

According to Susan Strauss, author of *Sexual Harassment and Teens,* sexual harassment becomes illegal (14):

- When the harassment is made a condition of employment or situation. A person cannot hire or fire another person based on whether or not she goes along with his/her sexual advances. This type of advance can be explicit (clearly stated) or implicit (understood but not directly stated). This can be applied in sports settings where a coach approaches a player sexually by saying she must go along with what the coach wants or she won't make the team or get a starting position.
- When the activity or language provides an uncomfortable work setting or learning environment. This tends to be the most common type of sexual harassment found in the schools. It can come from a teammate who is bigger than another player or has more friends or social status or an adult coach. When a person feels intimidated or offended as Kim did, she may be in a sexually harassing environment. Many factors go into determining whether the behavior by another is considered sexual harassment. These factors

include who the person is, what the relationship is with that person, whether that person has power over the other, and the time and place of the incident.

QUICK QUESTIONS

What are the effects of sexual harassment on the training environment?

Sexual harassment can significantly affect the training environment. As athletes become uneasy about attending practices, team morale may be altered. Relationships between teammates can become tense, and trust may be lost. As the athletic environment becomes increasingly uncomfortable, performance can suffer, and athletes may appear to be confused and distracted.

The uncomfortable learning environment must be ongoing in order to be considered harassment. The harassment must also affect the psychological well-being of the victim. This type of harassment can come from anybody, such as peers or subordinates. When deciding whether sexual harassment is indeed illegal, courts often use the test question, "Would a reasonable person be offended by the conduct?" One problem is that men and women may have different judgments about what is offensive, and this becomes especially difficult to judge when an adult and minor are involved.

Men may label fewer behaviors as sexual harassment and see sexual overtures from women as flattering. On the other hand, women may find sexual overtures from men to be insulting. Women are more likely to see subtle behaviors, such as gestures or looks, as harassment, and men are more likely to think that women will be flattered by behavior often labeled as harassment.(15)

It is imperative that we educate young women to seek out a trusted adult and speak out when feeling confused or "creepy" about adult behavior. Young athletes are praised for listening to and carrying out the demands of coaches. Sometimes in an attempt to prevent another from feeling hurt, young women withhold their own feelings. They may feel they should ignore sexual harassment because they don't want to be perceived badly by others. Young women may be frightened that others will

consider their report an overreaction or even try to blame them for pro-
voking the harassment. When a girl feels someone's behavior is harmful or
inappropriate, we must encourage her to trust her instincts and seek help.

In order for young women to speak out when sexually harassed, it's important parents make a commitment to understand, accept, and adhere to
ethical behavior. It can be helpful for parents to talk to their daughters and
make clear what is and is not appropriate behavior by a coach. They should
try and get to know the coach by attending practices and games and watching coach-athlete interactions as well as listen to how the athlete talks
about the coach. If concerns arise, action needs to be taken. First, talk with
the coach, and then if necessary, with the league, sport governing body, or
coaches' association.

Studies show that sexual harassment is most likely to occur in organizations where the administration fails to implement a strong philosophy and
policy letting people know that harassment will not be tolerated. Based
upon these findings, independent sports organizations should take the lead
from schools and adapt policies to prevent sexual harassment and lessen
the harm to athletes when it does occur. Policies stating that harassment
will not be tolerated need to be developed, distributed, and discussed with
athletes and parents. Athletes should be educated about whom to contact
for help, such as teachers, counselors, and administrators. These adult leaders must stay educated and aware of the issue of sexual harassment.

WHAT TO SAY WHEN SHE HAS BEEN
SEXUALLY HARASSED

Start by talking with your daughter about the specific incident. Find out
what happened, where it happened, when it happened, who did the harassing, and what action was taken. Reassure her that it's not her fault, and
let her know you will get the necessary help.

It's important to explain what sexual harassment is and why it is illegal.
Explain to her why victims of sexual harassment frequently don't report it.
Very often victims blame themselves, feel powerless, don't know how to report it, think they won't be taken seriously, don't trust their perception of
the event, want to protect the harasser, and feel afraid or embarrassed.

Be sure to investigate and receive a written copy of the school district or sports organization's sexual harassment policies. Share these with her to show that this type of behavior is not tolerated. You can explain that it's important to document the incident and that people will take the claim more seriously if the victim is clear on what happened, when it happened, and how often. When you are unable to provide the details, claims are taken less seriously.

Take time to discuss the options with her. Most victims just want the harassment to stop and don't want to file a formal complaint or take legal action. Some appropriate consequences for the sexual harassment are an apology to the victim, legal action, loss of job, loss of reputation, jail, and fines. A letter can be written to the harasser, which should include a description of the harassing behavior, how it makes the victim feel, the consequences the victim has experienced, and a request for the behavior to stop. Make sure another adult is present when giving the letter to the harasser, and keep a copy for your records. As parents you have the option of confronting the harasser and telling him or her how the behavior is affecting your daughter and to stop the harassment immediately. If you choose to confront the harasser, bring a trusted friend or official along for support. It will be up to you as a family to decide what action to take.

Here Are Some Options

1. Make sure she gets help from you as well as a counselor, school official, or other trusted adult.
2. Follow the sexual harassment policy and procedures used by the school district or sports organization.
3. Report the incident to a person in authority, such as a sports league director, school principal, counselor, or the police.
4. Document exactly what happened, when it happened, where it happened, who did the harassing, who the witnesses were, what she said or did in response to the harassment, how the harasser responded, and how she felt about the harassment.
5. If harassment persists, go to a person in higher authority, such as a member of the national governing body, school board member, athletic director, or superintendent of schools. Make sure an investigation proceeds in a timely manner.

6. Ensure that procedures for reporting harassment protect her privacy. Make sure to distinguish between informal and formal procedures for reporting the sexual harassment. During the informal procedures, confidentiality should be maintained. However, once a formal complaint is filed, there are some limitations to confidentiality that need to be clarified.

7. At any time, you may choose to contact the Office of Civil Rights, State Department of Education, State Department of Human Rights, an attorney, the police, or local program for victims of sexual assault.

FAST FACTS

➡ A sexual harassment questionnaire distributed to student leaders from thirteen school districts revealed that:

　80% of students said they were aware of sexual harassment in their schools.

　75% said they were aware of sexual harassment between students.

　50% said they were aware of sexual harassment between students and staff.

　26% said sexual harassment goes on all the time.

　50% said it happens to a fair number of people.

　6% said it doesn't happen.(16)

➡ Sexual harassment is illegal in the schools, as stated by the Civil Rights Act, Title IX of the Federal Education Amendments. It is illegal in the workplace according to the Civil Rights, Title VII. These are federal laws and apply to everyone in the United States.(17)

➡ In 1992, Christine Franklin, a high school student from a Georgia school district, became the first to win a Supreme Court case for sexual harassment under Title IX. She had been sexually harassed by her male science teacher for two years, with the harassment culminating in rape on three occasions.(18)

MY FRIEND SAYS I SHOULD TAKE STEROIDS

Tina is a fifteen-year-old softball pitcher who is immensely talented and has the potential to earn a college scholarship. She has been trying to lift weights and bulk up to help her reach the next level. An older friend pulled Tina aside one day and suggested that she begin using anabolic steroids to help her gain the muscle.

"Aren't they illegal?" Tina asked.

"Not if you don't get caught," the friend said. "And there's ways to take them now because you won't be tested until you're in college. By then you'll have gotten the muscle you need."

Tina was tempted. Many athletes are. Anabolic steroids are muscle-building drugs that are made of male hormones and designed to raise testosterone levels. Throughout history, the drugs have been used primarily by males who compete in body-building and weight-lifting contests and traditional physical sports, like football. However, they have been discovered by young girls, too, who now have many of the same pressures to succeed in sports as their male counterparts.

In fact, the number of young girls using steroids has roughly doubled over the past several years, with some studies estimating that 0.5 to 2 percent or more of high school seniors have used anabolic steroids; some began as early as sixth grade.(19)

Why?

Perhaps it's because as the number of athletic opportunities at the college and professional level have increased, so has the competition. Charles Yesalis, a leading researcher in the area of performance-enhancing drug use, says that many of these young women view steroid use as an investment in their futures. Females, like males for decades, now are being pressured to gain a competitive edge at all costs, especially when they are young enough that drug tests are not administered and detection is minimal. Tina's friend was simply pointing out a method by which Tina could, in her eyes, derive the benefits of taking steroids, get the scholarship, and then stop using the steroids before a test would be given. It is a procedure far too common for adolescent girls desperate to make it to the next level.

Even though they are illegal, like recreational drugs, they can be bought just about anywhere, from the Internet to a veterinarian or in Mexico.

They are typically taken in cycles lasting six to twelve weeks or longer, and can be taken orally, by injection, or topically. There are numerous effects from the use of steroids, some of which can be devastating. Women tend to get dramatic gains in strength. But keep in mind that these gains in strength do not always translate into better sports performance.

Athletes taking steroids hope to increase their muscle mass, increase strength and endurance, and speed recovery from intense training sessions. A study published in the *New England Journal of Medicine* in 1996 showed that men who received doses of testosterone experienced increases in muscle size and strength.(20) Research has also found the same effects among females and children. Possible unwanted side effects include liver and kidney damage, severe acne, deepened voices, increased facial hair, enlarged clitorises, and damaged reproductive systems. Some users have reported increased energy levels and aggressiveness.

Still, many people—millions, in fact—believe the benefits outweigh the risk.

"After every workout, I got a cocktail with vitamins," reported East German swimmer Kornelia Ender, a quadruple gold medalist at the 1976 Montreal Olympics.(21) In 1998, Chinese swimmer, Yuan Yuan, was caught at the Sydney airport with her thermos flask clearly labeled "human somatropin."(22) And East German shotputter Heidi Krieger claims that steroids effectively turned her into a man and had a sex-change operation to complete the process.(23)

"I think that there are a lot of athletes in danger," wrote former Denver Broncos and Oakland Raider Lyle Alzado in a 1991 article admitting long-term steroid use while in the NFL. "Almost everyone I know takes them. They are so intent on being successful that they're not concerned with anything else."(24)

Alzado died in 1992 of brain cancer he directly attributed to his steroid use.

Adults working with young athletes should have enough knowledge to recognize drug use and abuse and make appropriate recommendations for help. One factor to keep in mind is that some individuals working with athletes may place more emphasis on their own agendas, such as winning at all costs, rather than emphasizing the athlete's best interests. The physical, emotional, and mental health of athletes may not always be of the utmost importance to some adult leadership.

It is critical for adults involved with athletes to be able to recognize potential signs of drug use, but these people are not expected to be drug abuse experts. When they suspect drug abuse, they should refer the athlete to a trained professional immediately. Much as with eating disorders, coaches, friends, parents, and teachers should act quickly to secure the safety of the athlete and then remove themselves from the process. Trained professionals who can deal with drug issues include drug counselors, psychologists, psychiatrists, counselors, and physicians.

Very often a good place to start is either with a physician or the school counselor. If an athlete is in denial, a call to the school counselor expressing your concerns can get the ball rolling for treatment to begin. Also, an athlete who refuses treatment may be willing to go to her physician for a physical. The physician can then make the appropriate referrals.

For some, ceasing to take anabolic steroids may be difficult. Their body images and confidence in performance outcomes may be tied to the drug. Rather than seeking professional treatment, many users simply quit taking the drug when the effects become adverse.

Some of the warning signs indicating that an athlete may be using steroids include a marked drop in her voice which may be covered by whispering. She may get injuries to ligaments and tendons that have become weakened by muscle growth. Other signs to make note of are severe acne, mood swings, and rapid loss of body fat.

Some steroid users trying to quit may need to be treated with other drugs to handle withdrawal symptoms and to prevent them from returning to steroid use. Many times both medical and psychological care are recommended.

Many schools today provide drug awareness programming in the hopes of decreasing teen drug use. However, not many schools include anabolic steroid use in their education. One program, called Adolescents Training and Learning to Avoid Steroids (ATLAS), has been developed by a team of researchers at the Oregon Health Sciences University. Remember, there are healthy, legal, fair, and ethical ways to improve sports performance. Strength and conditioning training, paired with sound nutritional habits and mental skills training, can all help to enhance sports performance while also improving the health and well-being of the child.

The best way to assure that your daughter doesn't get caught up in the steroid craze is to make sure she has a healthy sense of the reasons why she participates in sports. Make sure you and her coaches value the process of sports achievement more than the product. Place emphasis on her health and well-being first and foremost. When you accept a "win at all costs" attitude, she will, too. Instead, reinforce through your words and actions that winning is a public validation of her talent, but what is truly amazing and awe-inspiring is not the win itself—people win everyday—it's how one wins. It's the process of achievement that lasts a lifetime.

How to Make Sure She Doesn't Adopt a Win-at-All-Costs Approach

1. Set realistic and achievable goals.
2. Value life lessons of sports.
3. Question her about the daily lessons she learns from sports. Let her know how important these are to you.
4. Talk openly and often about why she participates. Make sure there are reasons other than the winning, scholarships, and professional contracts.
5. Value and show interest in all of her pursuits and activities, not just sports.

FAST FACTS

➡ In November of 1998, the White House pledged unprecedented federal help to fight drugs in sports, including $1 million in research and pressure to award medals to athletes who lost because their opponents had used performance-enhancing drugs.

➡ The Justice Department's Office of Juvenile Justice and Delinquency Prevention distributes a guide, *The Coach's PlayBook Against Drugs*, to help coaches educate athletes about the dangers and problems associated with drug use.(25)

QUICK QUESTIONS

What about creatine? It's the latest rage, but is it safe?

Creatine is an amino acid that is in everyone's body; in synthetic form, it's a popular supplement used by athletes wanting to work out longer and more intensely. No studies have shown that it can increase muscles itself, but it does foster muscle growth, because the athlete is working out harder. There have been virtually no studies done on the long-term effects of creatine. However, doctors are now recommending that anyone still growing—usually under the age of twenty or twenty-one—refrain from taking the supplement, because it's not yet known how it affects a developing body. There also are no studies on the effects of creatine on female reproductive systems. Short-term effects include muscle cramping, gas and dehydration.

What is androstenedione, the stuff Mark McGwire took?

Androstenedione is a steroid that raises testosterone levels, similar to what an anabolic steroid will do. It is quite controversial, banned by the International Olympic Committee, the National Football League, and the NCAA, but not by major league baseball, which does not administer drug tests. It is legally classified as a food supplement and is readily available in many health food stores and over the Internet and in muscle magazines. Again, it is a very new drug and the long-term effects have not been studied. There is concern about the effects on adolescent athletes, and in adults, raised testosterone levels can trigger liver damage, increase the risk of stroke, and lead to mood swings and aggressive behavior.

Should parents allow their daughters to try these supplements?

No. The potential side effects and the unknown factor of the long-term effects should scare parents and athletes away on their own merits. Moreover, parents should teach their daughters that they can compete and find success without using a drug.

HE GRABBED ME

Tammy, a fifteen-year-old ice hockey player, made a mistake in practice. As she skated off the ice, her coach grabbed her by the arm and forcefully pulled her toward him, screaming: "You stupid, stupid girl. I've told you a million times not to do that and what do you do? What do you do?"

Tammy wasn't hurt physically and was able to leave the rink without bursting into tears. Later that night, however, she unloaded everything on her parents, who cringed at what the coach had done.

"What do we do?" they asked. "This can't be right."

Surprisingly, perhaps, this situation is not unsalvageable. While the behavior of Tammy's coach was awful and unacceptable, it was reparable. Tammy's parents respected the coach, and while it was difficult for them to see beyond the day's events, they did believe he was a good coach with a good mind and, basically, a good attitude. They had never before seen this type of behavior from him.

But they knew very little about him beyond that, which is normal and common. Many coaches are volunteers, and the only preparation and training they've had is from being an athlete's parent or an athlete themselves. Coaches very often may have their own silent agendas and approaches to motivating their athletes.

Often they are unaware of the emotional needs of young athletes, especially young female athletes. Many times, coaches used to dealing with boys cannot make the switch to dealing with girls. They believe in treating them the same, which is not logical, because boys and girls are far different. Sometimes coaches assume that athletes are emotionally developed beyond their age and that they are able to cope with certain situations without being taught how to do so.

At the worst extreme, they decide to adopt coaching methods from famous coaches who use abusive behavior but get good results. This "Bobby Knight syndrome" might work for the Indiana men's basketball coach, but won't work just about anywhere else, especially in dealing with young girls.

Tammy's parents immediately scheduled a meeting with her coach to address the abuse. They made it clear that physical contact was not acceptable and wouldn't be tolerated. They became more involved in her hockey by attending practices and setting up monthly conferences with the coach. If the coach's unacceptable behavior continued and became a pattern rather than a one-time event, they would report him to the league, the school with which he was affiliated, or the sport's national governing body.

Finally, I suggested they sit down and process this experience with Tammy. They were honest about their own feelings over the incident and the manner in which it was handled. They communicated to Tammy that their priority as parents was to keep her safe. Her parents informed her that they would be more involved and keeping a watchful eye on the coach. They congratulated their daughter on coming to them and speaking out.

Warning Signs of Emotional or Physical Abuse(26)

- Sudden aggressiveness
- Quitting the team or uncharacteristic lack of interest
- Sleep problems
- Appetite changes
- Sliding grades
- Fear of washrooms, locker rooms, closed doors
- Running away
- Sudden and disproportionate interest in sex for their age
- Reluctance to talk
- Frequent vomiting
- Bruises
- Scratches
- Inflammation
- Lesions
- Bleeding
- Genital injuries
- Sexually transmitted diseases
- Pregnancy

QUICK QUESTIONS

*My daughter has been diagnosed with attention deficit
hyperactivity disorder. Can sports help?*

Yes and no. Attention deficit/hyperactivity disorder, or ADHD, is a developmental disorder of self-control. The primary problems associated with ADHD are difficulties sustaining attention, impulsivity or inhibition, excessive activity, variability in responses to situations, and trouble following rules.

Children can also be diagnosed with attention deficit disorder (ADD), which presents different symptoms from ADHD. Children with ADD are often described as more fearful than other children, inattentive, slow-moving, and "out of it." Children with ADD seem to have problems sorting out relevant from irrelevant information, whereas children with ADHD seem to have more difficulty with impulsivity and distractibility.

In order to alleviate or even improve some of the symptoms of these illnesses, experts recommend enrolling children in organized activities that are very structured and supervised. Some children with ADHD have difficulty with peer relationships and therefore do better in small groups. If sports is the organized activity of choice, be sure to steer clear of sports that require a lot of sitting or standing around. For instance, a child with ADHD who plays softball may be highly distracted by playing in the outfield. She is better off up front where most of the action is taking place. Team sports provide the opportunity for children with ADHD to complete a task as part of a team and work toward a common goal. This can aid in developing peer relationships as well as reward behaviors such as attentiveness, completion of tasks, and adherence to rules.

To be successful in sports, children with or without ADHD need to learn to control their impulses and thought patterns. Some children with ADHD and ADD respond very well to strenuous sports activities but, as in other areas of their life, have trouble taking direction, attending to important cues, or having the patience to understand a coach's strategy or reasoning on issues. Sports is not a replacement for proper treatment of ADHD, but with the right adult leadership, sports can be a valuable tool in helping manage some of the symptoms associated with the disorders.

. . .

"She smokes and drinks, but thinks it won't hurt her because she plays sports. Is that right?"

No. And if she won't believe you, take her to a doctor who will counsel her on the dangers and consequences of alcohol and tobacco use. Sometimes teens respond better to information that comes from a health professional, but make sure you have made your values and thoughts on this topic perfectly clear. The information your child receives about alcohol and tobacco can be confusing. She is told by authority figures that drinking and smoking will kill her and she is told by peers that they are not harmful at all. We know that alcohol and tobacco are extremely toxic yet your child sees people smoking and drinking. Therefore, a discussion with your daughter on this topic needs to include a dialogue about making better choices. She needs accurate information about the consequences of her choices, and once these are understood, she may choose to act differently.

WHAT IF THEY TRY TO MAKE ME A LESBIAN?

Dana is a fourteen-year-old basketball player whose family recently moved to a new area. She began attending a new school, tried out for varsity basketball, and made the team. Several weeks into practice, however, she saw two of her new teammates kissing and holding hands in what they thought was a deserted locker room. She asked one of her friends at school about it and the friend replied, "That's nothing new. Everyone knows that's a dyke team."

Dana was so upset she wanted to quit the team.

"Everyone's going to think I'm gay, too," Dana explained to her parents. "What if they try to make me a lesbian?"

Dana's mother called me for advice on how to deal with this situation.

What I told her was that there are numerous lessons that can be learned through sports. This situation presents an opportunity for Dana's parents to teach their daughter about sexuality, tolerance, prejudice, and stereotypes. These lessons she will carry with her as she matures.

"She is likely to encounter lesbians and gays at some point in her life," I said. "I'd use this to teach her now about acceptance and tolerance."

I encouraged Dana's parents to talk with her so that she could understand how her parent's views and values fit with her own. Dana needed input from those important in her life so that she could absorb that information and feel good about forming her own value system. That kind of open discussion would help Dana form opinions about sexuality as well as develop self-esteem. Therefore, the process of dealing with the issue was as important as the issue itself.

When they talked with Dana, I told them to be up front about the facts. Yes, there are lesbian and bisexual athletes, and some teams may be composed primarily of lesbian players, just as others are not. But that should not scare her away from playing on those teams and with those players.

I suggested that they ask her to take a look at the reasons she plays basketball and the benefits she receives from playing and then challenge her to understand that she will find that many of those factors remain the same regardless of whether she is playing with lesbians or heterosexuals.

Dana was also facing the challenge that if she continued to play basketball, she might be in a position to have to defend her sexuality. In some cases, this happens with boys as well. Many boys are ridiculed by their peers for participating in sports such as figure skating and gymnastics. They are considered weak or soft unless they play so-called tougher sports, such as football or basketball. However, boys competing in more gender-neutral sports have come to defend themselves by noting that they are the ones who get to spend all of their time with girls. The moment the implication is made that a young woman playing a certain sport or playing for a certain school or a certain team is a lesbian, girls too often will then avoid sports entirely. These girls choose not to play because they don't want to go through life having people question their sexuality.

"The presence or absence of gays and lesbians is not the issue [in sports]," according to Donna Lopiano, president of the Women's Sports Foundation. "Any label applied to an entire group wrongly stereotypes every member of the group and is patently unethical. All football players are not dumb. All female athletes are not lesbians. All male dancers, artists, and designers are not gay. The bottom line is that we are educated people who must understand how homophobia is used by those who would like to destroy the reputation of a program or school or coach or to remove the opportunity to play or work."(27)

The worst action to take in Dana's situation would be to deny a problem exists or to simplify the problem as being that the team consists of lesbian players. An important part of the issue is Dana's fear and prejudice associated with lesbianism in sport. Dana can disagree with her teammates' lifestyle choices, but she has to learn that she has her own choice to make about whether to focus on her teammates' sexual preferences or on their strengths and rights as human beings.

Dana should be congratulated for her ability to acknowledge her own confusion about this issue, which can be used to help her learn about tolerance and respect for diversity. I suggested that she talk to the school counselor, who could educate Dana about the school's nondiscrimination policies and how those policies help to protect the rights of students. I also suggested Dana's parents talk with her coach to see where she stood in regard to this issue. Did the coach view sexuality as a priority? What were the coach's expectations of the athletes' behavior regarding sexuality? Did the coach expect the athletes to be tolerant of one another?

Before having Dana speak with the coach, I would want to find out if the coach had previously thought about this issue and how to deal with it. My guess was that Dana was not the only team member struggling with these issues. I would encourage the coach first to define her own personal policy regarding sexuality and then talk openly with the team, placing importance on respecting differences. In this situation, the coach would want to offer support services through the school counselor or outside professionals.

Questions a Coach Should Consider(28)

1. Do you use or allow others to use language or jokes that demean gays?
2. Do you use antigay language to motivate?
3. Do you expect gay players to keep their sexual orientation a secret?
4. Do you drop gay athletes or coaches if you find out they are gay?
5. Do you know of or use support services for gay athletes?
6. Do you discuss homophobia with your team?
7. How do you encourage kids to respect differences?
8. How would you react if someone on the team identified themselves as gay?

9. How would you react if a player brought a same-sex date to school or athletic function?

10. What are your concerns about having gay athletes on the team?

QUICK QUESTIONS

Why should a coach or parent address homophobia?

According to Pat Griffin, author of *Strong Women, Deep Closets: Lesbians and Homophobia in Sport,* there are several ways in which homophobia manifests itself in women's sports.(29) At times, people either deny that lesbians exist on certain teams or are silent about the issue for fear it may sour the progress women have made. Some coaches admit that secret antilesbian polices exist in their programs and that they impose informal quotas on the number of lesbians, or at least on the number of athletes they think look like lesbians, on their teams. The Fellowship of Christian Athletes distributes a free antihomosexual booklet to coaches and athletes entitled, "Emotional Dependency: A Threat to Close Friendships"; it discusses the symptoms of emotional dependency and how this supposedly leads to homosexual relationships. Many organizations have tried to place great importance on the feminine side of women's sports by promoting athletes who portray a feminine image or including marital and parental status in athlete biographies. One example is tennis player Anna Kornikova, who is described in press releases and articles as "beautiful," while other tour players are "athletic."

Women's sports can be affected by homophobia, and this is an important topic to address. Heterosexual athletes may have fears about homosexuals and bring these assumptions and misperceptions with them to the team. According to several studies, young men of high school and college age are among the most frequent perpetrators of hate crimes directed at lesbians and gays.(30) The Department of Health and Human Services reports that up to 30 percent of teen suicides are among lesbian and gay youth who are isolated and unhappy.(31)

In high school, students begin to explore sexuality, whatever it may be. By encouraging young women to discuss their sexuality, adults set an example of tolerance and social justice. Furthermore, discussion can help to dispel some of the fear that women have of being called a lesbian, which may cause them to choose not to participate in certain activities. By providing clear information that is accurate, adults can fight the stereotypes.

We must decide what we want our children to learn from sports and constantly reinforce these messages. Sports lessons can teach what is right and what is wrong. Young women must not be scared away from trying something because of our own or society's insecurities and prejudices. Certainly, fear of homosexuality should not be used as an excuse for nonparticipation.

HOW DO YOU TEACH TOLERANCE?

Parents need to investigate and inform themselves of any school or sport organization policies regarding discrimination. Many schools include sexual orientation as a category, like race and gender, for which discrimination is prohibited. Reinforce the inappropriateness of verbal or physical harassment and recognize the accomplishments of all groups of people regardless of race, gender, or sexual preference.

Discrimination against female athletes can come in many shapes and forms. For example, athletes who are known lesbians often will not be allowed on certain teams. Penn State's women's basketball coach, Rene Portland, has an unwritten rule of keeping lesbians off her team.(32) Other teams, however, will recruit only lesbian athletes. Make sure the team or club you choose for your daughter has a fair and up-front policy against discrimination based on sexual preference.

Racism is a form of discrimination that exists in society, and therefore it also exists in sports. You may feel your daughter isn't allowed onto a team or promoted or even played fairly because of her race. If you do, it's best to first discuss the situation with the coach or athletic administrator. If you still believe she is being held back because of her race, don't be afraid to take it to the next level.

Sometimes, athletes are dissuaded from joining a certain team or club because their family doesn't fit a certain economic profile. Some teams, by virtue of their geographic location, are naturally made up of athletes whose families fit into one general income level. Also, once on a team, girls from lower income families may be made to feel inadequate because they can't afford certain items that the other girls can, like elaborate costumes, or extra uniform items, or even travel. On the other hand, sometimes girls from higher-income families are wrongly labeled "arrogant" or "snotty" simply because of their family situation.

Discrimination can also occur simply because one is a woman. How many times do the boys get the gym or court time during the best hours of the day? How often are the girls' teams relegated to the second-rate fields or tracks? Make sure your daughter's school or sports program treats its boys and girls teams fairly and without prejudice. It's important that if you believe your daughter is being discriminated against for any reason, you bring those concerns to the governing body of her sport.

FAST FACTS

➡ Recent studies suggest that gay, lesbian, and bisexual young people are at increased risk of mental health problems, with these associations being particularly evident for measures of suicidal behavior and multiple disorders. One study found that gay, lesbian, and bisexual young people in New Zealand were at increased risk of major depression, generalized anxiety disorder, conduct disorder, nicotine dependence, other substance abuse and/or dependence, multiple disorders, suicidal ideation, and suicide attempts.(33)

10

Conclusion

Tomorrow's athletes will be stronger, more supported, better recognized. With more girls involved in sports, the next generation can only be better.

—Michelle Akers, member of the 1999 U.S. World Cup
Championship Women's Soccer Team

When I was near the end of my graduate training, I walked into the office of my advisor, Dr. Bob Rotella, and related to him a story about the work I had done with a young woman athlete who had made some major strides in her performance and in the way she felt and thought about herself. I thanked him for the knowledge and guidance he had provided that allowed me to do something that I truly loved. He told me, "I know you were pretty good at skating, but maybe sports psychology is the endeavor that will help you find greatness."

His comment stuck with me. When I made the decision to quit skating, one of my greatest fears was that I would never be as good at anything else in my entire life. It never dawned on me that I had yet to find what I could be great at. Why is it that sports has to be viewed as a means to an end? That a young athlete either wins and wins often or the experience isn't worth the money or the sacrifice? People don't treat academics that way. There are plenty of children who aren't outstanding scholars, yet school is seen as a critical part of their development.

What if sports were viewed as a springboard for some young woman to explore what her true talents might be? In 1996, I was a guest on the *Oprah Winfrey Show* and I listened to the audience express confusion regarding the value of the sports experience for girls. I left the show reflecting upon my work and trying to make sense of why so many young women who experience tremendous athletic success can walk away from the journey feeling as if they have failed and benefited little from the pursuit. Today, it is disheartening to listen to athletes who have devoted their time and energy to developing athletic talent yet can't identify one lesson learned from sports that they think might help them as they reach for new horizons. Many young women leave sports and distance themselves from the very endeavor that may have significantly shaped who they have become and aspire to be.

Someone once said, "Some people spend their whole life climbing the ladder of success only to get to the top and find that the ladder is leaning against the wrong building."

I believe this quote is applicable to sports. We as adults define for children what success means. Girls begin climbing the ladder trying to meet those expectations, and when they can't seem to get close to the top, they start to feel stuck, are afraid of falling off, and don't know where to turn. Do they keep climbing up or start walking down? Whom do they talk to about their dilemma? Why do they want to climb up if what's at the top of the ladder isn't a place they want to explore? And sometimes kids define success in a way that makes it impossible for them to see other benefits of the experience.

Very few girls will realize their ultimate sports dream of Olympic gold or professional status, but they will all be impacted by the sport experience itself. It is our responsibility to put the child first and the champion second by guiding and assisting her in identifying the many ways she can be successful even if she isn't the very best. Sports can be a wonderful and enriching life experience for young women. They can learn the obvious lessons about winning and losing, fairness, and competition. But they can also learn the lessons that will shape their character—lessons about perseverance, fortitude, dedication, work ethic, commitment, and responsibility. Furthermore, they can acquire mental skills such as focusing, self-talk, thought stoppage, goal setting, reframing, relaxation, and imagery. They can benefit from lessons about the body and the importance of seeing it as something useful, a tool to help them explore their talent, and not just something that's there for the sake of appearance. And what about the lessons of teamwork, friendship, rivalry, coaching, and parenting?

Sports holds the potential to teach valuable life lessons and help shape a young girl into a confident, self-approving, ambitious, hardworking, balanced woman. Yet sports also holds the potential to teach destructive lessons—ones about rule breaking, favoritism, winning at all costs, failure as devastation, drugs, thinness as fitness, and others' opinions being valued more than her own.

The one commonality between the enriching lessons and the destructive ones is that adults do the teaching. Sports is an activity brought to life by the adults who create the rules and enforce them. It is adults who teach kids how to play, and although not all adults share the same values or hopes for sports, it is the responsibility of every one of us to try to guide young women through the process.

Sports through the eyes of a young woman may be a mystery. We can easily get caught up in our own agendas for sports participation and neglect viewing it from the child's perspective. Isn't sport supposed to be an experience for the child? Aren't the adults supposed to be there to guide her through the journey, making sure she acquires some benefits and remains safe? How can we so easily allow sports to become about adult ideals and values?

We must always remember that the sports experience is helping to shape the way a young woman thinks and feels about herself. We must never lose sight of our obligation as adults to guide and support her through the process. How we measure success has an incredible impact upon a young woman. As adults we must be keenly aware of the lessons we are teaching and how we are using sports to help shape a young woman's life.

There are mistakes that we will make throughout the process. We'll sometimes let our personal emotions or ambitions cloud our judgments. These mistakes aren't irreparable as long as we are able to step back and acknowledge our errors and recognize where we became misguided. We must stay focused on putting the child first and the champion second. We must use sports to help a young woman shape a view of herself that is accepting and affirming.

Let us use sports to reinforce to a young girl that her feelings and thoughts are valuable, important, and worthy of being heard. We must teach her to accept her body and honor it as the place that houses her many talents. It is our adult responsibility to show our daughters how to turn obstacles into challenges and help them develop ways to respond to nervousness, fear, and anxiety.

Let us use sports to teach her how to clearly and honestly express herself, especially to adults. We need to help her to set personal boundaries and not allow anyone to invade her rights as a human being. During her sports participation, we must find moments to teach her to identify her needs and find effective ways in which to satisfy them. Furthermore, we must constantly encourage her to consider how the opinions of others fit with her own viewpoints.

Let us use sports to teach her how to be successful and encourage her to transfer these lessons to all areas of her life. We can help open her mind to new ways of seeing herself and her situation and reinforce that her thoughts and feelings are separate. Through sports, we can teach her how to put herself in control while also reinforcing the value of tolerance and fairness.

Let us use sports to teach her that even if she isn't the brightest, smartest, or prettiest, her thoughts, opinions, and feelings deserve to be heard and respected. We need to remind her that sports is a journey that will shape her physically and emotionally and help guide her as she explores her personal value, talent, and ultimately, greatness.

And let her always teach us that the sports journey may begin with a dream of becoming a champion, yet it always ends with the lessons learned by a child.

Appendix A

OLYMPIC SPORTS ORGANIZATIONS

Archery
Tel: (719)578-4576
Internet: www.USAArchery.org
E-mail: naa_ofc@ix.netcom.com

Badminton
Tel: (719)578-4808
Internet: www.usabadminton.org
E-mail: info@usabadminton.org

Baseball
Tel: (520)327-9700
Internet: www.usabaseball.com
E-mail: usabasebal@aol.com

Basketball
Tel: (719)590-4800
Internet: www.usabasketball.com

Biathlon
Tel: (802)654-7833
E-mail: USBiathlon@aol.com

Bobsled
Tel: (518)523-1842
Internet: www.usabobsled.org
E-mail: info@usabobsled.org

Boxing
Tel: (719)578-4056
E-mail: USABoxing@aol.com

Canoe/Kayak
Tel: (518)523-1855
Internet: www.applied.nct/usckt/
E-mail: USCKT@aol.com

Curling
Tel: (715)344-1199
Internet: www.usacurl.org
E-mail: usacurl@coredcs.com

Cycling
Tel: (719)578-4581
Internet: www.usacycling.org

Diving
Tel: (317)237-5252
Internet: www.usdiving.org

Equestrian
Tel: (606)258-2472
Internet: www.ahsa.org
E-mail: nlmigliarese@ahsa.org

Fencing
Tel: (719)578-4511
Internet: www.USFencing.org
E-mail: USFencing@aol.com

Field Hockey
Tel: (719)578-4567
Internet: www.usfieldhockey.com
E-mail: usfha@usfieldhockey.com

Figure Skating
Tel: (719)635-5200
Internet: www.usfsa.org
E-mail: USFSA1@aol.com

Gymnastics
Tel: (317)237-5050
Internet: usa-gymnastics.org

Ice Hockey
Tel: (719)576-8724
Internet: www.usahockey.org
E-mail: usah@usahockey.org

Judo
Tel: (719)578-4730
Internet: www.usjudo.org

Luge
Tel: (518)523-2071
Internet: www.usaluge.org
E-mail: usaluge@usaluge.org

Modern Pentathlon
Tel: (210)528-2999
Internet: www.uspentathlon.org
E-mail: usmpa@texas.net

Rowing
Tel: (317)237-5656
Internet: www.usrowing.org
E-mail: usrowing@aol.com

Sailing
Tel: (401)683-0800
Internet: www.ussailing.org

Shooting
Tel: (719)578-4670
Internet: www.usashooting.org

Skiing/Snowboarding
Tel: (801)649-9090
Internet: www.usskiteam.com

Soccer
Tel: (312)808-1300
Internet: www.us-soccer.com
E-mail: socfed@aol.com

Softball
Tel: (405)424-5266
Internet: www.softball.org

Speed Skating
Tel: (216)899-0128
Internet: www.usspeedskating.org

Swimming
Tel: (719)578-4578
Internet: www.usa-swimming.org

Synchronized Swimming
Tel: (317)237-5700
Internet: www.usasynchro.org

Table Tennis
Tel: (719)578-4583
Internet: www.usatt.org
E-mail: usatt.usa.net

Taekwondo
Tel: (719)578-4632
Internet: www.ustu.org

Team Handball
Tel: (770) 956-7660
Internet: www.usateamhandball.org
E-mail: info@usateamhandball.org

Tennis
Tel: (914)696-7000
Internet: www.usta.com

Track and Field
Tel: (317)261-0500
Internet: www.usatf.org

Triathlon
Tel: (719)597-9090
Internet: www.usatriathlon.org
E-mail: usatriathlon@usatriathlon.org

Volleyball
Tel: (719)228-6800
Internet: www.usavolleyball.org

Water Polo
Tel: (719)634-0699
Internet: www.uswp.org
E-mail: uswpoffice@aol.com

Weightlifting
Tel: (719)578-4508
Internet: www.usaw.org
E-mail: usaw@worldnet.att.net

Wrestling
Tel: (719)598-8181
Internet: www.usawrestling.org
E-mail: usaw@concentric.net

PAN AMERICAN SPORTS ORGANIZATIONS

Bowling
Tel: (414)421-9008 or
(719)636-2695
Internet: www.bowl.org

Karate
Tel: (206)440-8386
Internet: www.usankf.org

Racquetball
Tel: (719)635-5396
Internet: www.usra.org

Roller Skating
Tel: (402)483-7551
Internet: www.usacrs.com

Squash
Tel: (610)667-4006
Internet: www.us-squash.org
E-mail: ussquash@us-squash.org

Water Skiing
Tel: (941)324-4341
Internet: www.usawaterski.org
E-mail: usawaterski@worldnet.att.net

AFFILIATED SPORTS ORGANIZATIONS

Orienteering
Tel: (404)363-2110
Internet: www.us.orienteering.org

Rugby
Tel: (719)637-1022
Internet: www.usarugby.org
E-mail: info@usarugby.org

Sports Acrobatics
Tel: (916)488-9499
E-mail: USAAcro@aol.com

Trampoline and Tumbling
Tel: (806)637-8670
Internet: www.usat-t.org
E-mail: USATT@aol.com

Underwater Swimming
Tel: (650)583-8492
E-mail: usafin@aol.com

Appendix B

SOME GROUPS THAT PROVIDE COACHING EDUCATION

The National Youth Sports Coaches Association (NYSCA) trains more than 150,000 coaches each year. With chapters in every state, the NYSCA is able to provide programs administered by certified clinicians.

NYSCA
2050 Vista Parkway
W. Palm Beach, FL 33411
(800)729-2057

The American Sport Education Program (ASEP) provides training materials and conducts programs for coaches, parents, and administrators. The National Federation of State High School Associations selected ASEP as its coaching education program.

ASEP
P.O. Box 5076
Champaign, IL 61825
(800)747-5698

The Program for Athletic Coaches' Education (PACE) is administered by the Youth Sports Institute at Michigan State University and is active primarily in Michigan, Wisconsin, Indiana, and Hawaii.

PACE
Youth Sports Institute
Michigan State University
East Lansing, MI 48824
(517)353-6689

The National Institute for Child Centered Coaching offers videos, workshops, books, and speaker services for coaches, parents, and athletes.
National Institute for Child Centered Coaching
3160 Pinebrook Rd.
Park City, UT 84060
(800)688-5822

Appendix C

American Anorexia/Bulimia
 Association
c/o Regents Hospital
425 E. 61st St.
New York, NY 10021
(212)575-6200

Eating Disorders Awareness and
 Prevention, Inc.
603 Stewart St.
Suite 803
Seattle, WA 98101
(206)382-3587

National Association of Anorexia
 Nervosa and Associated Disorders
P.O. Box 7
Highland Park, IL 60035
(847)831-3438

The Renfrew Center
475 Spring Lane
Philadelphia, PA 19128
(215)482-5353
(800)736-3739

National Anorexia Aid Society
1925 E. Dublin Granville Rd.
Columbus, OH 43220
(614)436-1112

Overeaters Anonymous
P.O. Box 92870
Los Angeles, CA 90009
(213)542-8363

Appendix D

NUTRITION, MEDICAL, AND HEALTH ORGANIZATIONS

The United States Olympic Committee
Division of Sports Medicine
One Olympic Plaza
Colorado Springs, CO 80909
(719)578-4546

American Dietetic Association
National Center Nutrition and Dietetics
216 W. Jackson Blvd.
Suite 800
Chicago, IL 60609-6995
(800)366-1655

International Center Sports Nutrition
502 S. 44th St.
Room 3007
Omaha, NE 68105
(402)559-5505

**President's Council on Physical
    Fitness and Sports**
701 Pennsylvania Ave. N.W.

Suite 250
Washington, DC 20004
(202)272-3421 (general information)

**American Alliance for Health, Physical
    Education, Recreation and Dance**
1900 Association Dr.
Reston, VA 22191
(703)476-3405

**International Council for Health,
    Physical Education, Recreation,
    Sport and Dance**
1900 Association Dr.
Reston, VA 22091
(703)476-3486

**National Association for Girls and
    Women in Sports**
1900 Association Dr.
Reston, VA 22091
(703)476-3400

Sport Information Resource Centre
1600 James Naismith Dr.
Gloucester, Ontario
Canada K1B 5N4
(613)748-5658
(800)665-6413

**American Academy of Orthopaedic
  Surgeons**
6300 N. River Rd.
Rosemont, IL 60018
(847)823-7186

**American Academy of Pediatrics
  Committee on Sports Medicine
  and Fitness**
141 Northwest Point Blvd.
Elk Grove Village, IL 60007
(847)228-5005

American College of Sports Medicine
P.O. Box 1440
Indianapolis, IN 46206
(317)637-9200

**National Youth Sports Safety
  Foundation**
10 Meredith Circle
Needham, MA 02192
(617)449-2499

Appendix E

SEXUAL HARASSMENT NATIONAL HOTLINES

Equal Employment Opportunity
Commission
1-800-669-EEOC

Equal Rights Advocates
1-800-839-4372

National Victim Center
1-800-FYI-CALL

U.S. Department of Education's Office
of Civil Rights
(202)260-7250

FOR MORE INFORMATION, CONTACT

National Association for Girls and
Women in Sport (NAGWS)
1900 Association Dr.
Reston, VA 22091
(703)476-3450

National Youth Sports Coaches
Association
2050 Vista Parkway
West Palm Beach, FL 33411
(800)729-2057

The Women's Sports Foundation
Eisenhower Park
East Meadow, NY 11554
(800)227-3988

Mentors in Violence Prevention Project
Michelle King
MVP Coordinator
Northeastern University Center for the
Study of Sport in Society
wosportmrk@aol.com

National Federation of State High
  School Associations
P.O. Box 20626
Kansas City, MO 64195
(816)464-5400

National High School Athletic Coaches
  Association (NHSACA)
P.O. Box 1808
Ocala, FL 32678-1808
(904)622-3660

American Alliance for Health, Physical
  Education, Recreation and Dance
  (AAHPERD)
1900 Association Dr.
Reston, VA 22091
(703)476-3400

American Council for Drug Education
204 Monroe St.
Suite 110
Rockville, MD 20850
(301)294-0600

National Clearinghouse for Alcohol
  and Drug Information
P.O. Box 2345
Rockville, MD 20847-2345
(800)729-6686

Collegiate Consultants on Drugs and
  Alcohol
P.O. Box S241
St. David's, PA 19087
(215)688-5850

Hazelden-Cork Sports Education
  Program
1400 Park Avenue, D.
Minneapolis, MN 55404-1597
(800)257-7800

United States Olympic Committee
Department of Education Services
1750 E. Boulder St.
Colorado Springs, CO 80909-5760
(800)233-0393

End Notes

Introduction

1. Pipher, M. (1994) *Reviving Ophelia: Saving the Selves of Adolescent Girls.* New York: Ballantine Books.
2. Jaffee, L. and Sickler, H. (1998) "Boys and girls choices of equipment and activities on the playground, *Melpomene Journal.* 17(2), 18–23.
3. Bunker, L. K., Duncan, M. C., Freedson, P. et al. (1997) "Physical activity and sport in the lives of girls: Physical and mental health dimensions from an interdisciplinary approach." The Center for Research on Girls and Women in Sport: University of Minnesota.
4. Attanucci, J. (1988). "In whose terms: A new perspective on self, role, and relationship." In C. Gilligan, J. V. Ward, and J. M. Taylor (eds.), *Mapping the Moral Domain* (pp. 201–224). Cambridge, MA: Harvard University.
5. Brown, L. M., and Gilligan, C. (1992). "Meeting at the crossroads: Women's psychology and girl's development." Cambridge, MA: Harvard University.
6. Gilligan, C., Lyons, N. P., & Hammer, T. J. (eds.). (1990). "Making connections: The relational worlds of adolescent girls at the Emma Willard School." Cambridge, MA: Harvard University.
7. Stern, L. (1991). "Disavowing the self in female adolescence." In C. Gilligan, A. G. Rogers, and D. L. Tolman (eds.), *Women, girls and psychotherapy: Reframing resistance* (pp. 105–117). New York: Harrington Park Press.
8. Harris, L., Blum, R. W., and Resnick, M. (1991). "Teen females in Minnesota: A portrait of quiet resistance." In C. Gilligan, A. G. Rogers and D. L.

Tolman (eds.), *Women, Girls and Psychotherapy: Reframing Resistance* (pp. 119–136). New York: Harrington Park Press.

1. First Things First: Getting Her Started

1. Jaffee, L. and Manzer, R. (1992). "Girls Perspectives: Physical Activity and Self-Esteem." *Melpomene Journal,* 11, (3), 22.
2. Garcia, C. (1994). "Gender differences in young children's interactions when learning fundamental motor skills." *Research Quarterly for Exercise and Sport,* 65 (3), 213–225.
3. Bunker, L. K. Paper presented at the Sport Psychology Conference, University of Virginia, Charlottesville.
4. Schultz, D. L., (1991). *Risk, Resiliency, and Resistance: Current Research on Adolescent Girls,* Ms. Foundation, New York, NY.
5. Hellstedt, J.C. (1987). "The coach/parent/athlete relationship." *Sport Psychologist,* 1, 151–160.
6. Bunker, L.K. "Life-Long Benefits of Youth Sports Participation for Girls and Women." Paper presented at the Sport Psychology Conference, University of Virginia, Charlottesville, June 22, 1988.
7. Bloom, B.S. (ed.) (1985). *Developing Talent in Young People.* New York: Ballantine Books.

2. Now That She's Playing: Keeping It Positive

1. *Mental Readiness Video: 3 To Get Ready.* (1993) Indianapolis, IN. USA Gymnastics.
2. Bandura, A. (1986). *Social Foundations of Thought and Action: A Social Cognitive Theory.* Englewood Cliffs, NJ: Prentice Hall.
3. Duda, J. L. (1998). "The implications of the motivational climate in gymnastics: A review of recent research." In N. T. Marshall (ed.) *The Athlete Wellness Book,* Indianapolis, IN: USA Gymnastics.
4. Bunker, L. K., Duncan, M. C., Freedson, P., Greenberg, D., Oglesby, C., Sabo, D., Wiese-Bjanstal D. *Physical Activity and Sport in the Lives of Girls: Physical and Mental Health Dimension from an Interdisciplinary Approach.* (Spring 1997). Study under the direction of the Center for Research on Girls and Women in Sport: University of Minnesota supported by the Center for Mental Health Services/Substance Abuse and Mental Health Services Administration, U.S. Department of Health and Human Services.
5. Csikszentmihalyi, M., Rathunde, K., and Whalen, S. (1993). *Talented Teenagers: The Roots of Success and Failure.* Melbourne, Australia. Cambridge University Press.

3. Coaching the Coaches: Making Sure She Gets What's Right for Her

1. Duda, J. L. (1999). "The implications of the motivational climate in gymnastics: A review of recent research." In N. T. Marshall, (ed.), *The Athlete Wellness Book*: Indianapolis, IN: USA Gymnastics.
2. Borden, A. "Motivational Environments." Presented at the Athlete Wellness Course, New York, Oct. 17, 1999.
3. Weinberg, R. S., and Gould, D. (1995). *Foundations of Sport and Exercise Psychology*. Champaign, IL: Human Kinetics.
4. Ackerman, V. "Bringing in the male." *Washington Post*, Aug. 18, 1999. D-6
5. Allen, J. B., and Howe, B. L. (1998). "Player ability, coach feedback, and female adolescent athletes' perceived competence and satisfaction." *Journal of Sport and Exercise Psychology*, 20 (3), 280–299.
6. Kirk, W., and Kirk, S. (1993). *Student Athletes: Shattering the Myths and Sharing the Realities*. Alexandria, VA: American Counseling Association.
7. Black, S. J., and Weiss, M. R. (1992). "The relationship among perceived coaching behaviors, perceptions of ability and motivation in competitive age-group swimmers." *Journal of Sport and Exercise Psychology*, 14, (3), 309–325.
8. Barnett, N. P., Smoll, F. L., & Smith, R. E., (1992). "Effects of enhancing coach-athlete relationships on youth sport attrition." *The Sport Psychologist*, 6, (2), 11–27.

4. Parenting: When Mom and Dad Need Guidance

1. Kidman, L., McKenzie, A., and McKenzie, B., (1999). "The nature and target of parents' comments during youth sport competitions." *Journal of Sport Behavior*, 22(1).
2. Mihoces, G. "Silence on the sidelines." *USA Today*, (Oct. 1, 1999), Section: News, 1-A.
3. Mihoces, G. "Silence on the sidelines." *USA Today*, (Oct. 1, 1999), Section: News, 1-A.
4. Scanlan, T. K., Stein, G. L., and Ravizza, K. (1991). "An in-depth study of former elite figure skaters: III. Sources of stress." *Journal of Sport and Exercise Psychology*, 13(2), 103–120.
5. Gould, D., Jackson, S., and Finch, L. (1992). "Sources of Stress Experienced by National Champion Figure Skaters." Grant Report United States Olympic Committee Sports Sciences. Greensboro, NC: University of North Carolina.
6. White, S. A. (1998). "Adolescent goal profiles, perceptions of the parent-initiated motivational climate, and competitive trait anxiety." *Sport Psychologist*, 12(1), 16–28.

5. Effective Training: How to Help Her Get the Most Out of Practice

1. Van Raalte, J. L, Brewer, B. W., Rivera, P. M., and Petipas, A. J. (1994). "The relationship between observable self-talk and competitive junior tennis players' match performances." *Journal of Sport and Exercise Psychology,* 16(4), 400–415.

2. Kwan, M. *NBC Sports* television interview, March, 1997.

3. Robbins, A. "Women's teams hope on-site training pays off." *USA Today.* (June 2, 1999). Section: Sports, 6-C.

4. Weinberg, R. S., Burke, K. L., and Jackson, A. (1997). "Coaches' and players' perceptions of goal setting in junior tennis: An exploratory investigation." *Sport Psychologist,* 11(4), 426–439.

5. Weinberg, R. S. and Gould, D. (1995). *Foundations of Sport and Exercise Psychology.* Champaign, IL: Human Kinetics.

6. Silva, J.M. (1990). "An analysis of the training stress syndrome in competitive athletics." *Journal of Applied Sport Psychology,* 2,(1), 5–20.

7. Hall, H. K., Kerr, A. W., and Mathews, J. (1998). "Pre-competitive anxiety in sport: The contribution of achievement goals and perfectionism." *The Journal of Sport and Exercise Psychology,* 20(2), 194–217.

8. Jaffee, L., and Manzer, R., (1992). "Girls perspectives: Physical activity and self-esteem." *Melpomene Journal.* Autumn, 11(3).

9. Stephens, D. E., and Bredemeier, B. J. (1996). "Moral atmosphere and judgements about aggression in girls' soccer: Relationships among moral and motivational variables." *Journal of Sport and Exercise Psychology,* 18(2), 158–173.

10. *Mental Readiness Video: 3 To Get Ready.* Indianapolis, IN: USA Gymnastics.

6. Mind Games: Improving Performance as She Advances

1. Boeck, S. and Laird, B. "Mcdonald's 'Great Breaks' research." *USA Today,* Oct. 1995.

2. Defrancesco, C. and Burke, K. L. (1997). "Performance enhancement strategies used in a professional tennis tournament." *International Journal of Sport Psychology,* 28(2), 185–195.

3. Weinberg, R., Burton, D., Yukelson, D., and Weigand, D. (1993). "Goal setting in competitive sport: An exploratory investigation of practices of collegiate athletes." *Sport Psychologist,* 7(3), 275–289.

4. Moritz, S. E., Hall, C. R., Martin, K. A., and Vadocz, E. (1996). "What are confident athletes imaging? An examination of image content." *Sport Psychologist,* 10(2), 171–179.

5. Ievleva, L. and Orlick, T. (1991). "Mental links to enhanced healing: An exploratory study." *Sport Psychologist,* 5(1), 25–40.

6. Munroe, K., Hall, C., Simms, S., and Weinberg, R. (1998). "The influence of type of sport and time of season on athletes' use of imagery." *Sport Psychologist,* 12(4), 440–449.

7. Crunch Time: How to Help Her to Do Her Best When It Counts

1. White, S.A., and Zellner, S.R. (1996). "The relationship between goal orientation, beliefs about the causes of sport success, and trait anxiety among high school, intercollegiate, and recreational sport participants." *Sport Psychologist,* 10(1), 58–72.
2. Hanton, S. and Jones, G. (1999b). "The effects of a multimodal intervention program on performers: II. Training the butterflies to fly in formation." *Sport Psychologist,*13, 22–41.
3. Weinberg, R., Grove, R., and Jackson, A. (1992). "Strategies for building self-efficacy in tennis players: A comparative analysis of Australian and American coaches." *Sport Psychologist,*6(1), 3–13.
4. Weinberg, R. and Jackson, A. (1990). "Building self-efficacy in tennis players: A coach's perspective." *Journal of Applied Sport Psychology,* 2(2), 164–174.
5. Csikszentmihalyi, M. (1975). *Beyond Boredom and Anxiety.* San Francisco: Jossey-Bass.
6. Gilligan, C. (1982). *In a Different Voice.* Cambridge, Massachusetts: Harvard University Press.
7. Defrancesco, C. and Burke, K.L. (1997). "Performance enhancement strategies used in a professional tennis tournament." *International Journal of Sport Psychology,* 28(2), 185–195.
8. Jackson, S.A. (1995). "Factors influencing the occurrence of flow state in elite athletes." *Journal of Applied Sport Psychology,* 7(2), 138–166.

8. Her Changing Body, Her Changing Self: The Spectrum of Eating-Related Problems

1. USAG Task Force on USA Gymnastics Response to the Female Athlete Triad. (1995). *Technique,* 15(9), 16–22.
2. Nattiv, A., Agostini, R., Drinkwater, B., et al. (1994). "The female athlete triad." *Clinician in Sports Medicine,* 13(2), 405–418
3. *American Psychiatric Association Diagnostic and Statistical Manual of Mental Disorders: IV* (ed. 4), Washington, D.C., 1994.
4. Levine, M.P. (1987). *Student Eating Disorders: Anorexia Nervosa and Bulimia.* Washington, D.C.: National Education Association.
5. Sundgot-Borgen, J. (1994). "Risk and trigger factors for the development of

eating disorders in female elite athletes." *Medical Science Sports Exercise,* **26**(4), 414–419.

6. Sundgot-Borgen, J., and Corbin, C.B. (1987). "Eating disorders among female athletes." *Physician and Sports Medicine,* **15**(2), 89–95.

7. Kaye, W. (1999). "Altered dopamine activity after recovery from restricting-type anorerxia nervosa." *Neuropsychopharmacology,* 21(4), 503–506.

8. Cooper, K. (1991). *Kid Fitness: The Complete Shape-Up Program from Birth through High School.* New York: Bantam Books, pp. 2–3.

9. Levine, M.P. (1987). *Student Eating Disorders: Anorexia Nervosa and Bulimia.* Washington, D.C.: National Education Association.

10. Nattiv, A., Agostini, R., Drinkwater, B., et al. (1994). "The female athlete triad." *Clinician in Sports Medicine,* **13**(2), 405–418. For entire list of citations, see: Hecht, S. & Nattiv, A. (1998). "Gymnastics and the female athlete triad." In N. T. Marshall (Ed.), *The Athlete Wellness Book* Indianapolis, IN: USA Gymnastics.

11. Benardot, D. (1998). "Nutrition for gymnasts." In N. T. Marshall (Ed.), *The Athlete Wellness Book.* Indianapolis, IN: USA Gymnastics.

12. Loucks, A.B. (1997). "The female-athlete triad." *Gatorade Sports Science Institute Sports Science Exchange Roundtable,* 8(1) 1–7.

13. Hecht, S. and Nattiv, A. (1998). "Gymnastics and the female athlete triad." in N. T. Marshall (Ed.), *The Athlete Wellness Book.* Indianapolis, IN: USA Gymnastics.

14. Nattiv, A., and Mandelbaum, B.R. (1993). "Injuries and special concerns in female gymnasts." *Physician Sports Medicine,* **21**(7), 66–82.

15. Sharp, C.W. and Freeman, C.L. (April 1993). "The medical complications of anorexia." *British Journal of Psychiatry,* **162**, 452–462.

16. Nattiv, A., Agostini, R., Drinkwater, B., et al. (1994). "The female athlete triad." *Clinician in Sports Medicine,* **13**(2), 405–418.

9. Serious Issues: The Dark Side of Sports Participation

1. "As women's sports grow, so do harassment suits," (Mar. 7, 1999). CNNSI.com

2. Staff and Wire Reports, (Mar. 27, 1999). *The News Observer on the Web.* Newsobserver.com

3. Howard, J. "Betrayal of trust: The case against a top volleyball coach focuses attention on the sexual abuse of young athletes." *Sports Illustrated,* (Mar. 21, 1997), p. 66.

4. Schultz, J. "Historic gains, but also more pains." *The Atlanta Journal and Constitution,* (Sept. 20, 1998), p. A01.

5. Fish, M. "Accusations of lesbianism can ruin a coach's career, and even a hint can be used against them in recruiting." *The Atlanta Constitution,* (Sept. 23, 1998), p. D08.

6. Cronin, D. "Drug ban upheld on Irish swimmer." *USA Today*, (Jun. 8, 1999), p. 13C.

7. "Players file suit over coach." *The Washington Post*, (Oct. 17, 1999), p. D2.

8. Dickinson, L., Verloin deGruy, F., Dickinson, W.P., and Candib, L.M. (1999). "Health-related quality of life and symptom profiles of female survivors of sexual abuse." *Archives of Family Medicine*, 8(1), 35–43.

9. "The Women's Sports Foundation Education and Prevention Policy: Sexual Harassment and Unethical Relationships Between Coaches and Athletes" (1998). The Women's Sports Foundation, lifetimetv.com.

10. Greenfeld, L.A. (1996). *Child Victimizers: Violent Offenders and their Victims—Executive Summary*. U.S. Department of Justice and Office of Juvenile Justice and Delinquency Prevention. Annapolis, MD: Bureau of Justice Statistics Clearinghouse.

11. *Rape in America: A Report to the Nation* (1992). The National Victim Center. Arlington, VA.

12. *Rape in America: A Report to the Nation* (1992). The National Victim Center.

13. United States Equal Employment Opportunity Commission. (1999). Washington, D.C., eeoc.gov.

14. Strauss, S. (1992). *Sexual Harassment and Teens*. Minneapolis, MN: Free Spirit Publishing.

15. Strauss, S. (1992). *Sexual Harassment and Teens*. Minneapolis, MN: Free Spirit Publishing.

16. Strauss, S. (1992). *Sexual Harassment and Teens*. Minneapolis, MN: Free Spirit Publishing.

17. Strauss, S. (1992). *Sexual Harassment and Teens*. Minneapolis, MN: Free Spirit Publishing.

18. www.feminist.org, 8/26/99.

19. Yesalis, C.E. and Cowart, V.S. (1998). *The Steroids Game: An Expert's Inside Look at Anabolic Steroid Use in Sports.* Champaign, IL: Human Kinetics.

20. Bhasin, S., Storer, T., Berman, N., et. al. (1996). "The effects of supraphysiologic doses of testosterone on muscle size and strength in normal men." *The New England Journal of Medicine*, 335(1), 1–7.

21. Moore, K. "The U.S. Olympic women swimmers of 1976 swept into Montreal." *Sports Illustrated*, (Jul. 13, 1992), p. 54.

22. Owen Slot. "How China broke Stasi rules Owen Slot, in Berlin, fears for the Chinese after hearing graphic accounts of East German drug use. *The Sunday Telegraph*, (Jan. 18, 1998), p. 11.

23. Owen Slot. "How China broke Stasi rules Owen Slot, in Berlin, fears for the Chinese after hearing graphic accounts of East German drug use. *The Sunday Telegraph*, (Jan. 18, 1998), p. 11.

24. Smith, S., Huizenga, R. "Was Lyle Alzado's cancer caused by the performance-enhancing drugs?" *Sports Illustrated,* (Jul. 8, 1991), p. 22.

25. www.ncjrs.org/ojjhome.

26. *Fair Play Means Safety for All* (1997). Canadian Hockey Association.

27. Lopiano, D. (1998) "Homophobia in Women's Sports." The Women's Sports Foundation. lifetimetv.com.

28. Griffin, P. (1999). "Coaches: How safe and inclusive is your team for lesbian, gay, bisexual athletes and coaches." Griffin@educ.umass.edu.

29. Griffin, P. (1992). "Changing the game: homophobia, sexism, and lesbians in sport." *Quest,* 44(22), 251–265.

30. Griffin, P. (1999). "Why coaches need to address homophobia and heterosexism in athletics." Griffin@educ.umass.edu.

31. Griffin, P. (1999). "Why coaches need to address homophobia and heterosexism in athletics." Griffin@educ.umass.edu.

32. Longman, J. "Lions women's basketball coach is used to fighting and winning. Rene Portland has strong views on women's rights, lesbian players and large margins of victory." *The Philadelphia Inquirer.* (Mar. 10, 1991), p. G01.

33. Fegusson, D.M., Horwood, J., and Beautrais, A.L. (1999). "Is sexual orientation related to mental health problems and suicidality in young people?" *Archives of General Psychiatry,* 56(10), 876–880.